KU-518-481

REGULATING CYBERSPACE

The Policies and Technologies of Control

Richard A. Spinello

Q

QUORUM BOOKS
Westport, Connecticut • London

Library of Congress Cataloging-in-Publication Data

Spinello, Richard A.
Regulating cyberspace : the policies and technologies of control / Richard A. Spinello.
p. cm.
Includes bibliographical references and index.
ISBN 1–56720–445–7 (alk. paper)
1. Telecommunication—Government policy. 2. Cyberspace—Government policy. 3. Internet—Law and legislation. 4. Computer networks—Law and legislation. I. Title.
TK5012.5.S6633 2002
303.48′33—dc21 2001058931

British Library Cataloguing in Publication Data is available.

Library of Congress Catalog Card Number: 2001058931
ISBN: 1–56720–445–7

First published in 2002

Quorum Books, 88 Post Road West, Westport, CT 06881
An imprint of Greenwood Publishing Group, Inc.
www.quorumbooks.com

Printed in the United States of America

The paper used in this book complies with the Permanent Paper Standard issued by the National Information Standards Organization (Z39.48–1984).

10 9 8 7 6 5 4 3 2

Mark Spinello
May 13–14, 1960

Contents

Preface

In 1983 Ithiel de sola Pool wrote a highly influential book called *Technologies of Freedom* that dealt with the issue of preserving free speech in an electronic age. The Internet is the latest advance in the "electronic revolution," an admirable successor to the telegraph and the telephone. It too is a "technology of freedom." Some see it as the ultimate tool of autonomy. But because of the Internet's transformative power and its global reach, it presents unusual challenges. Countries, institutions, and individuals feel the need to control the Net and to curb its excesses.

This book deals with the architectures of control, those technologies like filters and rights-management protocols that attempt to tame the Net or protect property and privacy in cyberspace. These architectures can substitute for public policies, but some worry that this privatization of law can have detrimental consequences. Filtering, for example, can have a polarizing effect if it limits one's exposure to different points of view. Thus, we must reflect upon how these architectures can be used responsibly in order to prevent such collateral damage.

Policies still matter, of course, and this is primarily a book about those policies and laws that are designed to control the disorder of cyberspace. In the pages ahead we will conduct a tour of those emerging policies. As a "guide" for this tour we will also present and defend a credo or philosophy of Internet regulation. We will espouse an admittedly controversial viewpoint that the optimal form of regulation is self-regulation. A basic premise of the book is that thanks to powerful and flexible Internet architectures, a decentralized regulatory regime is a viable alternative to centralized structures and the uniformity they tend to impose. These architectures, however, must be used prudently, and this introduces an ethical dimension into our discussion. Our argument is that ethical self-regulation facilitated by technology is the most reasonable way to "control" and impose order on the Net. Technology transforms the regulatory landscape in cyberspace by lowering transaction costs and making it possible for individuals to deal with some negative externalities on their own terms.

On the other hand, we do not agree with an extreme libertarian perspective that argues for a simple "hands-off" approach by government. Government intervention is especially important when individuals lack the tools to deal with the negative by-products of cyberspace transactions or the problems involving the Internet infrastructure. Government intervention seems essential to preserve the original Internet design principles, such as end-to-end, which permit true open access on the Internet. And the government must ensure that Microsoft or some other monopolistic enterprise does not exert its dominance in a way that stifles innovation and ultimately hurts the consumer.

As we survey relevant policies, our main focus will be on five areas of social concern: fair competition in cyberspace, free expression, intellectual property, privacy rights, and security. The range of specific issues that emerge in each of these areas represents a fairly sizable portion of the political agenda in Washington. These issues demand creative and prompt responses, which are sensitive to jurisdictional ambiguities. But Washington, with a culture mired in special interests and bureaucratic paralysis, may be ill-equipped to handle all these matters expeditiously. Hence, the need for a more decentralized approach, whenever possible.

As one plunges into this book, it will also become apparent that we are embracing a centrist philosophy when policies are necessary. Regulating the Internet is about exercising control, and successful regulation is about achieving the proper level of control. In our estimation the center is usually the proper place to be, especially when dealing with contentious issues like free expression and intellectual property. We must eschew corporate extremism, which is sometimes hostile to democratic values and free expression on the Net, while it advocates exceptionally strong property protection. But we must also avoid liberal orthodoxy, which espouses few if any restrictions on speech and loose property protection. Balance or measure is the key virtue in both areas, especially in the case of intellectual property protection. In Aristotle's (1941) terminology, the goal of regulators should be to "hit the mark" and not to fail through excess (*hyperbole*) or defect (*ellipsis*); that is, to avoid excessive or feeble protections. In a world where intellectual property has such exceptional value, the challenge to "hit the mark" and get it right could not be more important.

Thus, if government intervention is welfare enhancing and architectures of control are deployed responsibly, we might be able to preserve the Net's core values and open architecture without anarchy and without allowing the Net to be smothered by superfluous regulations.

REFERENCES

Aristotle. (1941). *Nicomachean Ethics*, edited by R. McKeon. New York: Random House.

de sola Pool, I. (1983). *Technologies of Freedom*. Cambridge: Harvard University Press.

Acknowledgments

In this book I have incorporated a small amount of material from several articles or papers that have been published or presented elsewhere. Some of the discussion on ISP liability in Chapter 6 is derived from "Internet Service Providers and Defamation: New Standards of Liability," an unpublished paper delivered at the Fifty Annual Ethics and Technology Conference at Loyola, Chicago, July 20–21, 2000. I developed part of the section in Chapter 9 on digital identity from a paper called "Regulating Digital Identity," delivered at the ETHICOMP Conference in Rome, Italy, October 6–8, 1999. In Chapter 7, the discussion on linking borrowed several paragraphs from an article that originally appeared in *Computers and Society*, called "An Ethical Evaluation of Web Site Linking" (December 2000). Some of the material on Lessig's paradigm in Chapter 2 is derived from a review article of that book which appeared in *Ethics and Information Technology*, vol. 3, no. 2 (2001). Finally, several of the main themes of Chapter 3 were originally presented in an unpublished paper written for the ETHICOMP 2001 conference held in Gdansk, Poland, June 18–20.

The final task for any author is to offer thanks to those few people who have helped out in one way or another with the content of this book and with the logistics of its production.

Special thanks go to my editor at Greenwood Publications Group, Hillary Claggett, for her encouragement and enthusiasm and for her insightful comments on the first draft of the manuscript. I also want to thank all those involved in the production of this book, especially John Beck, for his patience in dealing with multiple editorial changes and alterations. I also owe a debt of gratitude to Joyce O'Connor of the Carroll School of Management at Boston College for helping me handle some of the mechanics involved in publishing this manuscript.

Finally, I am particularly grateful to my wife, Susan T. Brinton, for her prodigious efforts in typing and editing this long manuscript. I also thank her for the sustained interest that she has manifested in my work over these many years.

Thank you all.

1

Global Connectivity and Internet Access

In his extraordinary book, *The Future of Man*, the French Jesuit philosopher Teilhard de Chardin (1959) described a "thinking layer of the earth" and a "collective global energy" that would move "social Man towards ever greater interdependence and cohesion." We do not know precisely what Teilhard had in mind or how he thought this might be accomplished, but his remarks certainly anticipated the global connectivity and cooperative ethos made possible today by borderless electronic media and most especially by the Internet. Teilhard hypothesized a spiritual but tangible connectedness that would create a true world community or, in the words of another seer of the future, Marshall McLuhan, a "global village." McLuhan too was prescient in his ability to see how flexible electronic media would one day lead to the decentralization of power and information.

The emergence of this global information infrastructure (or GII) may well be the realization of Teilhard's intoxicating vision. It is the result of the merging or coming together of many national information infrastructures (NIIs). The GII has often been glibly referred to as a global *agora* (marketplace) or even a "superhighway." This highway is clearly hastening the forces of economic globalization and is radically reshaping the economic and political landscape of almost every major country in the world. While globalization is the result of many other forces besides the "connectivity" envisioned by de

Chardin and McLuhan, it would surely not be possible without technology; specifically, the technological advances that enable high-velocity transfers of our interconnected information resources.

While these references to thinkers like McLuhan may conjure up grandiose ideas about the transforming effects of the Internet, our aim in this chapter is a modest one. First, we review the costs and benefits of living in a network society. This concise discussion will set the stage for the policy and ethical issues to be covered in later chapters. Second, we focus on the information infrastructure, especially the physical layer of that infrastructure, that makes connectivity possible. One of our objectives is to suggest a proper role for the government to play in managing the development of that infrastructure and in ensuring open access.

In addition to its focus on the GII, this chapter will also introduce some of the broader themes of the book. As we review the ensemble of benefits associated with this information infrastructure, we will introduce one of the book's key arguments about the need to preserve the Net's open and distributed architecture so that it remains a truly universal network shaped by its users. A nonfragmented and open Net is the best stimulus for semiotic democracy; that is, for future creativity and innovation in the hands of the many rather than the few (see Fisher 2000). On the other hand, the impulse to control and renationalize the Internet, to introduce national boundaries into this virtual world, subverts the value structure that underlies the Net's unique ability to be an agent of change and a catalyst for innovation. The Internet has been a liberating technology, but if governments dismantle this ubiquitous, transnational network and rearchitect it so that it becomes as fragmented and enclosed as real space, the loss for global social welfare will be incalculable.

Much of this introductory chapter, then, will be about these issues of freedom and control, and about the interplay between those technologies and policies that have been developed to reassert control over the Net. When the Net first became popular there were many myths propagated about how it would level playing fields, undercut monopoly power structures, and even lead to the "twilight" of government sovereignty. We now know that this is hyperbole, and that it's a big mistake to write off the big corporations or the state. What we are less sure about is how well the state can balance its responsibility to promote the universality of the GII while it protects its own particular citizens from the Internet's excesses.

WHAT IS AN INFORMATION INFRASTRUCTURE?

Although there is probably no concise, univocal definition of the GII, it can be described in the most general terms as the synthesis of computer and information technologies with telecommunications. Before we elaborate on this definition, we must be clear on the relationship between the GII and the Internet. The Internet is an amalgam of networks that are interoperable thanks to the protocol known as TCP/IP.[1] The Internet is obviously a vital part of this information infrastructure, but the GII is a more expansive concept, including communications networks, content, computers, applications, and people. Nonetheless, the GII is often used as a synonym for the Net, and in this book, for the sake of simplicity, we will use the terms interchangeably. The GII can also be viewed as the merging or coming together of many national information infrastructures into a seamless whole that facilitates global information flows.

The GII, then, is a complex collection of systems that integrates several basic components:

- Communications networks or the conduits through which information is transmitted (e.g., telephone, cellular, wireless, satellite, and cable networks).
- Information equipment and appliances; this category includes computer workstations, televisions, and telephones.
- Information resources or the content that flows through these conduits. This information exists in many different media and in many diverse locations, such as government agencies, libraries, and so forth.
- Software applications that allow users to view and manipulate data. This category includes low-level protocols (such as TCP/IP) and interfaces (or browsers) that allow for interconnectivity and interoperation between networks.
- People, primarily in the private sector, who create the information, construct applications, and ultimately use this system.

Information infrastructures such as the traditional telecommunications system have been around for a long time, but we are now combining previously independent systems into this vast global network. And that network continues to rapidly expand with many new nodes and diverse information resources. Also, this infrastructure's capacities have been transformed by the simple power of digitization, the capacity to represent any form of information, including music and video, as bits; that is, as 1s and 0s. As Negroponte (1995) writes, "The information superhighway is about the global movement of weightless bits at the speed of light." Like all media, the Internet has its limitations, but it can connect more people to information and to one another faster and cheaper than any of its predecessors. And herein lies the seeds of its remarkable transformative power. Simple applications like e-mail and the Web have already revolutionized the way humans communicate and conduct business.

But despite its glorious success, we must be vigilant about the Net's future. Open competition and open access will be essential for preserving the GII's vitality as a breeding ground for new applications, services, and products that will create worldwide consumer value. It is important to underscore that this global information infrastructure has become an innovative force thanks to a regime of self-regulation and no regulation, and to the extent that a tendency to overregulate and balkanize the Net gains momentum, innovation and creativity could be adversely affected.

THE BENEFITS AND PERILS OF GLOBAL CONNECTIVITY

The enduring social and political impact of this evolving GII seems beyond dispute. It is reenergizing the economies of many countries, like Ireland, and ushering in a new area of "globalization." Globalization is a fuzzy term, but it can best be defined as the integration of world economic markets; that is, the fusion of separate national markets into a single marketplace. It recognizes the value of cooperation as economic interconnections are continuing to increase among countries around the world, and it tends to confirm the predominance of free-market capitalism. While globalization is viewed with a wary eye by some countries, there is no doubt that it is yielding many salutary effects in most sectors of the global economy.

Thanks in large part to the emergence of the GII and technologies like the Internet, globalization appears to be shifting the balance of power between individuals and the state and perhaps even undermining the power of the nation-state. According to Friedman (1999), "Because globalization has brought down many of the walls that limit the movement and reach of people, and because it has simultaneously wired the world into networks, it gives more power to individuals to influence both markets and nation-states than at any time in history." It also lowers the cost of entry into different media; thanks to the Internet it is easy to become a journalist or an investigative reporter with a global reach. This phenomenon could well subject governments and corporations to even greater scrutiny. In some countries, like Malaysia, some of the most objective and insightful reporting comes from a makeshift Web site, www.malaysiakini.com.

All of this leads many to conclude that the global information infrastructure with the Internet at its core is a "democratic" technology; that is, a technology with embedded democratic values. The U.S. Supreme Court has described the Net as a "vast democratic forum" that "is open to all comers" (*Reno v. ACLU*, 521 U.S. 844, 868 [1997]). We might even say that the Internet is a realization of Justice Holmes's vision in *Abrams v. United States* (250 U.S. 616 [1919]) of a society that supports "free trade in ideas." If this is so, if the greatest virtue of the Net is its promotion of democratic values and a free exchange of ideas, then this "democratic technology" has the potential to change the international political landscape and to undermine authoritarian, nondemocratic regimes.

This notion that the GII is democratic may seem like an indisputable proposition, since this information infrastructure makes so much diverse information available to so many. It also expands opportunities for "unmediated," horizontal communication between individuals and groups of individuals on a massive scale. But does this necessarily mean that democratic values are embedded in the GII and that its very architecture inherently supports those values?

In order to answer this question we must consider what we mean by "democratic values." According to Arblaster (1987), "At the root of all definitions of democracy . . . lies the idea of popular power, of a situation in which power and perhaps authority too, rest with the people." A democracy, therefore, is characterized by "popular sovereignty," where the ultimate political authority lies with a country's citizens. Does the GII promote or support such popular sovereignty? This is not so obvious. As Johnson (2001) argues, one might conclude that the GII is democratic according to the following reasoning: (1) democracy means power in the hands of many, (2) information is power, (3) the GII puts information into the hands of many, (4) and therefore the GII is democratic. While it is true that accessibility to information is empowering, Johnson points to countervailing tendencies, such as the selective filtering of information, an activity that usually does not support democratic values, and which, in fact, may pulverize those values. Governments like China are blocking more and more of the information sources in our information-rich culture in order to protect their authoritarian regimes and maintain control of their citizens. Filtering and digital-identity technologies could one day transform the GII into a hardwired version of an Orwellian society.

While it may be difficult to make a plausible case that the GII naturally embodies explicit democratic values, a stronger case can perhaps be made that the GII, as it is currently configured, is at least a threat to nondemocratic, authoritarian governments, especially those that callously tend to suppress free speech and other human rights. The expansion of horizontal, unmediated communication facilitated by the Internet is inimical to centralized controls that can take an extreme form in tyrannies and repressive political regimes. Also, Web sites in virtual space are much harder to censor and shut down than newspapers, so there is a greater opportunity for a free press and other information sources, even in the midst of oppression. This means that political information can be accessed more easily. The Internet tends to work against centralized controls because of its distributed and decentralized architecture—there is no central server to censor or suppress.

In addition, this global information infrastructure has been regarded as a democratizing force because it has enabled the creation of many new voices. It has created a "new marketplace of ideas," with "content [that] is as diverse as human thought" (*Reno v. ACLU*, 521 U.S. 844, 868 [1997]). It has unquestionably allowed many individuals to unleash their creative energies as writers, journalists, artists, and musicians. The fact that popular musicians can distribute their music online through their own Web sites may soon undermine the tyranny of the popular music industry. Thus, one might argue that the GII is empowering and democratizing because it has mightily expanded the opportunities for ordinary individuals to be producers of culture and to share in communicative power that was once reserved only for the elite. While undemocratic governments regard this tendency as inauspicious, this diversity and variety of expression made possible by the GII is considered by most citizens of the world as something to be celebrated and encouraged.

There is obviously some merit to these arguments. It must be emphasized, however, that even the Net's democratizing tendencies, such as its capacity to foster the emergence of "new voices" and to decentralize the production and redistribution of information, are not inherent in its architecture. To some extent the Internet is as malleable as any piece of software. Its open and neutral architectures are not a given; the Net has no fixed nature that reflexively supports democratic values or any other set of values. Its protocols can be changed to make the distribution of information more constrained, and new laws can be formulated or old ones recodified to stifle the creative efforts of those "new voices." There is also no guarantee that the Internet will remain a universal, global technology, or that some of these new voices will not be obstructed by filters and other software designed to block the flow of certain kinds of information. The insistence that jurisdictional laws be honored in cyberspace and the introduction of new applications such as geolocation software are examples of how computer code (software) and law can be used to transform the very nature of cyberspace. The GII will only promote democratic values and foster creativity if our laws and the technology allow it to do so. Thus, any claim that the GII is "democratic" must be qualified by an awareness that its democratizing tendencies could easily be altered.

Aside from its current ability to facilitate a "free trade in ideas," there are many other positive attributes associated with a robust and dynamic GII. It can provide unlimited and asynchronous access to public services and to a plethora of cultural, commercial, and educational opportunities. Thanks to venders such as amazon.com, the purchase of books from remote locations is now much simpler and convenient. Many argue that the Net is poised to revolutionize the educational process. This may be an exaggeration, but through distance learning the Net can certainly make educational opportunities available to far more people than anyone could have imagined just a decade or two ago. And the Internet should be able to enhance the availability of health information to remote locations so that medical knowledge and expertise can be shared more equitably and expeditiously.

The diffusion of network technologies also expands cultural openness and transparency. Through the World Wide Web, for example, we can learn about other countries and their citizens in a more immediate and direct fashion. Knowledge about other cultures that happens through the immediacy of Internet communication can help to deconstruct cultural barriers and prejudices. This can create a sense of proximity to diverse peoples throughout the world. Once again, this may not be a welcome development for repressive or authoritarian regimes, since they will find it more difficult to conceal the truth from their citizens or to dissemble the authentic features of other democratic cultures.

This wired world, then, holds out much promise for every country and for every individual fortunate enough to be "connected." But what about those who are not connected, who are left behind by the GII and by these inexorable forces of globalization? Many countries are skeptical about the great benefits of the GII. They are weary of expanding American hegemony as they watch the gap between per capita income of the world's richest nation and the poorest grow to 72 to 1 (Murray 1999).

This issue prompts us to consider the most conspicuous social costs of these globalizing technologies that constitute the GII. Many of these costs are quite predictable and some are possibly intractable. Social commentators have already expressed grave concerns about this widening "digital divide" and the deeper inequities that it spawns. If, as Friedman (1999) suggests, "the Internet has become an essential tool of life," what do we do about those who are excluded from this medium through poverty and ignorance? This exclusion may ultimately breed resentment that foments rebellions or acts of terrorism against the global superpowers.

Regrettably, we cannot treat the issue of the "digital divide" with the depth which it deserves, but a few remarks are in order. The chasm between industrialized and developing societies seems to widen each year, and a big part of the problem is the failure of developing countries to upgrade their infrastructures through technology. Estimates are that one-third of the world's population is technologically disconnected and disenfranchised. This includes people in regions like southern Mexico, most of Brazil, Laos, Cambodia, sub-Sahara Africa, and so on. According to Sachs (2000), the fundamental problem is that these developing countries are not prepared to absorb technologies from abroad: "[Technology] does not flow easily to remote mountainous regions (the Andean countries), landlocked developing countries (Central Asia), or regions that are far from seaports (inland China or northern India)."

Information technology (IT), however, does offer some hope in this otherwise bleak picture, since it can neutralize the disadvantages of geography. Poorly located countries that do not have an advantage in manufacturing and exporting physical goods might be able to develop some advantage in creating virtual IT-based products (such as software) or services (marketing). Information technology could be one way to help to close this widening chasm and connect marginalized societies to the global economy. Change of this magnitude, of course, will take a concerted and cooperative effort. Sachs (2000) suggests that a "first step would be a promise by international high-tech firms to increase their technological cooperation with developing countries." The Internet can provide universal access to information and communications resources, and this can become the foundation of economic growth even for impoverished countries, since in this world economy information is the most basic raw material. The Indian city of Bangalore, for example, has become a center for software development. Its citizens have acquired computer programming skills and now write programs for U.S. and European companies, which are indifferent to the location of their software developers. It will not be easy for other countries to emulate what Bangalore has done, but information technology may one day help many countries to overcome the gulf between wealth and poverty.

On the other hand, the digital divide may have certain advantages. Connection to a global information infrastructure can interfere with a country's unique traditions. And it can undermine national sovereignty. Thus, another source of friction for participants in the GII is the inauspicious threat it poses to a polity's cultural autonomy and political hegemony. While some countries (like China) may use that argument as a defense for the repression of legitimate free expression on the Internet, other countries experience real tension between the impulses to protect their cultures and to be participants in economic globalization. This clash between local values and standards and the Net's indifference to content may actually foment the greatest crisis for the GII. Consider, for instance, Germany's futile efforts to prevent CompuServe from carrying bulletin boards with anti-Semitic hate speech, which violates strong cultural norms and strict laws in that country. The German government realizes the need for connectivity through Internet service providers (ISPs) like CompuServe, but at the same time it does not want the complete openness and full range of content this connectivity provides to its citizens.

More recently, during the spring of 2000, two French antiracist groups filed suit against Yahoo, demanding that the company remove swastika flags and other Nazi memorabilia from its American Web site. Some of Yahoo's properties are auction sites that included such items for sale. French law expressly prohibits the display or sale of objects that incite racial hatred and this includes any World War II Nazi memorabilia. A French Judge, Jean-Jacques Gomez, ruled in favor of these two groups, concluding that Yahoo had violated French law and offended the "collected memory" of France. He ordered Yahoo to make it impossible for French users to access any auction site that contained illegal Nazi items.

Yahoo's lawyers claimed that the company was helpless in this regard, since it would not be technically feasible to accomplish such a task; that is, to identify Web users by national origin and block access to the contested sites. Nonetheless, after much haggling Yahoo was ordered to install a filtering system to block French citizens from these problematic sites. Yahoo eventually decided to remove these items from its auction site.

This unusual case triggers many difficult jurisdictional issues. On the one hand, France has the right to assert jurisdiction over its citizens and to enforce its own laws. But should it enforce its laws against a company located in the United States and impose them on this Web site with global reach? What about the precedent this case will set? As Alan Davison, a lawyer for the Center for Democracy and Technology, remarked, "We now have a race to the bottom. The most restrictive rules about Internet content—influenced by any country—could have an impact on people around the world" (Guernsey 2001).

In addition to threatening unique cultural traditions, the global information infrastructure is also menacing to privacy and property. How do we protect our privacy when business is transacted online and personal identity information is reduced to a cheap commodity? How can we be assured that sensitive financial or medical information will be adequately protected? This ubiquitous network also jeopardizes the right to act without being constantly monitored. The Web has made possible surveillance technologies such as cookies and Web bugs that only seem to accelerate privacy's steady erosion. But the privacy issue is not a simple one. If data flows are too restricted, the end result could be a negative impact on electronic commerce. And what about intellectual property, which seems so fragile in a network economy? The trouble with digital information is that it is so easy to reproduce and to circulate. Barlow's (1994) formulation of the digital property dilemma is the most pointed: "If our property can be infinitely reproduced and instantaneously distributed all over the planet without cost, without our knowledge, without its even leaving our possession, how can we protect it?"

Finally, the network is vulnerable to trespass and to assault from outsiders with malevolent motives. The Net's security breaches, made infamous through the "I Love You" virus, could one day be exploited to disrupt the world economy and the smooth flow of capital. The Internet is by nature an open and insecure environment, and as the economy depends more and more on this global network it becomes vulnerable to attacks, fraud, and other antisocial forms of behavior.

Telecommunications and information systems are vital components of a country's critical infrastructure, and their destruction would have a devastating impact on national security or national economic viability. The vulnerability of these systems seems beyond question, but most governments have not been proactive in dealing with the threat of a possible cyberattack. Yet the more dependent we are on the network, the more likely an act of sabotage will unleash global chaos. One of the challenges of coordinating security at this level is that the critical infrastructure is usually owned and controlled by the private sector, while responsibility for public safety belongs primarily to the government.

Even if a national government is able to deal with this issue and develop a comprehensive security scheme, there is no guarantee that other nations will do the same. This will mean that there are "weak links" in the chain of secure connectivity, and they expose the entire network to a disabling attack. The sovereign powers that constitute the GII have an obligation to keep their national systems safe, secure, and up to date so that the whole network will remain truly secure, but how can the global community deal with those weak links?

Thus, the global information infrastructure creates its share of social turbulence. But the response, even among democratic countries, has sometimes been disproportionate to the magnitude of that turbulence. Countries have begun to increase their regulatory oversight and restrict information flows.

Every country seems to have something about the Web or the Internet that it doesn't like or that it wants to control. In the United States the preoccupation has been with smut, while in Europe there has been a concerted effort to block hate speech no matter where its origins may be. South Korea's bête noire is gambling, and it has criminalized access to online gambling sites. The Yahoo case in France and the CompuServe case in Germany represent firm evidence of a tendency to assert national sovereignty even if it means nationalizing the GII.

This epic struggle between freedom and control in cyberspace, which has greatly accelerated during the last several years, will probably last for some time and could possibly lead to a more fragmented infrastructure with many virtual borders and information checkpoints. Unless countries like the United States resist this effort and embrace a universal and frictionless infrastructure, it is difficult to envision the forces of freedom eventually winning this battle.

INFRASTRUCTURE DEVELOPMENT POLICY

Each country must assume responsibility for the development and maintenance of its own information infrastructure. The major debate that has centered around infrastructure development focuses on the choice of managed versus free competition. In countries like Singapore and China the information infrastructure has evolved through carefully orchestrated, top-down planning. China, for example, has been centrally involved in the development of its infrastructure through its Golden Projects, large-scale networking applications coordinated by various government ministries. On the other hand, in the United States free competitive forces have shaped the information infrastructure with minimal government direction. The U.S. approach represents the "government as referee" model; that is, the private sector builds and maintains the infrastructure and the government ensures that everyone is playing by the rules. It seeks to make sure that there is open access, fair competition, and interoperability of the various systems.

Which of these approaches is preferable? While policy makers in the United States would understandably resist an infrastructure policy rooted in centralized planning, does the United States need a more coherent information infrastructure policy? What precise role should the government play? Should the private sector continue to lead so that policy *follows* technology and the marketplace? And what is the downside of the more directive policies and tight centralized planning associated with countries like China and Singapore?

If there is any national information infrastructure that exemplifies a managed or planning-based approach to infrastructure development, it is the NII of Singapore. Singapore is a small island at the northern tip of the Malaysian Peninsula. Despite its exotic location, Singapore is a sophisticated and prosperous city state with a population of about 3 million. One of the country's major advantages has always been its pivotal location as a key strategic port for those doing trade in the vicinity of Asia.

How did this small city-state come to develop one of the most admired and state-of-the-art IT infrastructures in the world? Much of the credit belongs to the leadership of Lee Kuan Yew, a central but controversial figure in Singaporean politics for three decades, whose clear vision and central planning enabled Singapore to build that infrastructure gradually in the 1970s and 1980s. Lee oversaw the development of educational, technological, and physical infrastructure in order to fulfill his vision of Singapore as an "intelligent island." This included the establishment of the Singapore Public Telecommunications Network, the automation of government services (the Government Computerization Project), and the creation of Singapore Network Services. These efforts in the 1970s and 1980s emphasized the crucial importance of information technology for the economic vitality of this country. Thanks to this infrastructure, Singapore implemented several key strategic applications, such as TradeNet, which automated and streamlined the country's trade procedures. This electronic data interchange (EDI) system has enabled shippers, insurers, port authorities, custom officials, and other relevant parties to move shipments in and out of Singapore quickly and efficiently (Applegate 1996).

There are many other sophisticated applications that have been built upon Singapore's comprehensive information infrastructure. Most of these have been constructed with the help of the government and its central planning efforts. Singapore's top-down approach relied on statutory boards (comprised of representatives from the business, government, and public sectors) along with government agencies and key network providers (such as Singapore Telecom) to develop these applications and unite them with the infrastructure. The Singapore government also provided significant funding for these projects. Thus, Singapore has chosen a path different from many Western countries by virtue of its role as a central player in the development of its NII.

Despite the effectiveness and the notable advantages of this approach, there is also a dark side to Singapore's laudable efforts to implement its vision of the "intelligent island." The Singapore government has so far taken great pains to control content on the Internet. For example, TechNet, Singapore's Internet service provider, was ordered by the government to check over 80,000 e-mail accounts of researchers and university faculty and professionals for the presence of pornographic material. Although recent evidence indicates that Singapore is easing up on some of its censorship laws, "the ruling party clings tightly to some information controls, raising doubts over how much impact the Internet will have in transforming this strait-laced, cautious culture" (Levander 1999).

In the United States infrastructure policy is markedly different from what happens in countries like Singapore. It has been aptly described as "order without design," where the private sector and not the government takes the lead in the development process. U.S. policy for its NII was first laid out in some level of detail in the Clinton administration's comprehensive white paper, "The National Information Infrastructure: Agenda for Action" (Clinton and Gore 1993).

The NII initiative in the United States actually has its roots in the High Performance Computing Act (HPCA) of 1991, which formalized the High Performance Computing and Communications Program (HPCC). The HPCC coordinated the work and investments of different agencies that were involved in advancing the country's computing and networking capacities. The HPCC was recognized in the federal budget, since the agencies it coordinated received funds designated for this purpose. The government's research and development (R&D) support during this period played a critical role in the Internet's development during the late 1980s and early 1990s.

But the Clinton administration took this approach a step further with its NII initiative, which became a federal project with an interagency task force. This initiative, however, involved no new programs, had no mention or support in the federal budget (in contrast to HPCC), and had no funding for policy development. The core of the NII initiative is explained in the principles and goals articulated in the "Agenda for Action." These include the following:

- promote private-sector investment.
- extend "universal service" concept to ensure that information resources are available to everyone at an affordable price.
- promote technological innovation.
- promote a seamless, interactive, user-driven NII.
- improve management of radio frequency spectrum.
- protect intellectual property rights.

The agenda served a useful purpose. It endorsed the private sector's lead in NII development and it asserted that government action would do no more than complement that leadership. However, as Kahin (1997) points out, the policy problems in some of the agenda's "ambitious items," such as universal service, "were never fully articulated let alone resolved." Nonetheless, Kahin also observes that "the NII initiative was successful out of proportion to its resources in focusing public attention on the massive changes in communication and information technology and the potential for economic and social change."

Surprisingly, the Clinton administration decided against creating a new government agency to implement its agenda. It relied instead on a team-based approach: Members of various government agencies came together to form the Information Infrastructure Task Force (IITF). According to Simon (2000),

"The IITF pushed the agenda throughout the government in the first Clinton administration and worked on major initiatives, especially telecommunications policy; it also focused on security issues and information policy, including intellectual property, privacy protection, and the use of government information."

For the most part, then, the U.S. approach to infrastructure development follows a free-market model, which is based upon minimal intervention and control by the state. The NII will develop through a cooperative effort between the private sector and government, with the private sector making the investments and taking most of the risks. The government provides only broad policy direction with minimal financial assistance. This is obviously quite different than Singapore's state-guided and more hierarchical approach to infrastructure development.

What are we to make of these contrasting visions of an NII? Should the United States move in the direction of Singapore and China and develop a more interventionist approach to infrastructure issues, especially as the NII grows in importance and as equity issues gain more prominence? Policy experts have cited the "Intelligent Island" vision as a classic example of how to achieve cooperation between the public and private sectors. According to the Harvard Policy Group on Network Enabled Services (2000), "Even though Singapore is small and quite different than us [the United States] in their political culture, they offer important lessons on how to use IT for economic development."

The Singapore experience is commendable and maybe it does have something to teach policy makers. There is more focus and efficiency along with greater potential for equity through directive policies that help ensure universal access. Universal access and other equity issues are not likely to be addressed by the marketplace, so they probably will need some government intervention if they are to be taken seriously. The biggest lesson for U.S. policy makers, however, is that synergistic partnerships between the private and public sectors are not impossible. If government leaders can unobtrusively mobilize stakeholders from both sectors to cooperate on specific projects, there could be substantial benefits.

But there are also some notable shortcomings to the planning-based approach of Singapore. There are certainly major risks in managing technology development primarily through centralized planning. Central planning and tight controls are undoubtedly necessary for major construction projects such as highway construction or the erection of a high-rise office building, where the final design and the outcome is obvious and predictable to everyone involved. But this is often not the case with information and communication technologies, where there are many unknowns and so much volatility. In these situations central planning can make one more susceptible to getting locked into the wrong technology or it could lead to the adoption of the wrong technological standard; that is, one that is eventually rejected by the marketplace.

The evolution of the Internet and adoption of technical standards are driven increasingly by market forces, not by governments or central planners. Given the rapid pace and unpredictability of technology's evolution, a top-down style of management that dictates direction and sets standards can be quite perilous.

Another advantage of privatization and the noninterventionist approach typified by the United States is that it tends to spur innovation. New content and applications, unforeseen by central planners, are more likely to emerge under this system, which encourages more diverse Internet usage. Consider the array of unplanned applications developed on the Internet such as e-mail, bulletin boards, or hypertext. It seems evident that the highest levels of private-sector innovation are found where market liberalization is in full force. Thus, there are significant advantages in allowing technology and the market to set the pace for policy.

To be sure, there are detriments and dangers entailed by the lack of a coherent infrastructure policy. Infrastructure development is more chaotic and progress in key areas is not always guaranteed. In the United States, for example, progress in unleashing broadband technology, or high speed access to the Internet, throughout the country has been disappointing. Also, the government is more at the mercy of the private sector, while cooperation appears to be a more formidable challenge. And the liberal market will probably not take steps to promote equity or help to make the goal of universal service a reality. Also, other important principles such as "open access" could be jeopardized by the private sector, which will always put its own interests first. There is no guarantee that the self-interest of private enterprise will coincide with the public interest.

But the privatization of infrastructure development and governance does not imply that the government's role is negligible. As we will see in the next chapter, the Internet was a product of government planning and guidance. The U.S. federal government invested heavily in this technology and helped foster the creation and adoption of standards like TCP/IP.

The Internet or the GII is now an essential quasi-public good, since to some degree, it satisfies the criteria of being nonrivalrous and nonexcludable (there is no additional cost in providing the good to another person and one cannot exclude others from deriving benefit from this good). And it has the same vulnerabilities as other public goods, like the physical environment. Public goods are usually neglected in the marketplace, since companies are rewarded for producing and selling private goods but not for preserving the integrity of public goods. Public goods like the Internet, therefore, need the right level of government protection and oversight. At a minimum, government must be involved to ensure open and fair access to the Internet, to maintain a level of vigorous competition, and to help ensure system interoperability. It is important, for example, that the GII is interoperable at critical interfaces, and that the United States support this objective by encouraging other countries to embrace market-driven standards. Polanyi (1944) argued that "the road to the free market was opened and kept open by . . . controlled interventionism." While the active interventionism of China and Singapore is anathema to most Americans, a philosophy of "controlled" or restrained interventionism seems suitable as a continuing basis for U.S. infrastructure policy.

COMMUNICATIONS NETWORKS AND ACCESS

Global connectivity and its associated benefits depend upon access. People must be able to make a connection to the Internet in order to take advantage of its abundant resources. Such basic access is a matter of social fairness, since being connected to the Internet is no longer a luxury. Given the high costs of computers, providing "universal service" at this point is unrealistic. But the U.S. government can fulfill a more modest goal of "equal access" by ensuring that public libraries and schools are wired so that those who cannot afford a computer will still be able to get online through these public institutions.

Aside from the issue of equal access, there is also a matter of the quality of access: Are we being connected in such a way so as to exploit the Internet's full potential? More specifically, how can governments and the private sector provide high-speed, broadband access to as many Internet users as possible? What is the optimum information connection? Given the central importance of this issue, it is instructive to consider some of the technical and policy issues surrounding the physical networks, the "pipes" that provide access, particularly since these issues will resurface in later chapters. The technology behind these physical networks is evolving rapidly. Perhaps the simplest way to understand the strategic functionality of a physical network is to consider its role in the context of a communications system. That system consists of three interdependent layers:

- Content layer: information and entertainment resources.
- Logical layer: the software, communications standards, and protocols.
- Physical layer: the telecommunications wires and fibers, computer hardware, routers, and so forth.

The physical-layer infrastructure includes the public telecommunications network that was first managed by the American Telephone and Telegraph Company (AT&T), the corporate giant founded in 1885. This company operated as a regulated monopoly until its historic dismemberment in 1984. The government refrained from breaking up this natural monopoly as long as AT&T made a good-faith effort to provide universal and affordable service throughout the country. In the 1960s and 1970s, however, the Federal Communications Commission (FCC) began to rethink AT&T's iron grip on its physical infrastructure and demanded that competing companies be allowed to interconnect with its network. AT&T's resistance led to the Department of Justice's antitrust case, which culminated in a modified final judgment whereby AT&T agreed to divest its Bell operating companies. According to the terms of the divestiture agreement, AT&T would be broken up into seven Regional Bell Operating Companies (RBOCs), such as NYNEX and US West. These RBOCs could only provide local telephone service to their regional areas. AT&T retained its long-distance service, which was now open to competition.

This cozy arrangement was in place until 1996 when the Telecommunications Act of 1996 became operative. This important piece of legislation essentially deregulated the telecommunications industry. The act allowed the RBOCs to enter the long-distance and equipment-manufacturing markets as long as they met fourteen criteria (e.g., their local markets had to be sufficiently competitive). It also allowed the long-distance carriers to enter the local telephone market, though again there were some conditions. Major long-distance companies like AT&T have so far focused on wireless and cable rather than on competing in this arena. This law encouraged more competition in local phone markets as it allowed competitive local exchange carriers (CLECs) to enter this market by leasing lines from the incumbents at wholesale prices. The act also acknowledged the universal service issue by creating the "E-rate" program, which would subsidize Internet access for schools and libraries.

The deregulation of the telecommunications industry, which became national policy thanks to this legislation, should greatly benefit consumers in the long run. The Telecommunications Act, however, had many flaws, including its broad scope and its complexity. This has necessitated more rather than less oversight by the FCC. As a result, the amount of costly litigation and regulatory decisions has steadily increased. In addition, this act paid little attention to the Internet and its unique issues. For example, there were no guidelines included about how to handle Internet services and especially Internet telephony.

There have been many changes in this dynamic industry since the Telecommunications Act was passed. The RBOCs have consolidated into four companies: SBC Communications, Verizon, Bell South, and Qwest/US West. CLECs such as NextLink have targeted medium and small businesses and have taken away 5 to 7 percent of local phone service from the Baby Bells, which have used their monopoly power to restrain the CLEC's progress by finding ways to delay switching customers to their new providers. Nonetheless, analysts predict that the CLEC's market share will rise to 25 to 30 percent in the near future (Whitman 2000). Long-distance companies such as AT&T and Sprint, on the other hand, have not fared so well. Their profits have declined and they have not yet been nimble enough to take advantage of the opportunities created by deregulation. As the Baby Bells begin to compete in the long-distance market, the deteriorating performance of the established long-distance rivals is unlikely to be reversed.

But despite this turmoil the Telecommunications Act along with President Clinton's white paper on the NII have given the country a vision for its national information infrastructure, putting in place the "right" network architecture that would support high-velocity communications and connect all of America by 2010. Like the telephone network, this network would have to be ubiquitous. But what is the right network architecture?

The current telephone network consists of copper wires that have significant limitations, such as exceedingly poor bandwidth. But in an effort to exploit their legacy infrastructure, telephone companies have promoted DSL (Digital Subscriber Lines) as a solution to the bandwidth problem. DSL provides high-speed Internet access by means of the local telephone network. DSL flows over copper telephone lines as an "always on" service that transmits bits continuously. In order for DSL to function effectively, customers cannot be located more than three miles from a telephone switch. As a result, only 60 percent of American households would be eligible for DSL services. Still, according to Romero (2000), "Because more than 95% of American homes have telephone lines, while fewer than 70% have cable television, analysts think DSL may eventually rival cable as the main way people get fast Internet access."

Nevertheless, since most U.S. households do have access to cable television services, this does provide another option for becoming a viable broadband pipe. Coaxial cable, which is currently used by the cable TV networks, has much more bandwidth than copper phone lines, but it is designed for one-way transmission of video programming. It has no reverse bandwidth capability, and it is optimized for the delivery of video services. As a result, this infrastructure is being upgraded to hybrid fiber-coax so that it can handle two-way broadband Internet access.

Another possible replacement with the most promise is fiber-optical communications, the transmission of textual data, video, and voice in the form of light over glass instead of electrons over copper. Long-distance companies have been using optical technology for a number of years, but their first-generation optical equipment cannot keep up with Internet traffic. This "fiber in the loop" technology used for upgrading the existing telephone network is different from hybrid fiber-coax for upgrading the cable network. Fiber optics offers much more bandwidth at a lower cost, and hence is preferred by many as the network of the future. The cost of bringing fiber to the home has so far been prohibitive, but that cost is coming down and telecom companies are poised to finally overcome the "last mile bottleneck." When they do, bandwidth will be plentiful even in densely populated metropolitan areas. According to Shinal (2000), "Analysts predict that optical equipment will continue to double the capacity it delivers at a given price every nine months—or twice as fast as the speed in improvements in semiconductor performance set out by Intel Corp.'s Gordon Moore [Moore's Law]."

Fiber in the loop also has advantages over hybrid fiber coax. According to Lalani (1996), "The fiber in the loop architecture terminates the fiber very close to the subscriber's home [whereas] hybrid fiber coax terminates the fiber at the neighborhood level, [and] fiber in the loop employs dedicated distribution to the subscriber, but in hybrid fiber coax architectures, distribution is shared." Finally, thanks to advances in technology the price of delivering capacity has dropped significantly. The telecom companies can employ wavelength-division multiplexing, which enables them to divide that fiber into 160 channels, with each channel able to carry as much capacity as the old single fiber.

Whatever the optimum network architecture may be, the physical layer of the infrastructure for accessing the Internet will be upgraded so that everyone can reap the benefits of high-speed broadband access. As this new infrastructure begins to take shape, policy makers must be particularly sensitive to the critical issues of open access and competitive neutrality, which would be jeopardized if one company controlled all three layers of the infrastructure. The debate over these issues came to the fore in the AOL–Time Warner merger, and we will defer a more in-depth treatment of that topic until Chapter 5. Suffice it to say at this point that we strongly support those who argue that open access to these physical infrastructures (for example, allowing competitive ISPs to interconnect to a cable network) is critical for sustaining the level of innovation that has been made possible by the Internet.

CONCLUSIONS

In this chapter we get a glimpse of the "big picture" as we begin to appreciate some of the benefits of global connectivity along with the potential social costs. Network technology seems to be a great equalizer, and many have suggested that the GII promotes democracy. But, as we have argued, there is nothing about the GII that inherently promotes democracy or any other ideology. The Net is currently an open and distributed architecture that has certainly democratized the creative process and encouraged "free trade in ideas." But it can easily be rearchitected to thwart the manifestation of such "democratic" tendencies. It would be difficult to argue that architectures that block copious amounts of information or engage in extensive covert network surveillance promote democratic values. A major concern of this book is that there are no guarantees about the future of the Internet; if it is to flourish as a technology of freedom and a universal global medium, governments will have to resist the temptation to impose upon it their own idiosyncratic rules and regulations.

We have also sought to explain and evaluate the different approaches for managing and controlling infrastructure development. These can be roughly represented on a continuum from controlled interventionism (United States) to heavy interventionism (Singapore and China). Although the latter approach seems to be more sensitive to equity issues, it runs the risk of dampening innovation along with the potential for "lock-in" to inferior technologies that are untested in the marketplace of competition. Open competition and infrastructure development in the hands of the private sector will optimize innovative applications and the creation of infrastructure technologies.

Last, we discussed the issue of access and the quality of one's connection to the Net. There are numerous possibilities for high-speed broadband access and different opinions about the optimum connection. The central policy issue is competitive access and the need to prevent all three infrastructure layers from being captured by corporate powers seeking to close the system to competitors. If the physical infrastructure becomes closed and proprietary, there will be negative consequences for the future of innovation in cyberspace.

Government must be a judicious referee and intervene only when necessary; that is, when key societal goals are being threatened. As we have argued, the state may be called upon sometimes to maintain the Internet's pro-competitive bias and to ensure that it remains an open and neutral platform where fair competition can flourish. Although we support strong government intervention for certain infrastructure issues (such as the preservation of open networks), for the most part this book is characterized by a presumption in favor of the market and self-regulation whenever possible.

What complicates all of this is the fast pace of technological change and the difficulty of knowing when and how the market's self-correcting mechanisms will work. Thus, the challenge for the state in this new millennium is to walk a fine line between premature regulation and procrastination. It must also make discrete choices about intervention, since not all government intervention is welfare enhancing. Maintaining this delicate balance will require that the state behave with prudence and restraint, which is a difficult challenge even for the most mature and well-intentioned democratic governments.

NOTE

1. This will be defined in the next chapter, which provides an overview of the Net's history and technology.

REFERENCES

Applegate, L. (1996). *Singapore Unlimited: Building the National Information Infrastructure*. Boston: Harvard Business School Publishing.

Arblaster, A. (1987). *Democracy*. Minneapolis: University of Minnesota Press.

Barlow, J. (1994). "Selling Wine Without Bottles: The Economy of Mind on the Global Net." Available: http://www.eff.org/pub/publications/John_Perry_Barlow/HTML/idea_economy_article.html

Clinton, W., and Gore, A. (1993). "National Information Infrastructure: Agenda for Action." Available: www.pub.whitehouse.gov

de Chardin, T. (1959). *The Future of Man*. New York: Harper and Row.

Fisher, W. (2000). "Digital Music." Available: http://eon.law.harvard.edu/Academic_Affairs/coursepages/tfisher/music

Friedman, T. (1999). *The Lexus and the Olive Tree*. New York: Farrar Straus Giroux.

Guernsey, L. (2001). "Welcome to the Web. Passport, Please?" *New York Times*, 15 March, E1.

Harvard Policy Group. (2000). *Eight Imperatives for Leaders in a Networked World*. Cambridge: JFK School of Government Publications.

Johnson, D. (2001). *Is the Global Information Infrastructure a Democratic Technology?* In *Readings in Cyberethics*, edited by R. Spinello and T. Tavani. Sudbury, Mass.: Jones and Bartlett.

Kahin, B. (1997). "The U.S. National Information Infrastructure Initiative: The Market, the Web, and the Virtual Project." In *National Information Infrastructures*, edited by B. Kahin and E. Wilson. Cambridge: MIT Press.

Lalani, H. (1996). "The First Hundred Feet." Available: http://ksgwww.harvard.edu/iip/doecont/lalani.html

Levander, M. (1999). "Singapore to Relax Censorship Laws as It Seeks to Expand Internet Access." *Wall Street Journal*, 1 September, A18.

Murray, A. (1999). "Trying to Make the World Safe for E-Commerce." *Wall Street Journal*, 18 December, A1.

Negroponte, N. (1995). *Being Digital*. New York: Alfred A. Knopf.

Polanyi, K. (1944). *The Great Transformation: The Political and Economic Origins of Our Time*. Boston: Beacon Press.

Romero, S. (2000). "High Technology Stew." *New York Times*, 28 December, C1.

Sachs, J. (2000). "A New Map of the World." *The Economist*, 24 June, 81–83.

Shinal, J. (2000). "At the Speed of Light." *Business Week*, 9 October, 145–152.

Simon, L. (2000). *Netpolicy.com*. Baltimore: Johns Hopkins University Press.

Whitman, J. (2000) "Battling the Bells." *Wall Street Journal*, 18 September, R17.

2

Creating and Regulating the Internet

The last chapter introduced us to the dark side of the Internet. The Internet has been called the ultimate tool of autonomy, but that autonomy is sometimes abused and social injury is the result. By now everyone is well aware of the social problems that have been engendered by this protean technology: the pervasiveness of harmful speech, the dilution of intellectual property protection, the persistence of contagious computer viruses, and the loss of privacy. The challenge is to find a way to address these problems without disrupting the Net's positive attributes.

Before reflecting upon that challenge, it is worth reviewing the highlights of the Net's development. As we shall see, we cannot separate regulatory regimes for the Internet from its technology and its underlying architectures. To understand those architectures we must appreciate the Internet's brief but eventful history.

The Internet has been aptly called an "accidental superhighway," reflecting the chaotic, decentralized, and even haphazard nature of its evolution. It is not the result of some grand design or coherent plan. Rather, the Internet as we know it today emerged from a loose confederation of networks that relied on leased telephone lines. According to Negroponte (1995), the Internet "is an example of something that has evolved with no apparent designer in charge, keeping its shape very much like a flock of ducks."

From these unremarkable and sometimes chaotic beginnings the Internet has experienced explosive international growth, especially within the last ten years. Yet the Internet's rapid growth is not completely a fluke, but a triumph of creativity and innovation. As Anderson (1995) describes this phenomenon, "If it were an economy, it would be the triumph of the free market over central planning . . . democracy over dictatorship."

The evolution of the Internet is not only a fascinating story about technical genius and ingenuity; it also offers a glimpse into the nature and complexities of the deepest controversies that surround the Net today. By reviewing the Net's history we can better comprehend the values embedded in its current architecture and how that architecture could be reconfigured. This cursory review of the Net's evolution may also help us to predict where this technology may be headed and what it might look like in the future.

The remaining portion of the chapter will be dedicated to a discussion of how the Net should be governed and regulated. We will rely heavily on the framework of Larry Lessig (1999b). His central insight is that the "code is the law"; that is, in cyberspace software architectures can have a greater regulatory impact than formal regulations. We will analyze the import and implications of Lessig's arguments. He is wary of most code-based solutions to correct the social harms in cyberspace, but we will contend that code should have a significant role to play in a responsible scheme of Internet regulation.

THE INTERNET: A HISTORICAL PERSPECTIVE

The Early Years

The origin of the Internet can be traced back to the paranoia fueled by the Cold War era in the 1950s and early 1960s. These Cold War fears led some scientists in the United States to contemplate the construction of a network that could function as a reliable and "survivable" communications medium, especially in time of a war or national emergency. The Rand Institute, a military funded research think tank, published a study "saying that this country's ability to survive a nuclear attack depended partly on the robustness of its communications system" (Miller 1996). Was it possible to make a more secure and reliable communications network in case of such a calamity?

Paul Baran and other engineers at Rand sought to find a way to make long-distance communications networks less vulnerable. The Rand study had called for a system that "was decentralized and had no single center of vulnerability" (Miller 1996). Baran proposed a design to the U.S. Defense Department that is quite similar to the current Internet architecture: a distributed network of 1,024 nodes that would carry encrypted voice and digital data; each node was a computer powered by a small generator and was connected to its closest neighbor in a string of such connections. At this point the Defense Department turned to AT&T for advice and assistance, but the idea of such a network met with strong resistance. For one thing, AT&T had always denied that its own network was vulnerable, so why should it get involved in building this new system, which was merely redundant. But as Naughton (1999) points out, "The most important reason for opposition was the simplest one, namely that AT&T's most senior engineers just did not understand what digital technology and computer-switching would mean for telecommunications in the coming decades." Jack Osterman of AT&T summarized the sentiment of the company's executives: "First it can't possibly work, and if it did, damned if we are going to allow the creation of a competitor of ourselves" (Naughton 1999). AT&T did not want to invest in a technology that might undermine its current monopoly, and so it resisted this uncommon innovation.

But Baran plunged ahead anyway, without AT&T's help, as he refined his ideas and developed a radically new system based on the principle of "distributed communications." Unlike conventional systems, a distributed system has many switching nodes and many links connected to each of those nodes such that any communication can take different paths to reach its end. In order to move data through this network, Baran developed the technique of "message switching," whereby each message is labeled with its origin and destination and is passed through the system from one node to another until it reaches that destination. Each node keeps track of the fastest route to each destination on the network. One advantage of this system is that it allows for more efficient use of the lines in the network, instead of holding one line open from one end to the other for each message.

Baran's message-switching technique ultimately evolved into "packet switching." This meant that messages could be broken up into smaller chunks (or packets) and sent across the network until they reached their ultimate destination, where they were reassembled. Packet-switching technology appealed to Baran and others at Rand because it seemed to realize the hitherto elusive goal of a "survivable communications" network. If one node was destroyed, others would still be available to move the packets along.

Coincidentally, Donald Davies, a researcher at the National Physical Laboratory near London, independently developed this same technology of packet switching. But for Davies, who was not searching for the key to a survivable network, the benefit of packet switching was that it would serve the purpose of interactive computing, since it would make optimal use of scarce network resources. Other parties cannot share telephone lines and other circuit-switched networks when two people are conversing; they require dedicated point-to-point connections during calls. Packet-switched networks, on the other hand, move data in separate chunks (or packets) based on the destination address in each packet. These packets seek out the most efficient route as circuits become available.

The first large-scale packet-switching network that was built using the insights of Baran and Davies was developed with the help of the Advanced Research Projects Agency (ARPA), a research agency of the Defense Department that financed high-technology research. In the late 1960s this agency provided generous grants to universities and corporations in order to develop a communications network between major research centers in the United States, including universities such as MIT and Stanford. It recruited Lawrence Roberts of MIT's Lincoln Laboratory to oversee the construction of the ARPANET, the first incarnation of what we know as the Internet.

This was an experimental project that put into practice the immature but promising technologies of packet switching and distributed networking. One of the challenges faced by ARPA and the team assembled by Roberts was how to connect different computers running different operating systems; that is, how to make networking functional in a heterogeneous computing environment. Some type of standard protocol network interactions would be essential to handle these incompatible systems.

In order to make this prototype network functional, Roberts and his researchers developed the strategy of *layering*. In a layered system the functions are organized hierarchically according to their "abstractness." The ARPANET would initially consist of two layers: the host and communications layers. The host would handle the user interface, while the communications protocol would handle the more abstract task of moving bits and bytes (i.e., the data) through the network using the technique of packet switching.

Once these and other conceptual hurdles were dealt with, work on the actual network was ready to begin. The basic infrastructure of the ARPANET would be simple enough: several time-sharing host computers, packet-switching interface message processors (IMPs), and leased telephone lines (with a pretty low baud rate). The host computers were already in place at the universities and research centers that would be part of the network and the telephone lines were being provided by AT&T. Thus, the main challenge was to build the IMPs. These IMPs were intermediary minicomputers that would perform key network functions such as sending and receiving data, error checking, and message routing. The interface message processors would do this by breaking up the messages into packets and adding the header information that would contain the source and destination addresses. The responsibility for building the IMPs was delegated to Bolt, Beranek, and Newman (BBN), a research and consulting firm in Cambridge, Massachusetts.

One other piece of the puzzle was the need to work out a set of conventions that would govern the exchanges between computers that were part of this fledgling network. The Network Working Group, a small group of graduate students, was charged with this task. They developed a symmetric host-to-host protocol, which eventually became known as the Network Control Protocol (NCP). This software program became the initial standard for communication on the ARPANET.

Once the NCP was written and the IMPs were delivered to sites like the Stanford Research Institute, the network itself was ready to be tested. By the end of 1971 the bugs were worked out and the ARPANET was up and running. Its debut was barely noticed by most of the world, but computer users were increasingly excited about its potential, and it was not long before its main function was reassessed and spontaneously transformed by an avid user community. The primary goal of the ARPANET was supposed to be resource sharing; that is, enabling connected sites to share hardware processing power, software, and data. But the network's users soon discovered another function: electronic mail. Instead of using the network primarily to leverage remote hardware resources, users began sending huge volumes of mail. As a result, this ad hoc application soon began to dominate traffic on the network. What was significant about the network, then, was not that it allowed researchers to use computers on other nodes but that it engaged people and encouraged a new form of human communication. It was much more than just another technology; it was a dynamic new communications medium. According to Abbate (1999), "Email laid the groundwork for creating virtual communities through the network. Increasingly, people within and outside the ARPA community would come to see the ARPANET not as a computing system but rather as a communications system."

During the 1970s, thanks to the great success of the ARPANET, new networks were developed that also relied on the technology of packet switching. These included the Alohanet, which used an Ethernet technology, and PRNET (packet radio network). The challenge now became "internetworking," allowing these networks to interact with each other. The question was what the optimal protocol was that could function even on unreliable networks such as PRNET. Was the NCP protocol up to the task?

Most researchers felt that the NCP was inadequate. At about this time, the Transmission Control Protocol (TCP) was proposed, and it eventually evolved into TCP/IP (IP stands for Internet Protocol or the network's address system). This universal protocol would now be responsible for passing packets through the network from host to host. Moreover, thanks to this universal protocol, the ARPANET was able to accommodate diverse networks with little difficulty.

From the ARPANET to the Internet

After converting the ARPANET to TCP/IP in the early 1980s, it was subdivided by the Department of Defense into two separate networks: the ARPANET and a military network known as MILNET. The MILNET was assimilated into a broader system of military networks known as the Defense Data Network. The ARPANET, now under complete civilian control, would still be used to experiment with network technologies. Furthermore, connections were developed so that users could communicate between the two networks. The interaction between these networks came to be known as the Internet.

In the late 1980s the ARPANET was showing its age and approaching obsolescence. It was decided that a replacement was necessary. This was the National Science Foundation Network (NSFNET) which relied on five supercomputers to link university and government researchers from across the world. It replaced the ARPANET as sites transferred their host connections from the ARPANET to the NSFNET. The regional networks were also connected in addition to the supercomputers, and the T1 lines, which connected these machines, became the initial Internet backbone.

At the same time, new networks were being developed. USENET, for example, was an informal network that came about thanks to a UNIX program called UUCP (Unix-to-Unix Copy) and allowed users to transfer data from one computer to another using basic modem technology. UNIX was an operating system developed by AT&T. It was not made for commercial purposes and was licensed to universities at a nominal rate. Thus, the UUCP program provided an inexpensive way for these schools to interconnect. It proved especially popular with universities that were not part of the ARPANET, and became known as the "poor man's network." This USENET network was used to create news exchanges and bulletin boards. Soon there were newsgroups forming all over this network, and it wasn't long before USENET was connecting thousands of host computers, including computer systems in Europe and other countries that had not been part of the original ARPANET.

The USENET story is significant because it represents the evolution of networking at the periphery, away from the more central and controlled approach of the ARPANET and its founders. This dynamic network was not in the hands of research scientists but of graduate students and novice computer users. The early Internet had no center of gravity, as it evolved from a research tool into a social and communications phenomenon.

Eventually, UUCP incorporated the TCP/IP protocol. In the late 1980s the NSFNET began to encompass many other lower-level networks, such as USENET and others developed by academic institutions, and gradually the Internet as we know it today, an amalgam of interconnected networks, was born. Abbate (1999) comments on the significance of this development: "This represented the convergence of two strands of network development: the users of grassroots networks adopted the Internet infrastructure, while the Internet community adopted newsgroups and other applications that had been popularized by the cooperative networks."

More and more people began to hear about the ARPANET thanks to a well-publicized security incident in 1988 know as the "Morris worm." Robert Morris, a student at Cornell University, wrote a self-replicating worm program that he unleashed on this young network. Approximately 10 percent of the systems connected to the ARPANET were overwhelmed and forced to shut down. The incident revealed the network's vulnerability and highlighted the need for effective security measures.

In 1989, shortly after the Morris worm incident, the ARPANET officially became the Internet. It had evolved into a fully operational network with over 100,000 connected computers. Because of the publicity generated by Morris's program, ordinary citizens began to hear about how this network might affect them one day.

In its earliest days, the U.S. government had generously subsidized the Internet, and as a consequence there were restrictions on any commercial use. The Internet was the exclusive domain of government researchers, the military, scientists, university professors, and others who used it primarily to share their research findings or other academic information. But in the early 1990s this all changed, as the Internet expanded beyond its traditional role as a research and educational tool. In 1994 the NSF terminated its subsidies for the Internet, commercial use exploded, and companies supplanted universities as the dominant users. At the same time e-mail providers such as MCI and CompuServe opened up e-mail gateways as this application quickly took off in almost every major corporation. Commercial use now accounts for a heavy percentage of all Internet traffic.

Finally, in 1995 the backbone of the Internet was sold to a private group of corporations, as government involvement in sustaining this network was being phased out. The privatization process went quite smoothly and the Internet passed another milestone. After several decades and a few transformations the Internet had finally come of age as a commercial and communications medium for the masses.

The global diffusion of Internet usage during this period was an extraordinary phenomenon. In 1983 there were a mere 500 computers connected to the Internet, but by 2001 there were over 100 million registered host computers connected (Internet Software Consortium 2001). It has now become a vast global "network of networks," connecting an estimated 300 million users in more than sixty countries ("Global Internet Statistics" 2001). And the more computers connected to this network, the more valuable the network becomes. According to Metcalfe's law, the power of computers on a network rises with the square of the total power of computers attached to it. Each new computer adds additional resources to the Net in a spiraling expansion of choices for all network users.

Progress in many developing countries, however, has been slow, in large part because of the poor telecommunications infrastructure. But this is gradually beginning to change, especially in countries like China. In China, for example, a fiber-optic grid has been laid across the entire country and major cities such as Beijing and Shanghai are quickly being connected through these high-capacity lines. In 1995 there were about 50,000 Internet users in China, but that number has already grown to 30 million in 2001 ("Caught in the Net" 2001). And Malaysia, following the lead of its savvy neighbors in Singapore, has also invested heavily in high-speed networks and created a "Multimedia Super Corridor" in its capital city of Putrajaya. Many experts predict that Internet penetration in the rest of the world will catch up with the United States, thereby further accelerating the forces of globalization.

The World Wide Web

The most recent surge in the Internet's popularity can be attributed to the emergence of the World Wide Web, which represents the last phase in the Internet's development. The earliest versions of the Internet interface were command driven and difficult to use. But the Web provided a more user-friendly interface that replaced commands with icons and mouse clicks. The Web now completely dominates the Internet. According to Barrett (1996), the Web is beyond any doubt a "killer application . . . that took the Internet from a relative handful of enthusiasts into the domain of serious, commercial and governmental users."

The Web is essentially a service that runs over the Internet. It was developed at the European Particle Physics Lab as a means of exchanging data about high-energy physics among physicists scattered throughout the world. Tim Berners-Lee, seeking to transmit images, data, and postscript files necessary for collaborative work in this field, developed a standard known as Hypertext Markup Language (HTML). HTML supports a procedure whereby "tags" or triggers are attached to a word or phrase that links it to another document located anywhere on the Internet. The documents created by HTML can be in a multimedia format, since they can include video, text, images, and even sound. Documents belong to a Web site that has a specific address, such as www.bc.edu. The last three letters represent a top-level domain (TLD) identification (for example, "edu" stands for education and "com" stands for a commercial enterprise), while the middle part of the name designates the actual site ("bc" stands for Boston College).

Net browsers such as Netscape's Navigator or Microsoft's Internet Explorer enable users to "explore" the Web rather effortlessly. They are highly versatile navigational tools that enable users to access, display, and print documents; they also give users the ability to link to other documents at any location on the Web. Hyperlinks can create a maze of interconnected documents and Web sites that can sometimes confuse users but also greatly expand opportunities for research and investigation.

Despite its brief history, the World Wide Web itself has already become a vast, tangled network. Web sites now proliferate throughout cyberspace at schools and universities, hospitals, corporations, and many other organizations. Even individuals and small businesses have established their own Web pages. These Web pages will undoubtedly be the vehicle for the acceleration of electronic commerce and many other network-based activities like education and fundraising. Web-based marketing is beginning to show significant results, and as a consequence ad banners and commercial messages can now be found in almost every region of cyberspace.

The plethora of Web sites has created a density of information that can make it difficult for users to locate a particular site. As a result, search engines developed by companies like Yahoo and Google began to grow in popularity. These tools applied Boolean search techniques to indexes based on HTML documents so that users could navigate the Web and locate the sites they wanted. But even search engines are sometimes ineffectual in the face of such voluminous data, sometimes returning too much or imprecise data. In addition, users are increasingly relying on the assistance of portals, which are gateways or starting points on the Web. These portals assist users in orienting themselves amid the welter of sites available on the World Wide Web. Portals such as Yahoo provide an array of services that include search functionality, categorized content, chat rooms, and access to "communities of interest." The premise of portal technology is that users should have a central point of access for all of their Web site surfing.

Regardless of the difficulties users encounter trying to navigate their way through cyberspace, the Web continues to gain in popularity. It is quickly becoming its own unique institution, taking the place of libraries, print catalogs, and even traditional news media for many users. It can be a rich source of research, news and information, and entertainment. As more and more users develop their own sites, the Web has helped to spawn a whole generation of online publishers and to generate innovative business models.

THE INTERNET'S CURRENT ARCHITECTURE

The history and general design of the Internet tells us a great deal about its present functionality and how it all works. As we have seen, there is actually little physical substance to the Internet. There are a few dedicated computers at key connection junctures, but "like a parasite, the Internet uses the multibillion dollar telephone networks as its hosts and lets them carry most of the cost" (Anderson 1995). Data are still transferred by means of the basic network protocol, TCP/IP, which allows for complete interoperability on the Internet so that computers can communicate with one another even if they have different operating systems or applications software. TCP/IP therefore makes the network virtually transparent to end users, no matter what system they are using, and it allows the Internet to function as a single, unified network.

TCP/IP consist of two pieces: The Internet Protocol establishes a unique numeric address (four numbers ranging from 0 to 255 separated by decimal points) for each system connected to the Internet. IP is a means of labeling data so that they can be sent to the proper destination in the most efficient way possible. The second piece, the Transmission Control Protocol, enables network communication over the Internet. The data are broken up into pieces called packets, with the first part of each packet containing the address where it should go. The packets are then sent by a router; that is, a server on the Internet that keeps track of Internet addresses. Packets may be sent through several different computers until they reach their ultimate destination. Once all the packets arrive the message or data will be reconstructed based on the sequence numbers in the headers to each packet.

On top of this lower layer of the Internet, which functions like its plumbing, we find the application layer. At this level there has been a proliferation of many other protocols, such as File Transfer Protocol (FTP) for transferring data files, Hyper Text Transfer Protocol (HTTP) for reading and publishing hypertext documents, and Simple Mail Transport Protocol (SMTP) for electronic mail.

The Internet's current architecture makes possible some important attributes that have some relevance for cybergovernance and deserve to be highlighted. To begin with, the Internet is *asynchronous*: Unlike telephone communication there is no need for coordination between the sender and recipient of a message. An e-mail message, for example, can be sent to a mailbox that can be accessed at any time by its owner. Second, the Internet permits *many-to-many communications* on a global scale: Many users can interact with many other users throughout the world through electronic mail, bulletin boards, Web sites, and other vehicles. Unlike traditional media, such as newspapers, the Net is interactive, since those users can speak back. Third, the Internet is a *distributed* network, relying on packet-based technology. As we have seen, it is a naturally decentralized environment. There is no center to the Internet, no central server or single controlling authority, since information can travel from one location to another without being transmitted through a central hub. This gives users more control over the flow of information. And because it is a packet-based network it is more difficult to locate and obstruct that information. The Internet is also highly *scalable*; that is, it is not directly affected when new computer links are added or deleted. Hence, it allows for much more flexible expansion or contraction than many other proprietary network technologies. Its basic architecture encourages universal access and participation.

Finally, the Internet's most distinctive feature is its *open architecture.* It is designed to maximize interoperability, to be completely independent of software programs, hardware platforms, and other technologies. Its flexible communications protocols, for example, enabled ARPANET to connect to thousands of local area networks. The Internet's open architecture is its greatest virtue since it encourages greater participation in the form of new technologies and applications that help shape and reshape the entire network.

While it is dangerous and difficult to speculate about how the Net's architecture will likely evolve, the shape of things to come is not completely obscure. The Internet's physical infrastructure is under strain due to the increased volume, and so it will need to be overhauled in the near future. In the last chapter we discussed how the physical layer was being upgraded, but it is also time for major changes to the logical layer; that is, the software protocols on which the Net is grounded. One problem is the shortage of IP addresses. This problem is resolved in a new version of the Internet Protocol known as Internet Protocol Version 6 (IPV6), an upgrade of IPV4. Version 4 supports 4 billion addresses, but IPV6 will support that number of addresses squared and squared again; the result will be more addresses than the Net needs for hundreds of years to come. Manufacturers of mobile phones have already adopted IPV6 as a standard. Switching to this new version of IP has been slow, but the use of IPV6 in these and other mobile devices should accelerate the migration process.

We are also apt to see more peer-to-peer computing on the Net, which can be concisely described as distributed file sharing. These programs enable two or more computers on the Internet to connect directly to each other so that they can communicate and share resources. The peer-to-peer movement has considerable momentum thanks to the success of grassroots systems such as Gnutella, which enable users to share digital music files. Unlike Napster, there is no central server, so it will be much more resistant to censorship. Wireless will obviously be another high-profile application: Projections are that by the end of 2002, "225 million people will use wireless services that bypass today's Web" (Ante 2001). Most of those services will provide selective bits and pieces of information on demand without relying on Web pages, which are time consuming to download. And perhaps the Net's so-called killer app, e-mail, will be rivaled by instant messaging, which is equivalent to online chatting or real-time e-mail.

The biggest wildcard in the Net's future is the growth of high-speed broadband connections and the corresponding need to scale up the network so it can handle the faster connections and the increase in data. Users are also demanding that such connections include a guaranteed level of service. According to *The Economist* ("Upgrading the Internet" 2001) this sets the stage for a showdown between "the harsh realities of economics" and the "lofty engineering ideals" that underlie the Net's original design philosophy, known as end-to-end (e2e).

THE END OF END-TO-END?

At the heart of the Internet's design is an architectural principle that was first articulated by Saltzer, Reed, and Clark in a seminal 1984 article entitled "End to End Arguments in System Design." According to the authors, the principle "suggests that functions placed at low levels of a system may be redundant or of little value when compared with the cost of providing them at that low level." In other words, the end-to-end principle suggested that application-level functionality should not be built into the low levels of the overall system; that is, into the network itself. According to Saltzer and colleagues, "The function in question can completely and correctly be implemented only with the knowledge and help of the application standing at the endpoints of the communications system." The authors believed that this type of design would have many advantages. First, it would ensure reliable and swift movement of data across this lean network. Also, by keeping the network general and free of specific functionality, it would be possible to add new applications in future years without reconstructing the network.

If a network is constructed in accordance with this end-to-end principle, intelligence in the networks is located at the ends, not in the network itself. The core of the network simply provides a data-transfer facility. This greatly enhances efficiency, but it also means that the network will be open and neutral with respect to the content it transfers. The network is dumb, and it has no idea whether it is transferring text files, photographs, or streaming video; it only knows that it needs to move packets of digital information from one destination to another.

Hence, this e2e design principle implicitly embodies certain values, such as freedom and equality: Users are free to use the network for any form of content or any type of application, and the network treats all packets equally. These values are embedded in this architectural choice. According to Lessig (2000), "What end-to-end meant was that the network was not in a position to discriminate. It was not capable of deciding which kinds of applications should run, or what forms of content should be permitted." The upshot was that this was an architectural principle that could easily foster innovation and heterogeneous applications. It could not have been foreseen at the time, but this principle of neutrality embraced in 1981 has had much to do with the Internet's remarkable evolution.

During the first stage of its existence the end-to-end design model served the Internet extremely well. But what does the future hold in store for this architectural principle? There are many pressures on e2e, and hence it may be seriously compromised in the future. Many claim that the Net's exponential expansion and increasing commercialization are incompatible with the end-to-end philosophy. Some of the pressures to move beyond end-to-end are certainly valid. For example, some functions can be handled better if they are done directly on the network and not at the ends. Technicians argue that broadband services demand that the networks be upgraded with security and "quality of service" (QOS). A network with QOS facility would supersede the simple service model now in operation known as "best-effort delivery." The problem with the best-effort approach for applications like video is that it's never clear if all the packets get sent and arrive at the same time. According to Clark and Blumenthal (2000), "A new set of applications is emerging, typified by streaming audio and video, that appear to demand a more sophisticated Internet service that can assure each data stream a specified throughput, an assurance that the best effort service cannot provide."

Without a guaranteed minimum level of performance these sophisticated applications would not be commercially feasible. One solution, which is antithetical to the end-to-end principle, is to introduce new protocols that would enable a user to initiate a connection with guaranteed quality of service. Clark and others are investigating QOS protocols that preserve some semblance of end-to-end, such as building a payment mechanism into the Internet Protocol. This may be an optimum solution, one that is acceptable to broadband providers yet still preserves key elements of end-to-end, since it would forestall the need for those providers to place limits on the services provided over their connections. Lemley and Lessig (2001) similarly argue that "we can preserve the possibility of e2e systems by keeping intelligence out of the hardware design, but building it into some software layers on an as-needed basis."

The demise of end-to-end would be tragic, but pragmatists like Clark and Blumenthal (2000) realize that some compromise, especially for QOS or for security features, may be inevitable. Many of the other pressures on the end-to-end principle come from untrustworthy or problematic communications in cyberspace. But most problems that result from lack of trust at the end points can be solved at those end points. Spam, for example, is a consequence of untrustworthy end points, since it is unwelcome and annoying behavior by one end point (the transmitter of spam). We could solve this problem in the network by embedding functionality designed to prevent spam from getting to the edges (or ends) of the network. But it is preferable to resolve problems like spam at the end points; that is, at the user's node, by means of a filter. This solution, which avoids building content-distinguishing capabilities into the network itself, will preserve the higher principle of end-to-end. Labels, filters, and metatags are some of the tools that can be used for the purpose of dealing with untrustworthiness and other externalities on the Net without involving the actual network.

The greatest threat to end-to-end, however, is most apt to come from commercial pressures, especially cable operations that bundle ISP services. If certain companies come to control all three layers of the information infrastructure (that is, the physical, logical, and content layers) there is a danger that they will close their networks to competing uses and providers. There is also a danger that content discrimination will ensue. We will elaborate on these dangers in the context of our discussion on the AOL–Time Warner merger in Chapter 5, but we tend to agree with Bar and Sandvig (2000) that there is need for "a new policy bargain between control and access, that allows non-discriminatory *ability to design* the architecture of a communication platform, not only for those who own and control network infrastructures, but also for end-users or third parties" (emphasis in original).

REGULATING THE INTERNET

The Libertarian Ethic

If anything is unarguable about the current architecture of the Net, grounded in this e2e design, it is its capacity to foster innovation. For evidence of this look at the explosion of "dot com" companies in the late 1990s, the emergence of digital music distribution models, Internet telephony, and novel business models such as online auctions. But what also fosters innovation is the absence of regulation and interference by the state. Since the Internet's great surge in popularity, much has been written about whether and how it should be regulated. Should we continue to support a philosophy of "hands off" the Internet lest we despoil this special place, or is it time for greater reliance on federal and state regulations?

It should be obvious from the previous discussion that the Internet's unique decentralized structure tends to defy centralized regulations. There is no central server that can be easily contained; there are many nodes on multiple networks, each transmitting and receiving data. Also, the Net's vast global reach, which transcends the jurisdiction of national governments, poses formidable problems for those governments that seek to impose laws on cyberspace activity. The possibilities for regulatory arbitrage are enormous. As Johnson and Post (1997) have observed, "The rise of an electronic medium that disregards geographical boundaries throws the law into disarray by creating an entirely new phenomena that need to become subject of clear legal rules but that cannot be governed, satisfactorily, by any current territorially based sovereign." Given its open structure and underlying protocols, along with its international scope, it seems logical to conclude that the Net will be an especially difficult medium to regulate.

This simple creed that the Internet is "unregulable" and will continue to thrive only if it remains unfettered by government regulations represents the core principle of *cyberspace libertarianism*. The world of cyberspace began as a libertarian utopia, the domain of academics and researchers, free of cumbersome rules and regulations imposed by the government. In the view of most cyberspace libertarians the Net should stay that way. This libertarian philosophy is idealistic, but it still exerts great influence over many of the Internet's stakeholders, who resist government intrusion into this special realm. Libertarianism is not a monolithic movement with a common value system or a coherent philosophy. We can, however, point out some of the general characteristics of this ideology that has become so entrenched among some influential segments of the online community.

In an essay in *Wired*, Jonathan Katz (1997) portrayed the emergence of a new "digital nation." He described the Internet and its community of users as a separate entity, careful to point out that this is not a political entity that should be subject to rules and regulations. Rather, its culture should be predicated on an ethos of individuality. Further, its dogma is "ingrained libertarianism, its wholehearted commitment to political and economic freedom, its fierce opposition to constraints on individual expression—from the chilling fanaticism of the politically correct to the growing movement to censor popular culture." The battle cry of the digital nation is a familiar refrain: Information wants to be free.

Libertarians who subscribe to this notion regard the Internet as an organic and powerful force that defies any forms of censorship or suppression and enriches those who seek out its various byways and tributaries. As John Gilmore has put it, "Information can take so many alternative routes when one of the nodes of the network is removed that the Net is almost immortally flexible. . . . The Net interprets censorship as damage and routes around it" (Rheingold 1993). How far this principle of free-flowing information should be extended is not completely clear. Some propose the elimination of most intellectual property laws that obviously constrain the free flow of information in cyberspace. The debate over Napster (see Chapter 7) has renewed contentions that these laws are irrelevant and outmoded in cyberspace. Information in digital form, including music and movies, cannot be easily enclosed: It is simple and inexpensive to reproduce and even easier to transmit that information across the network. Thus, the nature of the Net's content, digital information, poses yet another challenge for regulators. According to the libertarian ethic, information not only wants to be free, it *should* be free; that is, freed from the thralldom of property laws and the restrictions of censors. Hence, libertarians show implacable opposition to censorship or to government restrictions, even for harmful and offensive content on the Net.

Finally, the libertarian ideology is typified by a deep distrust and suspicion of authority, especially the authority embodied in the nation-state. Consider, for example, John Perry Barlow's (1996) observation that cyberspace "offers the promise of a new social space, global, and antisovereign, within which anybody, anywhere can express to the rest of humanity whatever he or she believes without fear. There is in these new media a foreshadowing of the intellectual and economic liberty that might undo all the authoritarian powers on the earth." The Net will in fact free us from the need to be so dependent on government. According to Boaz (1997), "One big reason that the future will be libertarian is the arrival of the Information Age . . . [which] is bad news for centralized bureaucracies. First as information gets cheaper and more widely available, people will have less need for experts and authorities to make decisions for them. . . . Second, as information and commerce move faster, it will be increasingly difficult for sluggish governments to keep up."

Hence, libertarians like Barlow and Boaz seem convinced that government regulations will be ineffectual, since the Internet will resist them. But they also believe that such regulations are inappropriate in the first place: To the extent those regulation succeed, they will only dissipate the creative energy of cyberspace. The absence of regulation combined with the nature of this technology will stimulate innovation. But it is important to underscore that libertarians do not accept that the absence of government regulation will necessarily doom cyberspace to anarchy. There has been a populist belief on the Net that ethics and enlightened self-interest will cultivate individual responsibility, and this, rather than the coercive force of government, will bring sufficient order and harmony to cyberspace.

Many are quick to point out that the libertarian perspective is too simplistic and idealistic. It seems to assume, for instance, that cyberspace is almost a separate utopia, disconnected and completely separate from the real world. Yet the Internet has indissoluble links to the worlds of government and commerce. Many libertarians seem to have forgotten that the technologies that make the Internet possible were developed with much government assistance and funding. Also, major corporations (like Cisco and AT&T) play a vital role in sustaining (at great expense) the Internet's infrastructure, while many others play a role in expanding products and services that have added such great value to the Web.

Further, libertarians seem to assume that regulation is a matter of just imposing laws. What they fail to appreciate is that there are other ways to regulate besides the law, and in order to appreciate how the Net might be subjected to other constraints beside the law, we turn to Professor Lessig's nuanced analysis.

Lessig's Paradigm

A growing number of legal scholars, such as Larry Lessig, now concur that the Net is far more "regulable" than the libertarian movement realizes or cares to admit. In his book, *Code and Other Laws of Cyberspace*, Lessig (1999a) points out that cyberspace was originally a place where people could move about and speak freely. It was a place without boundaries, unencumbered by the regulations and restrictions that typify the real world. But this anarchic and dynamic environment is changing thanks to the growing commercialization of the Web and the actions of certain governments. What could take its place is an Internet with some unattractive features: a depleted intellectual commons, pervasive hierarchical filtering, the disappearance of privacy and anonymity, and a preponderance of precarious virtual borders established by nervous sovereignties.

If there is one myth about cyberspace that Lessig seeks to expose, it is the facile assumption that the Net has a fixed and unalterable nature. According to libertarian orthodoxy, the essence of cyberspace is liberty itself. This is a place where packets of information can and should flow freely without discrimination or interference, and government should keep its hands off the Net to preserve that liberty.

But this sort of thinking assumes that the Net has some sort of irreducible nature or set of essential qualities that are independent of exogenous forces such as new technologies or the regulatory schemes of governments. Lessig argues that the Net's nature is not fixed. It is completely dependent on its underlying protocols and software architectures. The Net is no more or less than protocols, such as TCP/IP, HTTP, or SMTP (Simple Mail Transfer Protocol). The Net's properties are determined by code, which is written by programmers, and that code can be rewritten. In other words, human agents can easily rearchitect the very essence of the Net.

In order to appreciate precisely what Lessig means by "code," we must consider his analysis of how code has become the most effective regulator in cyberspace. He discusses the power of code in a broader treatment of what things regulate us. There are four distinct but interdependent constraints that regulate our behavior in the physical world: law, norms, the market, and architecture.

An example will best illustrate how these four constraints function. Consider how society attempts to deal with the problem of dangerous drugs, substances like heroin or cocaine. First, regulators and law-enforcement authorities rely on laws banning the sale and use of these drugs. These laws are supported by the threat of ex post sanctions, so if one is caught selling drugs, one will most likely be sent to jail or pay a fine. Second, the marketplace regulates the use of drugs by means of price. This is a conditional constraint imposed not ex post but immediately. If it costs $50 for a dose of cocaine, a high school student who cannot afford this amount of money will not be able to make the purchase. Drug users are also constrained by social norms imposed by the community. According to Lessig (1999a), "Those normative constraints [are] imposed not through the organized and centralized actions of the state, but through the many slight and sometimes forceful sanctions that members of a community impose on each other." There are unequivocal norms in families and communities against taking drugs, and those who do so might be punished or pressured to stop.

Finally, there is the constraint of architecture, simply the way the world is, or as architects themselves call it, "the built environment." It is a mixture of human and nonhuman constructs. Thus, architecture includes the laws of physics as well as physical constructs or technological innovations created by humans. There are countless examples of how architecture affects our life: Locked doors exclude us from certain places, the great arc of the Swiss Alps shut off the Roman empire on the north from many barbarian invaders, speed bumps slow down speeding automobiles. Unlike laws and norms, architecture is not an expression but a physical constraint imposed at the moment. In the case of illicit drugs there are architectural constraints imposed by the technologies or physical forces affecting their supply.

Each of these constraints is a "distinct modality of regulation." Each can support or oppose the others: Architecture, for example, could reinforce or undermine law; norms can also influence or support the law. Also, what differentiates the constraint of architecture from law, norms, and the market is its "self-executing" nature. People may be involved in constructing a certain architecture, but in the end it constrains immediately and directly without the mediation of another human being. The Swiss Alps impeded the progress of Hannibal and his elephants without the intervention of the Roman armies.

What does any of this have to do with the Net? Just as in real space, in cyberspace "regulations" are also a function of the interaction of these four constraints. Laws, such as those that provide copyright and patent protection, regulate behavior by prescribing or forbidding certain activities and by imposing sanctions for violators. Markets also regulate behavior in various ways: Advertisers gravitate to more popular Web sites, which enables those sites to enhance their services; also, the pricing policies of ISPs determine who gets access to the Internet and in the future those payments may determine one's level of service. And there are norms that regulate cyberspace behavior, including Internet etiquette and social customs. For instance, flaming and spamming represent violations of Net etiquette; they are considered "bad form" on the Internet and those who engage in these antisocial activities will most likely be shunned or rebuked by other members of the Internet community.

What parallels real-space architectures is described by Lessig (1999a) as "code"; that is, the programs and protocols used on the Internet, which also constrain and control activities. Lessig's recognition that this code is an instrument of social and political control is the principal insight of his book. The code writer, the software developer, emerges as the prime architect and the de facto regulator in cyberspace. And code controls or regulates more perfectly and completely than law, without loopholes and without ambiguities. According to Lessig (1999b), "The single most significant change in the politics of cyberspace is the coming of age of this simple idea: *the code is the law*" (emphasis added).

There are countless examples of how code controls our interactions on the Net. Code can limit access to certain Web sites by demanding a username and a password. Encryption code can help to protect the integrity and confidentiality of important communications. The introduction of cookie technology by Netscape has facilitated e-commerce by keeping track of transactions, but it has also compromised consumer privacy because cookies make it easier to track data about Web site visitors. Cookies are only one of several digital technologies that have been implicated in the deterioration of personal privacy. Software programs have also recently appeared that effectively filter out unsolicited commercial e-mail (or spam). Indeed, in cyberspace one could argue that we really don't need regulations about spam because the code is an efficient substitute for the law.

While the power of code is undeniable, Lessig reminds us that governments have not lost their ability to regulate by law. Law can still dictate how to behave with rules enforced by the threat of ex post sanctions. Or the function of law can be subtle and indirect when "it aims at modifying one of the other structures of constraint" (Lessig 1999a). Lessig uses the example of discrimination against the disabled to illustrate how the law operates indirectly. Besides making such discrimination illegal, government could insist on educating children about disabilities in order to change social norms, it could subsidize companies that hire the disabled (regulating the market), or it could mandate new building codes so that buildings are more accessible to the disabled (regulating architectures). In these cases, "the government is commandeering the power of another modality—another structure of constraint—to effect its own ends" (Lessig 1999a). Thus, we should not underestimate the power of law in cyberspace, which can also regulate there "indirectly" by influencing the market or by requiring the deployment of certain forms of code.

One example of this in the virtual world is the concerted efforts of the United States to regulate or control encryption code. Although U.S. policies were recently relaxed by the Clinton administration, for many years the U.S. government banned the export of strong encryption technology for fear that it would fall into the hands of terrorists or other criminals. It consistently demanded that this technology provide a back door so that law-enforcement authorities could tap into these communications if necessary. We see that while the code of cyberspace has sovereignty, it can still be decisively trumped at times by the entrenched interests and regulatory power of real sovereigns.

It seems clear then that the regulation of cyberspace goes well beyond the public-policy process of developing and imposing laws. In certain contexts cyberspace can be more effectively regulated by code than by law. But is this a positive development or is it something to be worried about? While Lessig has deep and legitimate concerns about this privatization of law, we are more sanguine that the regulatory impact of code opens up possibilities for an effective bottom-up regulatory structure in which order can be preserved without excessive government involvement. In the next chapter we will elaborate upon how this is possible and discuss other alternative models for Internet regulation.

"Norms" and Ethical Principles

My only quarrel with Lessig is that he does not pay adequate attention to ethical principles. In his presentation of the modalities of regulation, the category of norms includes customs, conventional community standards, and community-sanctioned ethical standards. But ethics, as it has been traditionally understood, goes beyond the mapping of conventions and customs. Ethical principles are enduring and transcend differences between communities and cultures. Hence, Lessig is mistaken when he lumps ethics together with the fleeting and impermanent norms of communities.

Is it really possible to identify a set of permanent core moral values? Several approaches have been suggested, but the work of John Finnis (1980, 1983), a contemporary natural law scholar, is particularly cogent and insightful. He argues that all human beings require certain premoral goods in order to achieve the ultimate end of happiness or self-fulfillment: life, knowledge, play, aesthetic experience, sociability (friendship), practical reasonableness (autonomy and authenticity), and religion. Each one of us participates in these basic goods, though we may participate in some goods more than others, and we do so in order to achieve "fullness of life." Moreover, from these core premoral goods Finnis (1980) deduces basic human rights such as "the right not to have one's life taken directly as a means to any further end; the right not to be positively lied to in any situation in which factual communication is reasonably expected"; and so forth. These basic human goods are not abstractions, but aspects of human personality. According to Finnis (1983), "Our fundamental responsibility is to respect each of those aspects in each person whose well-being we choose to affect; we never have sufficient *reason* to set aside that responsibility" (emphasis in original). In other words, we cannot let the worth of our rational projects and purposes supercede the worth of other human beings. As the German philosopher Immanuel Kant (1948) argued centuries before Finnis, our most fundamental moral obligation can be summarized in one word—*respect*—that is, respect for the needs, interests, and rights of others. Kant expressed that obligation more formally in his categorical imperative: "Act so that you treat humanity, whether in your own person or in that of another, always as an end and never as a means only."

Lessig's problem is that he fails to take into account the transcendent authority of ethical values, which are much different from culturally conditioned "norms." Individuals and organizations are moral agents, obliged to adopt the moral point of view, which is based on the principle of respect for the freedom and well-being of other human being. This moral point of view is the ultimate constraint and the most authentic grounding for the judgments we make about behavior in cyberspace. According to Midgley (1981), "Moral judgment is not a luxury, not a perverse indulgence of the self-righteous. It is a necessity. . . . Morally as well as physically, there is only one world, and we all have to live in it."

The relevance of this digression on ethics will become clearer in the next chapter. Our contention in this book is that self-regulation and self-ordering is preferable to centralized regulations and that code makes this feasible in cyberspace. But self-regulation itself can be prone to excess and must be tempered by a keen ethical awareness with sensitivity to these basic principles. Self-regulation, therefore, will not work unless it carefully and consistently takes into consideration the perspectives of others.

INTERNET GOVERNANCE

Although there are sharp disagreements on how the Internet should be regulated, there is consensus that it requires some type of governance and technical coordination. There must be some governing bodies that handle mundane matters, such as the setting of technical standards and the management of domain names and IP addresses. Two major policy groups that provide such governance are the World Wide Web Consortium, an international standards-setting body, and the Internet Engineering Task Force (IETF), which develops technical standards such as communications protocols. Both the IETF and the World Wide Web Consortium aspire to democratic ideals: They give all voices a hearing as they try to gauge consensus on key issues before making decisions. Anyone can propose a new standard to the IETF and thereby initiate a process that gives that proposal a full hearing.

The Domain Name System (DNS) also needs coordination. This system was formerly administered by a small private company called Network Solutions International (NSI); NSI charged $50 for the registration of a domain name and usually awarded the name on a first-come, first-served basis. The DNS maps the domain names of organizations, such as www.eBay.com, to the actual numeric Internet Protocol address. As the Internet grew in importance, stakeholders became more vocal about their disenchantment with the NSI arrangement. They believed that the authority to allocate domain names should not remain with a private company. As a result, the domain name system is now managed by the Internet Corporation for Assigned Names and Numbers (ICANN). The proposal for ICANN, initiated by Jon Postel, who developed the original DNS, was elaborated upon in a Commerce Department white paper published in May 1998. According to that white paper, the United States would enter into an agreement with ICANN to "coordinate the technical management of the Internet's domain name system, the allocation of IP address space, the assignment of protocol parameters, and the management of the root server system."

ICANN is an international nonprofit organization and it now has full responsibility for the coordination of the Domain Name System. ICANN has acted swiftly to deal with the issue of cybersquatting and other domain name disputes. In October 1999 it established the Uniform Dispute Resolution Policy for adjudicating such disputes (this is discussed in more detail in Chapter 7 on intellectual property). More recently, it has decided to create several new top level domains, such as aero, coop, biz, museum, and info. The implementation of these TLDs will undoubtedly trigger some contentious trademark disputes, but it will also relieve the burden on the existing TLDs. ICANN operates with at-large membership and three supporting organizations that deal with addresses, domain names, and protocol support. It is governed by a board of eighteen directors, nine of whom are elected by the at-large members through an electronic voting process. The remaining board members are appointed by the supporting organizations.

The governance model exemplified by ICANN has sparked some controversy. Skeptics say that ICANN is just a pawn of industry interests and that it is susceptible to capture. Also, the white paper calls for ICANN to be a representative body. But can it really represent all of the Internet's stakeholders and elicit agreement on controversial issues? Can its board be representative of the entire worldwide Internet community? Like the IETF, ICANN tries to operate by consensus, and the responsibility of ICANN's board is to ratify that consensus. It will probably always be difficult for ICANN to gauge the consensus of such a large and diverse group of stakeholders, though the use of online deliberative polls or online elections may help in this regard. According to Castells (2001), "The romantic vision of a global Internet community self-representing itself by electronic voting has to be tempered with the reality of lobbying, powerful support networks, and name recognition in favor of certain candidates."

ICANN's procedures for due process are also open to some criticism because there are too many mechanisms for appeals to review boards or constituency working groups. According to Zittrain (1999), there is "more process rather than less, without an overall sense of unifying structure." These due process procedures, therefore, seem to need some streamlining.

And there are broader questions about the source of ICANN's authority and its sources for future funding. Of course, ICANN does not have the same legitimacy as a democratic government; it is also hobbled because it is regarded as a uniquely American rather than an international organization. ICANN needs enhanced legitimacy, and perhaps this can be accomplished if its board members are more representative of the Internet community. But it should be remarked that ICANN has done some things right. It is to be praised for its open proceedings and deliberations: It posts full transcripts of all board meetings and even its telephone conferences. Last, we should bear in mind that ICANN is a young institution, and it deserves to be given a chance to manage the DNS and perhaps to serve as a model of Internet governance for the future.

THE FUTURE OF THE NET

We have seen in these two chapters that because of its plasticity and lack of substance it is naïve to assume that the Internet of today will necessarily be the Internet of tomorrow. The architectures of cyberspace could conceivably undergo a major transformation in the next few years. In particular, there is a danger that the Net can change from an open and borderless environment to one where there are tighter controls and an abundance of virtual fences. Moreover, as the Internet continues to become more commercialized, there will be enormous pressures for new protocols that conflict with its original design principle.

Can we prevent the slow transformation of the Net that is sought by some in the commercial sector? What's the right role for government in this impending conflict? How can we regulate and organize the digital frontier without destroying the special qualities of this place? Before we answer these questions we must explicitly identify those qualities and attempt to articulate a unifying vision of cyberspace that can guide our reflections and ultimately guide our policy choices.

As we saw in Chapter 1, the Net has many positive attributes, such as its ability to facilitate "free trade in ideas" and its potential for the expression of civil rights. But there are social harms and negative by-products as well: unwanted and offending forms of speech like spam and hate speech, privacy erosion, fragile protections for intellectual property, and so on. The challenge is to deal with these social harms reasonably and efficiently without impairing the integrity of the Net and without strangling it in oppressive regulations.

As we ponder our aspirations for the future of the Internet we must remind ourselves of the changes this technology has wrought in such a short time. The Net, as we have observed, has been an engine of innovation and creativity. It has become a vast repository of valuable information and a provider of instant communication. More important, it has decentralized the process of creativity and innovation. The Net enables entrepreneurial individuals with little capital to develop their own online businesses or start-up firms that are often in the forefront of digital innovations. It also enables artists, writers, musicians, and filmmakers to disseminate their work to a worldwide audience at minimal cost, thereby making culture more accessible for everyone. This decentralization is especially important in an economy where creativity and innovation have become the new elixirs of economic growth. According to Mandel and Hof (2001), the Internet has the potential "to boost the rate of innovation by increasing the speed at which ideas spread between companies, within economies, and across countries."

The Net has also been a place that has supported civil liberties, such as the right to anonymous free speech. It has promoted democratic values and given disenfranchised groups a chance to participate more fully in public debate and discussion. Recall the Supreme Court's observation that the Internet has created "a new marketplace of ideas." Finally, that marketplace of ideas has breadth and depth because of the Net's global reach. It is a universal medium that transcends physical boundaries.

In order to preserve this unique environment, we must be careful not to overwhelm the Net with regulations or yield to the impulses of local sovereignties. More specifically, we must safeguard the intellectual commons and eschew intellectual property protection that is too strong or too inclusive. If we enclose "ideas" by interfering with their diffusion by law or by code, the Net's capacity to spur innovation will be greatly impaired. Excessive enclosure can also lead to the dissipation of creativity or to its concentration in the hands of a select group of content providers. We must avoid cumbersome content regulations that would interfere with the Net's great capacity to promote and circulate new ideas. We must also sustain a level playing field for new commercial enterprises so that they will have the opportunity to compete against more mature businesses like Amazon.com, eBay, or Yahoo. Finally, the Net must remain a global universal medium. There would be something tragic about a fragmented Net that became mired in virtual borders and online restrictions where the net effect is that everybody is really not connected to everybody else. If we want to preserve a universal and global Net, we must guard against problematic changes in architecture or enforcement of laws that depart from this basic vision.

At a more abstract level, we can begin to discern the deepest values and underlying utilities of the Net: freedom of expression, empowerment of individual users, catalyst for innovation, and competitive neutrality and openness. According to Clark and Blumenthal (2000), these values constitute the Internet's "philosophy," and they suggest that the end-to-end arguments "fostered that philosophy because they enabled freedom to innovate, install new software at will, and run applications of the user's choice." But it is becoming increasingly difficult to sustain this simple philosophy, which often clashes with economic and social realities.

Also, what should be done about those social harms and network improprieties that interfere with this philosophy by undermining trust? If we leave the Net alone it could be overwhelmed by the harms that tend to polarize and disrupt the Net. Like other public or quasi-public goods, the Net is susceptible to a tragedy of the commons whereby individual actions, harmless in isolation, combine to damage the Internet's fragile ecology. But if we regulate these problems, such as various forms of harmful speech, we put curbs on freedoms and introduce restrictive controls that can cause havoc.

The solution favored by some libertarians is to ignore harmful speech and other manifestations of untrustworthiness. Some observe that problems such as harmful speech are often only in the eye of the beholder, and should be tolerated as long as the government keeps its hands off the Net. Others worry that in our zeal to deal with these social harms we will curtail them but cause negative political effects in the process. But the social and moral problems of cyberspace, such as pornography and spam, should not simply be ignored. They should be addressed prudentially and with sensitivity to human rights and moral values. There is a way to responsibly handle these problems without fatally undermining the most attractive qualities of the Net.

The option we propose is to put an emphasis on the use of technologies or code as a means for dealing with those by-products. These technologies would be implemented "downstream" by individuals and organizations seeking to protect themselves from untrustworthy endpoints elsewhere on the network. If these technologies are designed and implemented responsibly, they can contain some of the social harms in cyberspace without the need for an extensive regime of government regulations. Like all solutions, this one is imperfect. But, as we will argue in the remaining chapters of this book, ethical self-regulation is at least a path worth exploring and may be the optimal solution that maximizes social welfare. In this context self-regulation implies not only self-discipline but self-determination, allowing users and organizations to decide what is harmful and to take remedial action with the assistance of code, such as filters and firewalls.

REFERENCES

Abbate, J. (1999). *Inventing the Internet.* Cambridge: MIT Press.

Anderson, J. (1995). "The Accidental Superhighway." *The Economist,* 1 July, 4.

Ante, S. (2001). "In Search of the Net's Next Big Thing." *Business Week*, 26 March, 140–141.

Bar, F., and Sandvig, C. (2000). "Rules from Truth: Post Convergence Policy for Access." Working paper, University of California at Berkeley.

Barlow, J. (1996). "Thinking Locally, Acting Globally." *Cyber-Rights Electronic List*, 15 January.

Barrett, N. (1996). *The State of the Cybernation.* London: Kogan Page.
Boaz, D. (1997). *Libertarianism: A Primer.* New York: Free Press.
Castells, M. (2001). *The Internet Galaxy.* New York: Oxford University Press.
"Caught in the Net." (2001). *The Economist*, 24 March, 26.
Clark, D., and Blumenthal, M. (2000). "Rethinking the Design of the Internet: The End to End Argument vs. the Brave New World." *TPRC*, August, 19–35.
Commerce Department. (1998). "Management of Internet Names and Addresses." 63 Fed. Reg. 31. Available: http://www.icann.org/generla/white-paper-05jun.98.htm
Finnis, J. (1980). *Natural Law and Natural Rights.* London: Oxford University Press.
Finnis, J. (1983). *Fundamentals of Ethics.* Washington, D.C.: Georgetown University Press.
"Global Internet Statistics." (2001). Available http://www.glreach.com/globstats
Internet Software Consortium. (2001). "Internet Domain Survey." Available http://www.isc.org/ds
Johnson, D., and Post, D. (1997). "The Rise of Law on the Global Network." In *Borders in Cyberspace* edited by B. Kahin and C. Nesson. Cambridge: MIT Press.
Kant, I. (1948). *Groundwork of the Metaphysic of Morals.* Translated by H. Paton. London: Hutchinson University Library.
Katz, J. (1997). "Birth of the Digital Nation." *Wired*, April, 49–52.
Lemley, M., and Lessig, L. (2001). "The End of End-to-End: Preserving the Architecture of the Internet in the Broadband Era." *UCLA Law Review* 48: 925.
Lessig, L. (1999a). *Code and Other Laws of Cyberspace.* New York: Basic Books.
Lessig, L. (1999b). "The Code Is Law." *The Industry Standard*, 19–26 April, 18.
Lessig, L. (2000). "Cyberspace's Architectural Constitution." Lecture delivered at www9, Amsterdam, The Netherlands.
Mandel, M., and Hof, R. (2001). "Rethinking the Internet." *Business Week*, 26 March, 116–141.
Midgley, M. (1981). *Heart and Mind.* New York: St. Martin's Press.
Miller, S. (1996). *Civilizing Cyberspace.* New York: ACM Press.
Naughton, J. (1999). *A Brief History of the Future.* New York: Overlook Press.
Negroponte, N. (1995). *Being Digital.* New York: Alfred A. Knopf.
Rheingold, H. (1993). *The Virtual Community: Homesteading on the Electronic Frontier.* Reading, Mass.: Addison-Wesley.
Saltzer, J., Reed, D., and Clark, D. (1984). "End to End Arguments in System Design." *ACM Transactions on Computer Systems* 2: 277–288.
"Upgrading the Internet." (2001). *The Economist*, March, 32–36.
Zittrain, J. (1999). "ICANN: Between the Public and the Private." Comments before the Subcommittee on Investigations and Oversight of the House Commerce Committee, July.

3

Decentralizing Regulation

Our limited experience of the new economy has given us a glimpse into the novel market failures we can expect as electronic commerce and online interactions become more widespread. The most typical market failure is an externality (or "spillover"), which involves costs borne involuntarily by society that are not reflected in the price of the good whose production has generated those costs. According to Coase (1960), these externalities or social costs are the result of the "actions of business firms which have harmful effects on others." Some of the social harms we have been discussing can be viewed from this perspective; that is, as harmful by-products of certain Internet transactions. Clearly, the erosion of privacy that may ensue when information is exchanged between two parties or the transmission of disruptive forms of speech like spam would fall into this category. According to some economists (Arrow 1962), there are even social costs entailed in the enforcement of intellectual property rights; that is, the cost to society of losing access to the proprietary information that is protected.

The ubiquitous nature of externalities suggests the high cost levels that must be anticipated if regulatory remedies are consistently imposed by the government. Hence, there has been an intense and ideological debate about the optimal means of rectifying market failures such as externalities. As more economic activity shifts to cyberspace, so too will the focus of that debate. Is there something qualitatively different about cyberspace that would enable us to handle these externalities in a different manner? Can the market be a more effective constraint in this virtual world, or do we still need big doses of government intervention?

In this chapter we will carefully examine whether these market failures should be left to the marketplace, which will eventually effect some resolution and impose its own discipline on the disorder of the Net, or if the answer should come from carefully crafted policies and laws that curb excesses and require companies to internalize the costs of the externalities they cause. In Lessig's (1999) terms, should it be the market or the law that functions as the primary constraint? We will argue that both of these approaches are problematic.

It is dangerous to rely exclusively on market forces in any context, and reliance on the regulatory apparatus of government becomes more difficult and challenging in the context of a global technology without boundaries such as the Internet. Instead, we will argue that ethical self-regulation is a far more efficacious approach, which will preserve individual choice while still engendering social order and protecting the Net as a public good. What makes self-regulation feasible in the context of cyberspace is the power of software code, tools like filters and tags that allow users to protect and order their virtual environments as they see fit. Sometimes, however, code works too perfectly and can cause its own harmful effects, so it must be used circumspectly. We will offer some principles that delineate how code should be deployed and developed in a prudent manner. Only the prudential use of code will help to mitigate the distorting effects of code-based solutions to market failures and thereby yield a welfare-enhancing result.

THE INVISIBLE HAND

In the virtual world as well as the physical one, market failures and imperfections are inevitable. But how should we address these failures? What are we to do about injurious speech like spam or the assault on personal privacy? One possibility is to turn to the market for relief. We can be patient and wait for the "invisible hand" of the market to unleash its self-correcting mechanisms. Free-market enthusiasts and even some cyber libertarians argue that the market will bring about the most efficient use of economic resources in the long run, which, in their view, is the socially optimal result.

A corollary of this free-market ideal is the belief that the right level of social and ethical responsibility is programmed into the marketplace. If corporations mistreat employees, infringe on consumers' privacy rights, or produce unsafe products, they will be punished in the marketplace. Adam Smith, Milton Friedman, and other free-market economists implicitly embrace this viewpoint. Friedman (1970) has contended that "in a free society, there is one and only one social responsibility of business—to use its resources and engage in activities designed to increase its profits so long as it stays within the rules of the game." It's not safe to stray from market forces even when social issues are at stake.

In European countries this philosophy is often described as "liberalization" because of its focus on keeping markets free from regulatory constraints. Advocates of liberalization, for example, contend that commercial freedom must take priority over consumer rights. The underlying assumptions of liberalization are well summarized by Venturelli (1997): "The basis of the liberal model, by contrast, is the argument that modern market societies require little or no political–legal intervention, thereby creating a favorable climate for capital investment and private innovation through which social needs will be automatically and naturally addressed."

However, while the market can bring about some progress in eliminating certain imperfections, it is not the best forum for encouraging attentiveness to noneconomic values such as privacy or free-speech rights. The history of capitalism has demonstrated that a hypercompetitive marketplace does not include the necessary mechanisms for compelling organizations to focus their energies on moral and social issues. Markets reward the efficient production of private goods, but they rarely reward firms for preserving the integrity of public goods such as the natural environment, the intellectual commons, or the information infrastructure. Corporations have often been oblivious to "social costs" in real space and there is no reason to think that this will change in cyberspace. Certain forms of e-mail marketing entail such costs, but that has not stopped some companies from exploiting this marketing strategy. To be sure, there are market pressures for companies to avoid significant ethical lapses and untoward behavior and to respect the concerns and interests of their customers. But as Goodpaster (1984) writes, "The pressures on the other side are also significant, pressures for single-minded pursuit of profits and even for relatively short-term gains that run rough-shod over moral convictions."

Thus, as many economists have argued with some insistence, economic actors do not have the discipline to transcend their own self-interest and to work out welfare-enhancing arrangements that handle these social costs. Many economic actors in cyberspace have no problem selling data collected about consumers without notifying those consumers or even considering the impact on their privacy. These negative third-party effects represent an imperfect functioning of the market. Economists like Pigou (1962) firmly reject the viability of market-based solutions to these externality problems: "No 'invisible hand' can be relied upon to produce a good arrangement of the whole from a combination of separate treatments of the parts. It is, therefore, necessary that an authority of wider reach should intervene and should tackle [society's] collective problems." The marketplace will always function as an important constraint on behavior, and it will have some role to play in resolving social problems. But the liberal market approach cannot be consistently effective in addressing negative externalities, and it cannot be relied upon to produce a fair outcome without assistance or guidance from other sources.

The market constraint, therefore, should not take priority over other regulatory forces such as law, norms, and code.

THE VISIBLE HAND

As an alternative, Pigou (1962) and others advocate greater reliance on the "visible hand" of government. The coercive force of law will be used to secure values such as privacy rights, fair competition, or protection from unwanted forms of speech. In this case we ask policy makers to intervene and correct the market failure or to force the internalization of social costs imposed on others. The implication is that many corporations are loath to fix these problems themselves, since their performance would be negatively impacted by such corrective action. Hence the need for legal sanctions that will curtail social harms and force recognition of basic values (such as privacy).

One example of a visible hand approach is what Venturelli (1997) calls the "public service" model, which has become popular among some European countries like France. This model represents a major departure from the assumptions of market liberalization. According to Venturelli, "The public service model requires that the central principle of modern free societies comprises not merely the rights of private investors, competitors, and the functioning of the communications market, but also the rights of citizens to comprehensive information services and access to the communications network." This public service model not only mandates universal service but also requires consumer protection through laws that will restrict certain forms of offensive content and protect consumer privacy. This model presumes the existence of the beneficent state controlling the economy.

For an example of this approach that relies heavily on the visible hand of government to protect its citizens, we need look no further than the comprehensive privacy laws that have been formulated throughout most of Europe. The European Union Directive gives citizens significant rights to access, correct, and withhold the transfer of their personalized information. Prior to the enactment of this directive, many European countries were proactive about privacy protection. Sweden, for example, enacted the world's first data-protection legislation in its 1973 Data Act, which was designed to prevent "undue encroachment on personal privacy" (Paine 1992).

Also, many scholars and jurists in the United States favor a robust regime of government regulation, since without such regulation derived from the democratic collective, laws will be privatized and democratic values will be compromised in the process. Collective decision making, they argue, will do a better job of protecting these values (privacy, free speech, due process) than the marketplace. According to Lessig (1999) there are many choices to be made about cyberspace, and "some of these choices are collective—about how we will collectively live in this space." The purpose of government is to make these collective decisions through a deliberative and democratic process. As Post (2000) summarizes Lessig's position, "Contra the Net libertarians, we need more, not less, government in cyberspace if those collective values are to prevail."

While there are clear benefits to deferring to this visible hand, there are also some liabilities with this approach. There is always the risk that vested economic interests will capture policy makers and persuade them to develop policies that are inconsistent with the public good. There is little guarantee that regulators will act in the public interest, especially as they come to view the issues of the industries that they regulate in those industry's terms. Government regulators are also self-interested, and hence government lacks the impersonal nature of the market, which at least on some occasions can channel self-interest to the public good. And bureaucratic regulatory agencies have repeatedly demonstrated a tendency to be wasteful and grossly inefficient. One reason for this is the result of their more centralized decision-making style. According to Coase (1962), "The attempt to control everything from the center is liable to lead to paralysis." Citizens begin to feel powerless in the face of a highly centralized political bureaucracy. As Taylor (1992) remarks, "The operation of the market and the bureaucratic state . . . favor an atomist and instrumentalist stance to the world." The more we regulate and create necessary enforcement mechanisms for those regulations, the more dominant and burdensome that bureaucracy becomes. Bureaucracies tend to concentrate power as they extend their control. This makes people even more alienated from the public sphere, and it reinforces those feelings of impotence that contribute to political paralysis.

Moreover, it is even more difficult for the state to exercise its power in cyberspace. For example, the threat of regulatory arbitrage is greatly magnified there, since jurisdictional issues are so complex and companies can move from one jurisdiction to another by simply switching the location of their servers. The global Internet cannot be easily governed by the traditional practices of local sovereignties. The German and French governments can legislate against the dissemination of hate speech in their respective countries, but it is not so easy for them to exercise jurisdiction over purveyors of hate speech located in the United States, even though they have attempted to do just that in several recent cases.

Furthermore, what the "Pigouvian" approach fails to adequately consider are the high transaction costs associated with government regulation. Taxation, strategic subsidies, or other regulations may not yield the most efficient solution in all situations where there are harmful effects triggered by market transactions. Governments do not function without costs, and the costs of imposing certain regulations may sometimes outweigh the benefits. For instance, it is obviously quite expensive for Sweden to carry out its extensive regime of privacy regulations. The country has had to establish a bureaucratic infrastructure to enforce the act. This includes a Data Inspection Board, which licenses and controls the owners of databases with personal information. These costs of enforcement and compliance are a burden on the taxpayers and probably on the growth of online commerce and innovation in Sweden. This is not to suggest that the problem of privacy should be ignored, but only that there may be a more optimal solution that minimizes costs.

In addition, law is reactive and slow, especially in the face of rapidly changing technologies. It is often incomplete and vague, formulated quickly to "fix" a problem of public concern that has caught the public's attention. For evidence of this we need only consider the hastily crafted U.S. Communications Decency Act (CDA) of 1996, which was quite vague and in clear violation of the First Amendment. As Stone (1975) writes, the solution to this vagueness is more precision, "but once we have unleashed the regulators to make finer and finer regulations, the regulations become an end in themselves, a cumbersome, frustrating and pointless web for those they entangle." Thus, while law too has a significant role to play in resolving market failures, it is certainly not a panacea. We surely should not abolish government's regulatory role in cyberspace, but we should avoid excessive regulation and give the Net's stakeholders a chance to responsibly correct some of the Net's market failures without external assistance, as long as they have the tools to accomplish such a task.

THE THIRD WAY: DECENTRALIZATION AND SELF-ORGANIZATION

Despite the notable shortcomings of government regulation, many economists and ethicists still embrace the Pigouvain philosophy and the primacy of government resolution of externality problems. Other economists, however, such as Ronald Coase and his followers, question the wisdom of such heavy reliance on the visible hand. Coase has argued that this simplistic approach often ignores the reciprocal nature of externalities. For example, in the case of noise pollution an externality exists because of the polluter and those in the vicinity who hear the noise. We cannot necessarily conclude that A is harming B, since if B were not present there would be no harm. According to Coase (1960), "The real question that has to be decided is: should A be allowed to harm B or should B be allowed to harm A? The problem is to avoid the more serious harm." Coase is echoing the work of Hohfeld (1913), who recognized that in these conflict situations both A and B have a set of interests, and those interests that are considered "rights" are protected by the state.

The Coase theorem argues that in the absence of transaction costs (the costs of coordinating and bringing together the affected parties, negotiating contracts, etc.) the preferred solution to externalities when rights are properly assigned is to allow the relevant parties to negotiate a private arrangement. According to Coase (1960),

> It is necessary to know whether the damaging business is liable or not for damage caused since without the establishment of this initial delimitation of rights there can be no market transactions to transfer and recombine them. But the ultimate result (which maximizes the value of production) is independent of the legal position if the pricing system is assumed to work without cost.

Quite simply, when rights are specified and there are no costs to using the pricing system, private parties can work out arrangements that maximize the value of output. In the pollution example, if the factory has the right to pollute, then its neighbors can pay the factory not to pollute; and if the neighbors have a right to unpolluted air, the factory can pay them a fee for waiving that right. In either case, a deal is made that leads to the optimal level of output for society.

Of course, in most cases it is impossible to work out such a deal due to the high transaction costs of negotiating a settlement and enforcing the results. When these transaction costs are substantial, social efficiency is unlikely to be realized by means of private arrangements. Under these circumstances, government intervention through some type of regulatory mechanisms may be the only solution.

The Coase theorem is controversial and this is not the place to debate its strengths and deficiencies. Regardless of its shortcomings, there seem to be some key insights here that have some relevance for regulating externalities in cyberspace. First, Coase's insight regarding the reciprocal nature of externalities is apposite. Harmful effects like pollution are not pure evil but the by-products of valuable actions; that is, the production of certain goods that society needs. The problem with the perspective of economists like Pigou is that it compels only one party, the source of the harmful effect, to take that harmful effect into account. But we must consider both sides of this question—that is, whether the cost to society of generating the harmful effect is worth the benefits received—and determine the least costly remedy. For example, in cyberspace the loss of privacy is an externality. When consumers provide information to a commercial Web site, that information is sometimes sold to a third party. There are obvious economic benefits in this transaction, but there is also a social cost (the loss of privacy) for the consumer whose information has been sold. Do the discrete economic benefits outweigh the costs? If we assume that information is a factor of production, we can consider whether producers have the right to generate these harmful effects (loss of privacy) in their "production" process. In cases like this we must come to terms with the reciprocal nature of the problem and appreciate that both parties need to be taken into account in effecting a resolution.

Second, we must not jump to the conclusion that government intervention is the optimal solution, since there may be a less costly way of solving the problem. Government regulations generate positive transaction costs, and we need to carefully evaluate the effects of taxes, regulations, and enforcement, and "attempt to decide whether the new situation would be, in total, better or worse than the original one" (Coase 1960). The operative principle is that the presence of a market failure does not necessarily imply a welfare-enhancing government solution.

Third, when the transaction costs of working out a mutually agreeable deal are low, a private arrangement may be more efficient than turning to the government for a solution. In this context, privatization has the potential to maximize social welfare, which should not be narrowly understood in terms of output maximization. Social welfare is more than a function of the value of output produced by society. Rather, social welfare should be regarded more broadly as the aggregate well-being of society's members and that well-being involves things other than economic output (Medema 1993; Veljanovski 1981).

Externalities abound in cyberspace, just as they do in the physical world. But the possibility of working out private solutions, the equivalent of negotiated deals in the physical world, is much greater in cyberspace. The reason for this is that Internet users are far more empowered than their counterparts in the real world to resolve these social costs independently, without the need of government regulation. The big difference is software code, which can embody rules and other mechanisms that protect users from harmful effects. As Lessig (1999) reminds us, the most potent regulatory force in cyberspace is not the market or the law, but code (i.e., the protocols and software programs that comprise the architecture of the Internet). Recall Lessig's essential insight: The code is the law. For example, users and organizations have at their disposal many software tools to control and regulate their environment: filters for unwanted speech, rights management systems for intellectual property protection, encryption software to help ensure confidential communications, and even technologies that make it easier to compare the privacy policies on Web sites with one's privacy preferences. There is also copious "metainformation" in the form of labels and tags that concisely describe a Web site's main attributes so that users can avoid troublesome sites or deflect unwanted junk mail.

Consider the asymmetries between the physical world and the virtual one. If a steel mill pollutes the environment and affects 1 million people in its environs, there is no way for the mill to negotiate a private agreement with each of these individuals. Unless government gets involved as a proxy acting on their behalf, they are impotent to do anything about this pollution (short of taking drastic measures like moving far away from the plant). But in cyberspace many problems like pornography or other forms of unwanted speech can be handled expeditiously by individuals who can simply choose to install a filter. Thanks to code, it may be possible to prevent young children from looking at pornography without the high transaction costs of negotiating a "settlement" that make government intervention inevitable. Software code, therefore, alters the regulatory landscape and enables more externalities in cyberspace to be remedied in a cost-effective way by private parties.

Let us turn to an example of how this privatization and "implicit deal making" might work with the help of code. When *Penthouse* magazine creates its Web site, penthouse.com, it is exercising its free speech rights and creating something of a certain economic value. There is, however, a serious harmful by-product or externality. The site's indecent material is legally acceptable for mature adults, but that material might also be viewed by young, impressionable children. Congress was justifiably concerned about this and passed the Communications Decency Act, which made it illegal to transmit indecent material to minors. Users would need to show an ID before entering penthouse.com, but how could such an ID be authenticated? The Supreme Court ruled that the CDA was unconstitutional: The state had a compelling interest in protecting children but could not do so in a way that interfered with the rights of adults and of *Penthouse*. The more efficient solution, which respects penthouse.com's right to speech and the rights of adults to view this material while still dealing with the harmful by-product of minors' accessibility, appears to be the private use of filters. The responsible use of filters (or an equivalent technology) by parents or schools protects children, but at the same time adults are not prevented from viewing the site. Reliance on code then would appear to be an optimum solution when all costs and benefits are evaluated. Filters are inexpensive and reasonably effective. This is by no means a perfect solution, since the use of filters does have its drawbacks. But it seems preferable to more costly alternatives that fail to consider the reciprocal nature of the externality involved here and that put too much of the burden on the source of this indecent speech.

There are other benefits to privatization. As Clark and Blumenthal (2000) have argued, the resolution of problems like spam or pornography at the endpoints also has the added virtue of helping to sustain the end-to-end philosophy. "End node modification" by means of filters or the use of labeling schemes (such as PICS, Platform Internet Content Selection, a protocol that will be discussed in Chapter 6) can be used to efficiently control access to pornography by minors. This makes the network more reliable, safe, and trustworthy, without disrupting end-to-end design.

Thanks to code and its ability to provide users with an adequate level of self-protection, we argue that this third alternative of self-regulation has much more viability. According to this model, the primary burden of regulating the Net falls on its diverse stakeholders, assuming, of course, that rights like speech are reasonably well-defined and clearly assigned. For example, companies might have the free-speech right to send unsolicited e-mail (or spam), but recipients can respond to this nuisance accordingly, without the intervention of the regulatory authorities. This model encourages both self-restraint and self-determination. Users refrain from harmful conduct and make their own decisions about how to handle the harmful conduct of others.

We certainly do not suggest that government intervention is always inappropriate or that it is always an ineffectual solution for externalities and other market failures. It may be necessary, for example, for government to safeguard the confidentiality of highly sensitive information, such as one's medical history. The preservation of medical privacy may be too important a responsibility to be delegated to individual users. And in certain areas where individuals are impotent in the face of corporate power, government intervention will also be essential. We have already argued that government must be responsible for keeping access open on the Net and preserving fair competition. Hence, in our estimation, it was perfectly legitimate for the U.S. government to insist that AOL–Time Warner provide access to other ISPs for their cable systems. The Internet has been an innovative force because it is a neutral and competitive network, and any efforts by cable-owned ISPs to make it a more closed or proprietary environment should be viewed with suspicion. Moreover, antitrust law also continues to be relevant in the digital age so that dominant companies like Microsoft do not engulf the Net.

However, government regulations in other areas like speech or consumer privacy should only be invoked when truly necessary; that is, when privatized solutions cannot work due to the high transactions costs of negotiating an agreement or other overriding factors. Also, if regulations are imposed they should be "predictable, minimalist, consistent, and simple" (Clinton and Gore 1997). Aside from minimizing overall transaction costs, such a decentralized regulatory scheme with minimal government intervention is preferable for several reasons. First, it will continue to allow the Net to realize its potential as a liberating technology. The more government regulation we have in cyberspace, the less likely the Internet will be able to function as a democratizing force that encourages the open exchange of ideas. What has allowed the Net to flourish up to this point has been the right balance of regulation and self-regulation. If governments and other vested interests clutter cyberspace with excessive and burdensome regulations, the liberties we currently enjoy in cyberspace will be seriously attenuated. A decentralized approach can help to preserve the structures of individual choice in cyberspace while still providing for an appropriate level of order and social cohesion.

Second, self-regulation is more consistent with the Net's evolving architecture, which still tends to defy centralized controls. Even those committed to a philosophy of "command and control" must admit that peer-to-peer networks will make it exceedingly difficult for authorities to control the flow of information on the Net. FreeNet, for example, is designed to spread copies of documents or other digital data all over the Web so they no longer belong to one central location. In cases like Yahoo's confrontation with the French government over the sale and display of Nazi memorabilia, we have seen that the state has begun to exert jurisdiction over cyberspace, but the Net is resilient, and any inordinate exertion of control will be met with technological resistance.

Finally, it seems evident that individual and institutional autonomy, which are preserved by this scheme of decentralization, represent important countervailing powers to government authority. The principle of separation of powers pertaining to government institutions, which is embodied in the U.S. Constitution, has a much broader applicability. As Selznick (1992) indicates, this principle "might be traced through the whole history of human affairs, private as well as public." Preserving autonomy in cyberspace helps maintain a critical balance of power between the public and private sectors that undoubtedly serves the common good. The more online regulations we have, the greater the state's influence in the affairs of cyberspace, and this will inevitably mean more centralized structures of choice.

Software code, which embodies its own rules and regulations, has the potential to dramatically reduce the need for government-imposed regulations that fix externalities. It does not replace government, but when used properly, it provides another option to resolve harmful effects. What is needed is an open approach to various regulatory possibilities that explores alternative arrangements and structures. Of course, the misuse of code can have harmful effects and lead to distortions in the market. How can we be sure that code-based solutions do not do more harm than good, and do not create disproportionate distortions in the marketplace? The following section examines this question.

THE PATH TO ETHICAL SELF-REGULATION

Critics of self-regulation facilitated by reliance on code are quick to point out that such decentralized rulemaking is fraught with risks and obstacles. Sometimes code developed by programmers, such as filtering devices to block pornographic Web sites, masks a certain political agenda. Or code can be utilized to stifle legitimate forms of free expression and to unduly narrow one's perspective. There is also the danger that commonly accepted traditional values will be ignored or swallowed up in a code-based solution. Trusted systems, which function as intellectual property enforcement systems, may obviate the need for copyright laws, but will they adequately preserve important values such as fair use and limited term?

Given these problems, should code be a surrogate for the laws and public policies that originate with democratically elected officials? Shapiro (1999) argues that "increasing reliance on code is . . . perilous." He worries that "the precision of digital interactive technology" will make possible "total filtering, the ability to exercise nearly absolute personal control over experience that once was subject only to very approximate control." The problem is that code sometimes regulates too completely and too thoroughly. Sunstein (1995) argues that filters tend to be much too exclusive and end up dangerously narrowing the user's perspective, sometimes without his or her awareness. He writes that "each person could design his own communication universe; each person could see those things that he wanted to see, and only those things; insulation from unwelcome material would be costless." Hence, if we were to follow the advice of these scholars, we must eschew centralized structures of choice but also beware of structures that are too individualized and too narrow.

Obviously, the concerns of Shapiro and Sunstein are valid: Untempered self-regulation and self-organization of the Net is inadequate and even dangerous, since it can solve some of these market failures but lead to other distortions, especially when stakeholders act only in accordance with their own rational self-interest. What we need, therefore, is ethical self-regulation, whereby rational self-interest, even when it is being used to deal with Internet externalities, is linked with respect for the needs and concerns of others and, above all, respect for the common good of the Internet community. Self-determination without these limits can never become the basis for a regulatory system that enhances social welfare.

How then is this ethical self-regulation to be achieved? Can it be implemented in a way that is not disruptive or counterproductive? We must first appreciate that there are three key issues involved in a decentralized scheme of regulation. First, users and organizations who frequent cyberspace must exercise proper self-restraint. They must abide by commonly accepted moral principles and respect the needs and interests of others even when the law is not yet formulated or is ambiguous. For example, while it may be legal to transmit spam (unsolicited, commercial, automated e-mail), there is certainly a compelling moral imperative against doing so. Self-regulation begins with the responsible moral conduct of all Internet users, including individuals and corporations.

Of course, we must confront the reality that this utopian environment where everyone in cyberspace respects the rights of others will never be actualized. Some individuals and organizations will not exercise self-restraint or curb their opportunistic impulses, and they will seek to further their own interests at the expense of others. As we have seen, this sort of activity produces harmful effects on others. However, instead of turning to government intervention as the automatic solution to a problem, it is often possible to let individuals decide what to do about these harms and to take steps to control their own environments. Through this decentralized decision making, order will still be imposed, but from below. However, there is one critical proviso: Internet stakeholders must regulate or order their environments with care and ethical sensitivity. They must seek to avoid or at least minimize the collateral damage that can sometimes accompany code-based solutions designed to handle externalities (such as filtering pornography or blocking out junk e-mail.) For example, if a private library is seeking to purchase a filter for the express purpose of screening out pornography, it must take pains to avoid filters that screen out other sites that may be useful to its patrons. Prudent self-regulation, then, will often involve choosing the right software and implementing it responsibly. Users must be circumspect about how code can alter their environment and even inadvertently infringe on the rights of others.

Finally, this system of self-regulation cannot succeed without the cooperation of those who develop the tools that counter antisocial behavior on the Web. A large burden falls on software developers, ISPs, and other gatekeepers that facilitate Internet access. They develop and execute the code that regulates the Net and enforces this bottom-up social order. They are shaping the Internet's future architectures and are obligated to do so in a way that is attentive to basic moral values and the rights of Internet stakeholders. If self-regulation is to function effectively, they must aspire to greater accountability for their work and must demonstrate a "moral competence" in developing code as carefully as lawmakers craft laws. If code is law, it follows inexorably that it must be designed and applied with the same care, publicity, and fairness as the law itself. But what constitutes prudent use and development of software code that has some regulatory impact? Can one develop basic principles that will offer some guidance to both users and developers of this code?

PRINCIPLES FOR RESPONSIBLE DEPLOYMENT AND DEVELOPMENT OF CODE

We have argued that self-regulation has a chance to be a welfare-enhancing resolution to cyberspace externalities thanks to the power of software code. If self-regulation works it can preserve structures for individual choice while curtailing harmful conduct and maintaining some semblance of order. Thus, software code can positively transform the regulatory landscape of cyberspace as long as it is deployed and developed prudentially. Otherwise it will produce distorting, harmful effects that may exceed its benefits. We do not have a great deal of experience in this area, so it is difficult to articulate what it means to use such code in a morally responsible manner. Both the developers and users of this code need to develop moral competency with code that embodies its own rules or regulations. In this final section we suggest some broad parameters for how users should behave when ordering their environment and how developers should behave when writing the Net's code, especially code that has the same force as law. The principles proposed here by no means represent an exhaustive list. This is merely a preliminary presentation of the moral competencies required for the development and implementation of code when that code is a surrogate for the law.

Let us first consider this matter from the perspective of developers. What principles should guide their development of code that has regulatory impact? First, code should be as open and transparent as possible so that the user's autonomy and capacity for informed consent is fully respected. This first principle acknowledges that one of the most serious problems endemic to the use of code is that its regulatory impact is often occluded, hidden in lines of obscure, proprietary source code. When parents buy a filtering program to protect their children from pornography, they may be unaware that the program also blocks out sites dedicated to feminist causes or sites where sexual education issues are presented. Code is usually hidden and nontransparent, but law is public. As Lessig (1999) suggests, we should be worried about forms of "invisible regulation." This puts users at a great disadvantage and opens the way for all sorts of subtle manipulations. We would surely have major difficulties with any laws or a legislative process that lacked transparency. According to Fuller (1969), the "internal morality" of legislating or of a rule-making process requires generality, publicity, intelligibility, and constancy; thus, "no statute should become law until it has been given a specified form of publication." This means, for example, that purveyors of filtering products must provide users some indication of the sites being filtered so that an informed decision can be made about the suitability of the particular product.

Second, code should be written so that it preserves universally shared social and moral values such as anonymous free speech and personal privacy. There is reasonable consensus about the values and rights that are widely observed in cyberspace, since they are the same ones that have been enshrined by most democratic governments. For example, in the area of intellectual property the values of "fair use" and first sale have a long tradition in copyright law. This implies that rights-management systems, software applications that allow content providers to determine the conditions under which users may gain access to their digital works, should respect those values and not simply exclude them from the code, even if it is convenient to do so. Also, code that facilitates covert surveillance or code that surreptitiously collects information is equally problematic, since at the very least it violates the principle of informed consent. The Internet's social order cannot be achieved at the expense of traditional moral values.

Third, opportunity should be provided for independent review and dialogue for pieces of code that appear to have some regulatory force. Purveyors of filters or rights-management systems should seek out ethicists and other disinterested third parties to render an objective opinion about the efficacy of their products. Does the product respect traditional values and does it provide enough transparency so that end users can make informed judgments? By providing these independent reviews, these vendors will go a long way toward holding themselves accountable for their products.

Finally, there must be reasonable proportionality between the harm that is being corrected and the benefits of the code-based solution that corrects this harm. For example, software developers must avoid overreacting to problems like cyberspace pornography or hate speech in ways that threaten other forms of valuable online speech or infringe on other important rights. If a rights-management system could not be built in a way that ensures "fair use," we might reasonably conclude that the loss of fair use is too steep a price to pay for the protections and convenience afforded by this system.

What about the users of this code? How should we consider these questions from the perspective of the user community? What constitutes responsible use of code in support of their private efforts to contain social costs? First, users must make well-informed and conscientious choices about software. They must also make every effort to implement and utilize that software in the most responsible way possible. For example, in the case of rights-management systems it would be incumbent upon users to choose systems that preserve fair use and manifest respect for other limits on copyright protection. Also, the choice and implementation of filters has created problems for many institutions. For example, in the U.S. case of *Mainstream Loudon v. Loudon County Library* (see Chapter 6), the library purchased a filter called X-Stop to protect children from pornographic Web sites. The library installed the filter on all of its computers so that even adults could not view the material, which was considered to be harmful for juveniles. It could certainly be argued that the Loudon County Library has not been judicious in its use of this code, since it restricted the access of adult patrons just because the material was unfit for minors.

Second, users must be circumspect about using code in a way that might excessively narrow or bias their experience. Code such as filters should be adopted and implemented for a determinate and specific purpose, such as preventing one's children from getting access to online pornography. It should not be used to privatize or customize one's experience or to prevent children from enjoying the diversity of content on the Web. Open-mindedness is an important virtue, especially in a democratic society, and code should not be used in a way that undermines that virtue (Sunstein 2001).

Third, whenever feasible, regulations should be imposed downstream rather than upstream, at the level of the end users (i.e., at the ultimate "endpoints") or in some cases the organization, but preferably not at the level of the ISP or the state. One of the problems with software programs like filters is that they can be imposed anywhere in the vertical chain of communication: the state, the ISP, an organization, and so on. The use of code upstream is problematic, since it prohibits and undermines individual choice in most cases. There is something disturbing about a major ISP filtering content for pornographic material or even for odious hate speech. But it is quite a different story when parents use a filter to shield impressionable young children within their household. Also, consider the case of spam, where developers have devised two code-based defenses: the black hole and the filter. The most famous black hole is MAPS–RBL (Mail Abuse Prevention System–Realtime Blackhole List), which maintains a list of network service providers that are spam friendly. Subscribers to MAPS–RBL will block all e-mail coming from the network providers on this list, not just the e-mail of the spammer. One problem with the black hole approach for spam is that the decision about whether a particular e-mail account will receive messages from RBL-listed servers is not made by the owner of that account. The decision is made by the service provider for the owner's account. Should these service providers be making such decisions about the mail their clients should not see? With spam filters properly deployed, the decision about this nuisance mail lies with the individual account holder, who can preserve his or her choice, and, all things being equal, this is a far more preferable solution.

In Lessig's terms, then, the solution to harmful by-products we favor is a combination of code and ethical principles. Code developed and used responsibly, code implemented at the endpoints of the network, should take priority over law or restrictive regulations whenever possible. This solution empowers end users, as it helps to keep the network open and unfettered by government rules. It will also avoid the costs and inefficiencies that sometimes accompany government intervention.

CONCLUSIONS AND A LOOK AHEAD

In this brief and all too theoretical chapter we have sought to defend a decentralized approach to resolving the ubiquitous externalities in cyberspace against two alternatives: heavy reliance on free-market forces or on the top-down, "command-and-control" policies of government. The market itself is an inadequate mechanism for encouraging attention to the public interest, and heavy reliance on the visible hand of government is fraught with difficulties, from the possibility of industry capture to the lack of efficiency that often typifies government bureaucracies. More important, government regulation is not cost free: There are sometimes heavy transaction costs that can outweigh the benefits of regulations. Economists have pushed the visible-hand approach because they overlook the inefficiencies inherent in many government bureaucracies. Coase (1964) often refers to this bias among economists: "In economic analysis we have 'market failure' but no 'government failure.'"

For externalities in the physical world, government intervention has often been the only choice. This was due to the transaction costs of coordinating a resolution between the disputed parties, such as the polluter and the dispersed victims of pollution. But in cyberspace, thanks to the power of software code, the transaction costs entailed in making a deal disappear in many situations, and this makes privatization a more feasible alternative. We recognize that the use of this code may sometimes have its own harmful effects. Hence, software code that has a regulatory impact must be used and developed prudentially.

Code should not always be a surrogate for law, but code can be a valid self-regulatory mechanism when it is deployed in a conscientious manner to protect individual rights or to constrain antisocial behavior. We have provided some general guidelines for the proper use of code, but we admit that much more work needs to be done in this area. If software code can be prudentially developed and applied to certain externalities, it will have an opportunity to alter the regulatory landscape of cyberspace. It is our contention that the role of government can be diminished, though certainly not eliminated. In many cases ethical self-regulation can effect socially optimal results by preserving the structures of individual choice while keeping transaction costs low and curtailing the harmful effects associated with market externalities.

In the chapters ahead we will attempt to apply this framework of ethical self-regulation to various topics of debate, such as speech, intellectual property, privacy, and security. Among other issues, we will attempt to sort out when government regulation is essential and when self-regulation supported by technology could be an effective substitute.

REFERENCES

Arrow, K. (1962). "Economic Welfare and Allocation of Resources for Invention." In *The Rate and Direction of Inventive Activity: Economic and Social Factors* 609. Washington, D.C.: National Bureau of Economic Research.

Clark, D., and Blumenthal, M. (2000). "Rethinking the Design of the Internet: The End to End Argument vs. the Brave New World." *TPRC*, August, 19–35.

Clinton, W., and Gore, A. (1997). "A Framework for Global Electronic Commerce." Available: http://www.iitf.nist.gov/eleccomm/ecomm.htm

Coase, R. (1960). "The Problem of Social Cost." *Journal of Law and Economics* 3: 1–44.

Coase, R. (1962). "The Interdepartment Radio Advisory Committee." *Journal of Law and Economics* 5: 17–47.

Coase, R. (1964). Discussion of "The Effectiveness of Economic Regulation: A Legal View" by R. C. Campton. *American Economic Review* 54: 194–195.

Friedman, M. (1970). "The Social Responsibility of Business Is to Increase Its Profits." *New York Times Magazine*, 13 September, 1–7.

Fuller, L. (1969). *The Morality of Law*. New Haven: Yale University Press.

Goodpaster, K. (1984). "The Concept of Corporate Responsibility." In *New Introductory Essays in Business Ethics*, edited by T. Regan. New York: Random House.

Hohfeld, W. (1913). "Some Fundamental Legal Conceptions as Applied in Judicial Reasoning." *Yale Law Journal* 23: 16.

Lessig, L. (1999). *Code and Other Laws of Cyberspace*. New York: Basic Books.

Medema, S. (1993). "Is There Life Beyond Efficiency? Elements of Social Law and Economics." *Review of Social Economy* 51: 138–153.

Paine, L. (1992). *Note on Data Protection in Sweden*. Boston: Harvard Business School Publications.

Pigou, A. (1962). *The Economics of Welfare*. London: Macmillan.

Post, D. (2000). "What Larry Doesn't Get: Code, Law, and Liberty in Cyberspace." *Stanford Law Review* 52: 1439.

Selznick, P. (1992). *The Moral Commonwealth*. Berkeley and Los Angeles: University of California Press.

Shapiro, A. (1999). *The Control Revolution*. New York: Century Foundation Books.

Stone, C. (1975). *Where the Law Ends: The Social Control of Corporate Behavior*. New York: Harper and Row.

Sunstein, C. (1995). "The First Amendment in Cyberspace." *Yale Law Journal* 104: 1757.

Sunstein, C. (2001). *Republic.com.* New York: Free Press.
Taylor, C. (1992). *Ethics and Authenticity.* Cambridge: Harvard University Press.
Veljanovski, C. (1981). "Wealth Maximization, Law, and Ethics—On the Limits of Economic Efficiency." *International Review of Law and Economics* 1: 5–28.
Venturelli, S. (1997). "Information Liberalization in the European Union." In *National Information Infrastructures: Vision and Policy Design*, edited by B. Kahin and E. Wilson. Cambridge: MIT Press.

4

Electronic Commerce and the Network Economy

There is no industry in the world economy that has remained unaffected in some way by what is happening on the Internet. Consider the sleepy newspaper industry, where change seems to happen at a glacial pace. Even in this industry the Internet has emerged as a minatory force, threatening to undermine the traditional economics of this business. Because of the physical infrastructure necessary to print and distribute a newspaper there have always been significant barriers to entry in this industry. But thanks to the Web, those barriers have fallen, and one can enter various aspects of the newspaper business either to provide selective content or classified ads. The newspaper is really an amalgam of "businesses" or distinct products combined in a single edition: weather, sports, financial news, the classifieds, and property listings. Niche publishers can choose one of these areas and specialize in delivering that content.

It is not surprising, therefore, that a big problem for the newspaper industry is the migration of classified ads to the Web. Newspapers need this lucrative piece of business, but classifieds work better on the Web than they do in print. While the reach of newspapers is usually confined to their local audience, the Web has a much broader reach. As a result, classified advertising has become extremely popular on the Net. Major newspapers in the United States are seeing sharp declines in revenues for classified advertising. No one is predicting that newspapers such as the *New York Times* or the *Chicago Tribune* will be replaced by Web-only news sites, but the old business model of these newspapers will need radical revision: Major newspaper brands may need to invest in Web-based businesses that provide property listings or other content traditionally found only in newspapers. On the other hand, local newspapers, which are far more dependent on classified revenues, may have trouble surviving the Internet revolution.

The newspaper industry is one of many confronting the threats and opportunities of digital technology and Internet commerce. These technologies are compelling companies to modify how they deal with their customers and suppliers and how they organize work patterns. Some of these changes are minor, but others have the potential to be revolutionary.

The primary purpose of this chapter is to provide an extremely brief introduction to electronic commerce and to the business models that have proliferated in the Internet economy. This discussion is quite limited, and it is only meant to serve as a cursory overview in preparation for the extensive treatment of antitrust and other policy issues in future chapters.

E-BUSINESS MODELS

Electronic commerce refers to the process of conducting transactions by electronic means. More simply, e-commerce is just trade that occurs on the Internet. Why is there so much interest in electronic commerce even after the dot-com debacle in 2000? The euphoria about the Net has faded, but no one is dismissing the likelihood that this global network will be a main thoroughfare of commerce. What are some of the general benefits of e-commerce? First, it eliminates the constraints of time and space and thereby provides extraordinary convenience for consumers. Most Web sites are asynchronous, so users can do their browsing and shopping at any time. Second, the Internet is a low-cost communications technology, so it can greatly reduce overhead and transaction costs. According to Mandel and Hof (2001), "The Internet is a tool that dramatically lowers the cost of communication, [and] that means it can radically alter any industry or activity that depends heavily on the flow of information." Thanks to the Net, most organizational bureaucracies can be scaled back. Third, e-commerce can also reduce distribution costs, especially for those goods and services, such as software, books, or financial services, which can be delivered electronically. Finally, e-commerce can appreciably increase liquidity; that is, the ability to translate corporate resources into value. Exchanges, for example, increase liquidity by bringing buyers (demand chain) and sellers (supply chain) together in ways that create many new opportunities.

The bottom line is that the Internet is fundamentally deflationary, and this deflation will have a long-term economic impact. When costs are lowered in this systematic way, there is an increase in the equilibrium level of production and a fall in price. This is illustrated in Figure 4.1. As a result of these lower

Figure 4.1
Internet's Impact on Aggregate Supply and Demand

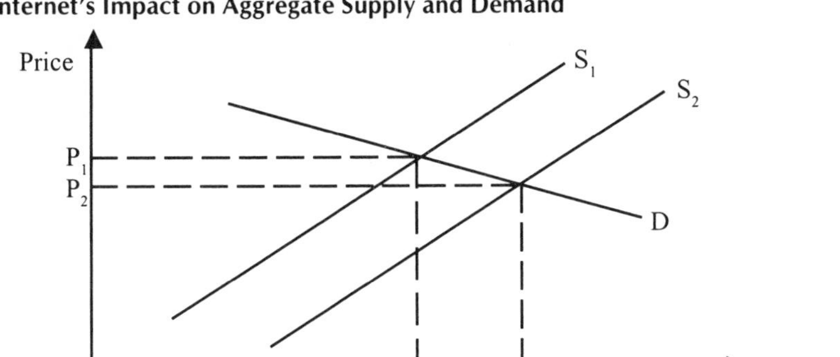

costs, the aggregate supply curve is pushed out to the right (from S_1 to S_2), and, assuming stable aggregate demand, this leads to a rise in aggregate production from Q_1 to Q_2 and a drop in price from P_1 to P_2.

There are many types of electronic commerce, and for the sake of clarity it makes sense to think of the broad category of e-commerce in terms of different business models. Before we can categorize these models, it is instructive to review the generic value chain for all businesses. Porter (1985) introduced the value-chain concept, which regards "every firm as the collection of activities that are performed to design, produce, market, deliver and support its product." Porter's model is especially well suited to describe the value chain of traditional manufacturing firms. But in today's economy there is much more emphasis on products whose primary value lies in intellectual property: software, pharmaceutical products, movies, and so forth. Hence, with these companies in mind we might depict the value chain a little differently. According to Applegate (2000), the value chain consists of those who create information (or other products), those who produce and package the work of these creators, and those who distribute the end product to the customer. It might be depicted as follows:

Creators → Producers → Distributors → Customer

Creators develop ideas and innovative products, and they include artists, authors, inventors, and research scientists. Producers include manufacturers, such as the pharmaceutical company Merck, or service providers, such as United Airlines, along with suppliers of information and news services. Distributors "may connect suppliers to business customers, forming what is often called a *supply chain*, or they may connect producers to consumers forming what may be called a buy chain" (emphasis in original) (Applegate 2000).

The customer is either another business or an individual consumer, the actual end user of the product or service.

There are two broad categories of business models on the Internet. According to Applegate (2000), the first category consists of firms that provide the infrastructure for the Internet itself and for the companies that want to do business there. In this category we find software firms such as Oracle and Microsoft, hardware manufactures such as Dell and Apple, or infrastructure portals such as AT&T and America Online. The second category consists of digital businesses that exploit opportunities in distribution channels by linking businesses to consumers or even consumers to consumers. In this category we find "focused distributors": familiar online companies like Amazon.com, eBay, Schwab.com, and Webvan, the now defunct online grocer, and we also find portals like Yahoo and AOL.com. Our concern is with this second category of digital businesses: the focused distributor and the portal. These online companies rely heavily on their ability to organize the distribution of information on the Internet. As Castells (2001) points out, "There is a shift in the value chain of the e-commerce industry toward the information distribution systems at the expense of the value of information itself."

A MAP OF DIGITAL BUSINESS MODELS

Focused Distributors

Among these focused distributors, there are four basic types of digital business models. While business to consumer (B2C) receives most of the attention, business to business (B2B) has the greatest potential to revolutionize the global economy. The dynamics of the Internet have changed the value chain so that the focus is less on the supply side and more on the demand side, as buyers set the price and drive the creation of new products and services. This makes possible other models like consumer to business (C2B) and consumer to consumer (C2C). Let us consider each of these basic models in some detail.

Business to Consumer

One of the most famous online businesses selling directly to consumers is Amazon.com, based in Seattle, Washington. The online bookseller and general retailer has yet to turn a profit, as its CEO, Jeff Bezos, continues to expand the company's horizontal scope into new product lines. But Bezos still insists that he will attain profits in all sectors despite the need to fight off many aggressive and more focused competitors.

Given the problems that have plagued Amazon and other e-retailers, one wonders how to make the B2C model more viable. How can these companies build a sustainable competitive advantage and create enough added value to generate consistent streams of profit? What would be the building blocks of such a sustainable advantage? What are the most salient characteristics of the B2C model?

According to Bezos, "The thing a lot of people don't understand about e-commerce is the degree to which it is a scale business" (Hamilton 2000). Economies of scale (and scope) are easier to achieve in an online business. While conventional offline retailers have to increase capital spending in order to increase sales, such investments are not necessary online. If Starbucks aims to sell more cups of its cappuccino coffee it needs to open more stores, and this is a pretty expensive proposition. But a single Web site can serve customers all over the world. An online business, therefore, is *scalable*; that is, it can get bigger and bigger without a significant increase in costs.

Second, running an online business entails lower operating costs than a bricks-and-mortar business. There are no rental expenses, and there are quicker inventory turnovers along with much lower labor costs. Expenses are even lower when the end product is fully "digitizable," since there is no need to invest in an infrastructure to store and deliver goods. As a result, operating expenses will be far lower for online brokerage business like Charles Schwab than for companies like Walmart.com or Amazon.com, which must deliver a physical product. Finally, there are lower working capital requirements, since online retailers typically get paid by the consumer before payment is due to the distributors. The bottom line is *enhanced capital productivity*: Capital is substantially more productive in a low-cost, scalable Internet business.

Third, data can be more easily collected and exploited on the Net. A customer's every transaction can be recorded, along with what banner ads the customer clicks on. This enables personalized marketing such as customized ads or special offers tailored to a consumer's interests. This information can also be used to generate extra revenue, since it can be sold to advertisers or to interested third parties.

Finally, there is the distinct advantage of *interactivity*, the ability to cultivate feedback mechanisms and to communicate directly with customers and suppliers. The Internet enables a company's constituencies to circumvent vertical communication channels, and this should improve the quality and timeliness of its information resources.

Despite these distinct advantages, there are significant pressures on online businesses. Economists once suggested that Internet competition would be virtually "frictionless." Price increases are difficult to sustain, since consumers can easily search the Web, perhaps with the help of shopbots, to find the lowest price. There are still predictions that Web-based search engines will provide buyers with more data about products, and equipped with these data, consumers will be able to exert greater bargaining power. In addition, low capital costs should translate into lower entry barriers. This will mean more competitors entering the market, and the presence of these new industry incumbents leads to greater price competition.

But just how "frictionless" is this economy? To a great extent this characterization is more myth than reality. For most industries with a presence in cyberspace, there are still some economies of scale that deter entry. Also, as brands become established it will be increasingly difficult for new competitors to gain a foothold in certain businesses. Online bookselling, for example, is now dominated by two entrenched brands: Amazon.com and bn.com (Barnes & Noble). Although there may be profitable niches in this market, it will be difficult for aspiring mainstream competitors to contend with these branded products. In addition, there are first-mover advantages. As *The Economist* points out, "If an early mover gets it right—its web site, its order fulfillment, its distribution—a newcomer might find it much harder to knock it off its perch than would be in the physical world" ("Shopping Around the Web" 2000).

But what about traditional retail stores, so-called legacy businesses like Home Depot, Wal-Mart, or Sears Roebuck? Won't they challenge the pure plays or dot-com companies and steal their business? These legacy firms should have more major advantages over their counterparts in the virtual world: established brand identity, substantial base of customers, mastery of logistics and distribution, in-depth industry knowledge, and well-established supplier and customer relationships.

There are complications, however, for legacy firms that the pure players do not have to worry about. For example, there is the potent threat of cannibalization. Will selling the same goods and services online, often at lower prices, merely reduce revenues for goods sold through traditional channels?

Then there is the problem of channel conflict. In anticipation of the busy Christmas season, Mattel began selling a wide array of toys and clothing on its Barbie.com Web site. Thesc are the same products it sells at retail stores such as Toys "R" Us and Kmart. According to Bannon (2000), "Mattel says the initiative is designed to boost the popularity and awareness of its brands—not to compete with retailers." The Web site is certain to cause tension, however. Retailers are bound to lose sales when their suppliers begin selling directly to consumers, and that will cause considerable friction in their relationships.

None of these difficulties are insurmountable, and while some offline giants like Wal-Mart and Levi-Strauss have stumbled in their efforts to build Web-based businesses, many predict that bricks-and-mortar companies, thanks to their formidable assets, will be the biggest winners of the B2C e-commerce battle in the long run.

Consumer to Business

The unique technology of the Web has enabled radically new business models such as the consumer to business approach, which has been popularized by the Priceline.com Web site. Priceline introduced its innovative "name your own price" model in 1998. Customers could specify the price they were willing to pay for an airline ticket to a certain destination or for a hotel room. According to Priceline's founder, Jay Walker,

In the traditional model of commerce, a seller advertises a unit of supply in the marketplace at a specified price, and a buyer takes it or leaves it. Priceline turns that model around. We allow a buyer to advertise a unit of demand to a group of sellers. The sellers can then decide whether to fulfill that demand or not. In effect, we provide a mechanism for collecting and forwarding units of demand to interested sellers. (Carr 1999)

Priceline has therefore inverted traditional pricing structures by allowing the customer to set the price he or she is willing to pay for a product or service.

Despite the attractiveness of this approach, it has limitations. Of course, one is not "naming" a price, one is "proposing" a price and hoping someone will accept that proposal or bid. Some skeptics have begun to raise questions about the long-term viability and efficiency of this model. They see it as a form of haggling, which is usually an inefficient way to buy most goods. While Priceline may work for big-ticket items, the name-your-price approach does not make sense for most low-priced or commodity products. The company found this out when it tried to extend this model to groceries with its WebHouse club venture. WebHouse was abruptly discontinued in October 2000 at a loss of $360 million for its investors.

Another C2B pricing model is employed by so-called aggregators like Mercata.com. These sites accumulate bids from price-sensitive consumers and offer the lowest bid to a group of buyers. If the bid is accepted by a vendor, all of the consumers receive the product at that price. While Priceline.com's pricing model is one to many, Mercata's is many to many.

Although these pricing models have not yet been a rousing success, they are not likely to disappear from the landscape of the Web. However, their use will most likely to be confined to certain types of products: big-ticket items such as airline tickets, hotel rooms, and automobiles. But reverse auctions and aggregators are inherently global in scale and clearly have not yet reached their full potential.

Consumer to Consumer

This third model is epitomized by consumer auctions, where consumers sell goods to other consumers. The most successful consumer to consumer site is eBay, the online auctioneer. Users can buy and sell almost any legal good on the eBay site. In 2001 eBay boasted over 23 million customers ("Internet Pioneers" 2001). eBay acts as an intermediary for these buyers and sellers; it charges a 7.5-percent commission on most sales, which is far less than most bricks-and-mortar auction houses like Southeby's.

eBay's success illustrates the Net's potential to create radically new markets where none previously existed. And the company is only an intermediary: The buyers and sellers do all the work. Sellers pay the company for the privilege of auctioning their products and buyers make the bids. If a bid is accepted, the seller ships the product after receiving payment, and eBay never gets involved in collection of payment or in shipping. Here again there are also strong scale economies: There are few limitations on the number of auctions eBay can handle, since they are only the intermediary. This is the perfect virtual business.

Part of eBay's success story can be attributed to the power of "network effects": The more people that use an auction Web site, the more useful and valuable it becomes. Sellers want liquidity; that is, they want to auction off their wares where there are the most bidders so they can get a quick sale. This also means that there is a significant first-mover advantage for a successful auctioneer like eBay.

A variation of the eBay model is consumer to consumer swapping, where users trade goods but usually do not purchase them. SwitchHouse operates one of the largest personal swapping sites. Since this company does not levy a trading fee, it depends on advertising and the sale of users' data in order to generate revenues.

Online auctioneers like eBay are more than just a temporary fad. They have truly redefined the business of consumers selling to other consumers, an activity normally confined to weekend yard sales or flea markets. eBay is a much more efficient forum for fragmented groups of buyers and sellers to come together. As Guernsey (1999) puts it, "They have created ways for everyday people to connect with other everyday people who have the same interests, needs, and must have obsessions for items like coin operated video games, circa 1980." eBay calls its broad base of customers a "community," and by reinforcing that sense of community through online discussions of particular items, it cultivates customer loyalty. However, its efforts to increase its scope and its base of registered users will be in tension with its aspirations to be a true online community.

Business to Business

The Internet is bringing about fundamental changes in the way almost every business controls its value chain, from procurement and manufacturing to selling and marketing. For one thing, it is helping companies to lower costs across their value chain by automating supplier deliveries or refurbishing customer-service operations. Gartner, Inc., an IT research company, has lowered its estimates for online business to business transactions but still projects close to $6 trillion by 2004 (Totty 2001).

Perhaps the greatest potential in the B2B market is the remarkable growth of trading sites, which range in complexity from online catalogs to public exchanges and online collaborative design. At the simplest level, a vendor can establish its print catalog on a Web site; customers can search the entire product line and make purchases electronically. Another possibility is public exchanges; that is, a public e-marketplace where buyers and sellers come together to exchange goods. Ventro, formerly known as Chemdex, was a public exchange for the medical equipment industry. These exchanges are open to a much larger group of buyers than a private network, and this greatly enhances the potential market for the sellers.

However, Ventro and other public exchanges are struggling due to lack of interest and lack of liquidity. This has not been the case with industry-specific consortia, which have great promise of success. Unlike a public exchange, access to these consortia is more restricted. Sellers can market their products over a Web site and buyers can purchase goods directly; buyers can also use the private network to post their own bids for products. According to *The Economist*, "Unlike independent public exchanges, [consortia] have the clout and the backing to define and impose standards" ("B2B Exchanges" 2001). One of the largest such exchanges in the auto industry is known as COVISINT (connectivity, collaboration, visibility through the supply chain, combined with international scope). The exchange is supported by the world's leading automobile manufactures, such as GM, DaimlerChrysler, Ford, and Nissan, and is expected to include about 40,000 parts suppliers. The benefit for the automobile manufacturers is that their concentrated buying power will save them billions of dollars when they purchase raw materials and preassembled components that are used to assemble automobiles.

Manufacturers expect that CONVISINT will save on average between $1,500 and $3,600 in the production costs for each automobile (Meredith 2001). It will also mean much better just-in-time inventory and less inventory stockpiling. In the future, thanks to COVISINT, auto manufacturers will have in place a system that will let consumers customize their cars: They can choose the engine size, the upholstery color, along with other amenities, and expect delivery within a week after the order has been placed.

The B2B marketplace is evolving quite rapidly. Some e-exchanges are struggling with sophisticated technologies or even the mechanisms of cooperation, and others like COVISINT worry about whether they can live up to the promise and the hype. But online exchanges will radically change the way business gets done as they also unalterably affect the competitive landscape for many different industries. These exchanges and consortia do have drawbacks, however. They raise the specter of collusion and invite unwelcome scrutiny from regulatory agencies. Also, some fear that these consortia or exchanges will be used by big firms to squeeze the margins of their suppliers.

Finally, there are private exchanges, which have the same clout as industry-specific consortia and probably the same potential to be lucrative in the long run. In a private exchange or trading network a single company establishes a network for a specially invited group of suppliers or partners, who may become privy to sensitive information about prices or inventory levels. The benefit, according to Harris (2001), is that these companies "don't have to give over control of their precious supply chains to third parties that are also serving their competitors." General Electric, IBM, and Wal-Mart operate substantial private exchanges. GE, for example, does about $20-billion worth of business buying and selling products through its private exchange, called Global Supplier Network (GSN), and estimates savings of $1.6 billion in 2001 (Wilson 2002).

Portals

The second major digital business model is the portal. Yahoo, AOL.com, MSN.com, and Lycos are all examples of horizontal portals catering to consumers in cyberspace. Portals such as Yahoo began as search engines. But Yahoo quickly transformed itself into a media company as it added considerable content and communication facilities. Yahoo's primary services are called "properties." These properties included navigational services that help users find Web sites and other information more easily. There are also e-commerce properties for shopping or making travel arrangements. Millions also use Yahoo for e-mail, instant messaging, chat rooms, scheduling, and personal Web pages. The portal business model is based on generation of revenue primarily through advertising fees, so portals seek to attract large numbers of repeat visitors in order to enhance the value proposition for their advertisers.

Portals provide a single focal point from which users can connect to various Web pages or track down necessary information. They help users impose their own personal order on the chaotic structure of cyberspace. In addition to horizontal portals such as AOL.com, there are vertical portals, which specialize in information about a particular industry. Quicken.com and Healtheon/WebMD are prime examples of such portals.

The importance of horizontal commercial portals should not be underestimated, but it may begin to wane in future years. While it is true that Web-site access has become increasingly channeled through portals like Yahoo and MSN, users have many viable substitutes. As they become more familiar with the Web and build a portfolio of bookmarks, users may be able to navigate cyberspace without the aid of a portal. Vertical portals are also a threat since they provide better information resources for specific topic areas. Portals like Yahoo have sought to build up end user switching costs by offering "sticky" applications such as e-mail and personal Web pages.

There has been some convergence of these two digital business models as the functions of focused distributors and portals merge together. Yahoo now competes directly with Amazon.com and eBay. It has auctions and has also moved into the financial-services business. All three of these companies now host storefronts for other companies (such as zShops.amazon). Each is trying to leverage its broad customer base by horizontal-scope expansion into new businesses.

TRUST AND INNOVATION

Before we conclude, a few brief words on the theme of trust are in order. We have already alluded to the loss of trustworthiness on the Net and to some potential remedies. The Internet economy's need for trust is beyond dispute. For example, unless an atmosphere of trust is established and sustained, we will not be able to exploit the most adventuresome of the B2B exchange models, the public e-marketplace. In this model many buyers come together with many sellers and the possibilities can be endless. Metcalfe's law (attributed to Robert Metcalfe, known for his work in network computing), which states that the value of a network is equal to the square of the number of users ($v = n \times n$), applies to exchanges as well as to network connections. The benefit of belonging to an exchange or consortium increases exponentially with the number of connections. According to Koulopoulos and Palmer (2001), this creates the possibility of "N:N communities," where "the degree of value creation is directly related to the level of connectivity between community members."

Public exchanges or semipublic exchanges with multiple and diverse members have more potential to increase aggregate welfare, therefore, than private exchanges that restrict membership and limit information flows. In many-to-many situations like this, massive collaboration can be achieved as the supply-chain members work in different permutations to meet the requirements of the demand chain. The potential for innovation becomes enormous. As Romer (1989) reminds us, "We consistently fail to grasp how many ideas remain to be discovered. The difficulty is the same one we have with compounding. Possibilities do not add up. They multiply."

But public exchanges have floundered due to a lack of trust and concerns about the need to surrender proprietary data or reveal the elements in a firm's supply chain. According to one executive, "Everybody believes their supply chain is a competitive advantage—Why would I want to *share* that with a competitor?" (Mandel and Hof 2001, emphasis added).

Unless businesses can become more accustomed to information sharing they will never be able to take full advantage of the new business models the Internet makes possible. We might look at a company such as Safeway in Britain, which allows its suppliers access to its data warehouse so that they have real-time access to how their products are selling. With this information these suppliers can tailor their production to demand and do a better job of making sure that Safeway has adequate inventory. The lesson here is that companies can no longer see themselves as isolated and independent entities. Rather, according to *The Economist*, they "must be willing to bring suppliers and customers deep into their processes and to develop a similar understanding of their business partners' processes, [and] that implies a degree of openness and transparency which is new to most commercial organizations" ("The Net Imperative" 1999). An atmosphere of trust is therefore critically important, since there is no place for reticence or reservations about what to reveal to one's partners.

There is no magic formula to engender a higher degree of trust, but trusting relationships have a tendency to build upon each other. Moreover, responsible moral agency, acting from the moral point of view, is the most vital element in creating and solidifying bonds of trust. Architectures can only take us so far in building a trusting environment. Also, as we will argue in the next chapter, responsible management of these exchanges will be essential for avoiding untimely and potentially repressive government regulations.

If a public exchange can create an environment that eschews exclusivity and collusion, it will have a much better chance for sustained commercial success. Any successful public exchange will be a stimulus for innovation thanks to the "multiplying" of possibilities. But we must keep in mind that the sheer novelty of these exchanges is not conducive to the quick formation of trust and credibility, and so this is likely to be an evolutionary and slow process.

REFERENCES

Applegate, L. (2000). *Overview of E-Business Models*. Boston: Harvard Business School Publishing.

"B2B Exchanges: Time to Rebuild." (2001). *The Economist*, 19 May, 55–56.

Bannon, L. (2000). "Selling Barbie Online May Pit Mattel vs. Stores." *Wall Street Journal*, 17 November, B1.

Carr, N. (1999). "Redesigning Business." *Harvard Business Review*, November–December, 19.

Castells, M. (2001). *The Internet Galaxy*. New York: Oxford University Press.

Guernsey, L. (1999). "Night of the Living Bid: Four Tales from an Hour of eBay." *New York Times*, 22 September, E7.

Hamilton, D. (2000). "The Profit Puzzle in Electronic Retail." *Wall Street Journal*, 22 May, A1.

Harris, N. (2001). "'Private Exchanges' May Allow B-to-B Exchanges to Thrive After All." *Wall Street Journal*, 16 March, B1.

"Internet Pioneers." (2001). *The Economist*, 3 February, 69–71.

Koulopoulos, T., and Palmer, N. (2001). *The X-Economy*. New York: Texere.

Mandel, M., and Hof, R. (2001). "Rethinking the Internet." *Business Week*, 26 March, 116–141.

Meredith, R. (2001). "Harder than the Hype." *Forbes*, 16 April, 188–194.

"The Net Imperative." (1999). *The Economist*, 26 June, 17–21.

Porter, M. (1985). *Competitive Advantage*. New York: The Free Press.

Romer, P. (1989). "Increasing Returns and New Developments in the Theory of Growth." Working paper no. 3098. Washington, D.C.: National Bureau of Economic Research.

"Shopping Around the Web (A Survey of E-Commerce)." (2000). *The Economist*, 26 February, 5–6.

Totty, M. (2001). "The Next Phase." *Wall Street Journal*, 21 May, R8–9.

Wilson, T. (2002). "GE Expands Private Hub to Woo Users." *Internet Week*, 7 January, 38.

5

Competition and Antitrust Issues in Cyberspace

For over two months in a Washington, D.C., courtroom the Department of Justice (DOJ) sought to prove to the world that Microsoft was an evil monopoly that harmed American consumers and stifled competition. Microsoft's defenders argued that the company's aggressive competitive spirit should not be the cause for its dismemberment. It was procompetitive, its lawyers contended, not anticompetitive as the government had alleged. In the end, however, the government's lawyers, led by David Boies, were more persuasive, convincing Judge Thomas Penfield Jackson of Microsoft's culpability. The remedy imposed by Judge Jackson could not have been more drastic: dividing the company into two separate entities, an operating-system unit and an application provider. No one was quite sure whether this would ultimately benefit consumers, but it seemed like a fitting punishment for Microsoft's nefarious behavior, even if we ended up with two big monopolies instead of one. Fortunately for Microsoft, a federal appeals court overturned this decision, while not completely exonerating the company. The two sides have reached a settlement which awaits court approval.

What does this case tell us about the import and future of competition policy in the United States? The precise role of antitrust policy in this network era assumes new prominence thanks to the seemingly pervasive presence of network effects and the aggregated buying power of emerging e-marketplaces.

There are also questions about the ownership of the information infrastructure and open access, which received some attention in government deliberations about the America Online–Time Warner merger. Some type of government intervention is clearly essential, but what is the optimal regulatory scheme in a network economy? What set of competition policies best suits the Internet era? If the U.S. government chooses to remain faithful to the principles of open competition for infrastructure development, it must still function as a referee, but there are no easy formulas that dictate the conditions for intervention in the markets.

We grapple with these difficult questions in this chapter by examining in some depth three specific case studies:

- The Microsoft antitrust case and the problems generated by the need for interoperability and by network effects
- The antitrust concerns provoked by aggregators and B2B exchanges such as COVISINT.
- The issue of open access and the America Online–Time Warner merger.

In the area of antitrust policy, the government faces a delicate balancing act. If it waits and moves too slowly it may be too late to fix things before considerable damage is inflicted on the market. It is easier to take actions ex ante, since the cost of undoing the damage caused by exertion of monopoly power is often high. But if it tries to be proactive and aggressive, it could run the risk of stifling innovation and putting a potential e-commerce endeavor at a serious competitive disadvantage.

Although we embrace the philosophy of deregulation when consumers and users have the ability to regulate their environment with minimal transaction costs, we support a more interventionist approach for certain forms of anticompetitive behavior that could harm the information infrastructure. Government, for example, must strive to preserve open access, or the vital principle of end-to-end will be threatened. Regulators must also maintain a reasonably level playing field in a way that promotes fair competition without dampening innovation. The ideal policy path is to fine tune a regulatory regime that supports competitive markets without intervening inappropriately.

THE LEGAL FRAMEWORK

The Sherman Antitrust Act of 1890 seems highly irrelevant and anachronistic in these earliest years of the twenty-first century. This act, which was passed to combat the power of individual trusts threatening to control essential facilities like the railroad, bans anticompetitive mergers and predatory tactics. It states that "every person who shall monopolize, or attempt to monopolize, . . . any part of the trade or commerce among the several States, or with foreign nations, shall be deemed guilty of a felony." The main objective of the Sherman Act was to fight against price fixing, which was becoming rampant in the early stages of the industrial economy in the United States.

The railroad and its trusts were a great threat to free markets, but can the same be said for high-technology industries like software? Do we still need Senator Sherman's antiquated "smokestack" laws in this digital age? On the surface, it surely appears that this legal framework has some applicability. Microsoft's Windows operating system (OS), for example, has about an 80-percent share of the world's personal computing market, assuming that one includes the Macintosh OS in this category. Microsoft is also the leading supplier of personal computer software applications. Given its power, what's to stop Microsoft from devouring the Net?

But is the dominance of a company in a market such as operating systems equivalent to the monopolistic control of a railroad company? It is certainly difficult to equate these two situations. In this digital era it is much harder to determine where markets begin and end. Likewise, the boundaries of fair competition are murkier. Also, Microsoft and other dominant firms in digital technology face constant market threats in the form of new technologies, which railroad and oil companies did not confront.

Before we examine the Microsoft case it would be instructive to consider the broad goals of antitrust policy. Economists generally regard antitrust regulations as "a set of laws designed to promote competition and, therefore, economic efficiency" (Viscusi, Vernon, and Harrington 1998). Economic efficiency is defined as the maximization of total surplus, which is equivalent to maximizing producers' plus consumers' surplus. And "maximizing total surplus is equivalent to selecting the output level at which price equals marginal cost [P = MC]" (Viscusi, Vernon, and Harrington 1998). For example, for a manufacturer of screwdrivers the marginal cost is the cost of producing and distributing one more screwdriver. Consequently, under normal conditions antitrust policies and initiatives are in the public interest when they lead to an increase in total economic surplus.

In the past two decades antitrust policy has been dominated by the more laissez-faire "Chicago School" approach, which originated with a group of economists at the University of Chicago. The Chicago School adheres to the theory that the goal of antitrust policy is economic efficiency, and its focus is primarily on the price that consumers pay for a product. It accepts that a price equal to marginal cost is efficient from the producer's and the consumer's point of view. As long as P = MC, it doesn't matter whether the industry structure is a monopoly or something closer to perfect competition. Thus, it is acceptable for companies to dominate their markets, but they must eschew any use of their market power to manipulate prices.

Chicago School proponents worry more about mergers between "horizontal" competitors, while they give considerable leeway to vertical mergers or relationships. Companies have horizontal relationships when they compete in the same market. Consequently, a merger between Ford and General Motors might set off alarm bells at the Justice Department. Companies have a vertical relationship when they have different positions on the value chain within an industry and therefore are not direct competitors. For example, the Justice Department did not seem concerned about the AOL–Time Warner merger, since AOL is an Internet service provider and Time Warner is a cable company and a content provider. The reason is that this merger represented a set of vertical relationships. When horizontal connections create substantial economic power there is a need for scrutiny, since this could have a negative effect on competition and pricing policies. The Justice Department and the European Commission, for example, concluded that a horizontal merger between MCI/WorldCom and Sprint should not be allowed, since the result would be a reduction of competition in the long-distance market and probably higher prices in the long run.

The Clinton administration was more aggressive about enforcing antitrust laws than previous administrations, and some economists detected a moderate change in policy. According to the assistant attorney general in charge of the Justice Department's antitrust division, "Antitrust law is now . . . focused on identifying where there might exist a particular competition problem in the sense of creation of economic power in certain markets" (Schiesel 2000). What is most troublesome to economists like Becker and Murphy (2001) is this "focus on avoiding 'market dominance' and [on] 'market engineering' through the imposition of structural remedies." They argue that the heightened scrutiny and stricter standards for companies that have achieved a dominant market position are unwarranted. A presumption against dominance is unfair because it "penalizes companies for achieving market success." They also argue that the tendency to impose structural remedies that reshape boundaries of markets and industries is misguided because of the "enormous potential for unintended and adverse consequences." It remains to be seen whether the Bush administration will continue with this policy direction.

But we are still left with the question of how to apply antitrust regulations to software companies in an information-based economy. If we examine the economics of this industry we get a better sense of why such application might be so difficult. The structure of the software industry is shaped by three interrelated factors: network effects, systems, and standards. In the information age we depend on networks, physical networks to communicate and virtual networks allowing us to communicate on the same platform. This leads to network effects: The benefits accruing to each user of a product (such as an operating system or a browser) increase with the number of users. The more people that use the same operating system, the easier it is for users to communicate and share files. Also, that operating system will attract more software applications. A network therefore is different from traditional markets, since in a network the more people connected, the more everyone gains. One could argue, for example, that Microsoft's alleged anticompetitive actions (such as tying together its browser and operating system) actually stimulated the network's expansion and that this expansion benefits everyone else connected to the network.

Although information-age products may be used in isolation, they are often more valuable as parts of a system where each component is interdependent with the others. Operating systems require application software, some application software requires Internet access, and so forth. In addition, networks and systems need common standards, since they facilitate interconnections along with the user's ability to communicate.

These characteristics of the software market often lead to a "winner-take-all" or at least a "winner-take-most" dynamic. Once users settle on a standard, the winner commands the lion's share of the market. Microsoft's Windows' standard has won out over competitive standards such as the Apple OS or IBM's OS/2. What also complicates matters for economists evaluating antitrust concerns is the different rules for pricing. These products typically entail huge fixed costs and almost zero marginal cost. Microsoft estimates that it cost $500 million to develop the Windows operating system, but once the code has been written, the marginal cost of producing a disk with a copy of that operating system is negligible (Khanna and Yoffie 1995). Its huge market share enables Microsoft to charge a low price and yet still recoup its investment and generate substantial profits.

But does Microsoft's monopoly still pose a problem for free markets? Is there real harm to consumers? Once again the answer appears to be unclear. Although Microsoft has a monopoly position in the operating-system marketplace, there is no history of price manipulation for consumers who have purchased PCs. As a result, if one approaches the Microsoft case from the Chicago School perspective, a case can be made that its dominance has not really hurt consumer welfare.

These peculiarities of the software business may lead some to conclude that antitrust policy has a diminished role to play in the new economy where various networks prevail. Some economists have argued that in these increasing-returns industries, monopoly does not lead inevitably to a negative outcome for society. In their estimation this is because the dominant companies like Microsoft are not conventional monopolies. Rather, they are serial monopolies, where one monopoly (or near monopoly) gives way to another. In other words, these monopolies are inherently transitory. The rate of innovation is so great that market leaders are regularly leapfrogged by new competitors. Consider, for example, how WordStar gave way to WordPerfect, which then gave way to Word. This is a socially desirable and efficient outcome given our dependence on standards in a network economy where there is a need to communicate or interconnect (Liebowitz and Margolis 1999). These companies need time to recoup their investment. According to former Treasury Secretary Larry Summers, in the Internet economy "the only incentive to produce anything is the possession of temporary monopoly power—because without that power the price will be bid down to the marginal cost and the high initial costs cannot be recouped" (Murray 2000). But as technology evolves, these temporary monopolies become vulnerable and will eventually be overthrown by rivals with new technologies also striving for monopoly status. In this Schumpeterian world of creative destruction, innovation spurs new waves of economic growth and monopolies like Microsoft are eventually dethroned.

Some economists like Romer (2000), however, argue that strong antitrust enforcement is still needed in order to ensure a high level of innovation. He worries that powerful industry incumbents could erect barriers to innovation in order to preserve their monopoly status. According to Romer, healthy industry competition is much more likely to stimulate innovation than a monopoly.

What most concerned some economists and U.S. antitrust officials in the Microsoft case was not price manipulation but Microsoft's attempt to stifle innovation. They seemed to agree with Romer, rationalizing that government intervention was necessary because innovation would be more likely to thrive in a competitive market rather than in one dominated by one company like Microsoft. This focus on innovation is a new thrust for antitrust policy, which, as we have seen, has been more preoccupied with preventing price manipulation and promoting choice in static markets. According to Mandel (2000), "The government's focus on promoting innovation . . . is likely to form the basis of antitrust policy in the New Economy."

There is significant debate among policy makers and economists as to whether or not an innovation-based approach to antitrust is feasible. This new antitrust philosophy surely raises many questions. What are the key success factors that foster innovation in the "new economy"? Do small companies or large companies exhibit a better track record? How important are substantial resources and scale economies? Until these and other questions are answered with more empirical evidence it will be difficult to develop criteria for government intervention in the marketplace for the sake of this new principle.

UNITED STATES OF AMERICA V. MICROSOFT CORPORATION

The significance of this case cannot be overstated. According to Lipsky and Sidak (1999), "The Microsoft litigation is widely regarded as the most consequential case prosecuted by the federal government since the IBM and AT&T cases." Obviously, not everyone agreed that just because network effects bias certain industries to monopoly power that the outcome is benign and efficient. There were many economists who argued that these network effects create a serious threat of anticompetitive behavior that must be dealt with before too much damage is done. The U.S. Department of Justice, swayed by this logic along with its dismay at Microsoft's behavior as a monopolist, decided to pursue legal action against Microsoft. This epic confrontation commenced in 1993 and culminated in the famous antitrust trial, which got underway in October 1998.

The government's case focused on four distinct violations of the Sherman Act:

1. Microsoft's monopolization of the market for PC operating systems and its maintenance of monopoly power by anticompetitive means, especially in its efforts to combat the browser threat (the browser was viewed as a possible future partial substitute for the operating system). This is in violation of Section 2 of the Sherman Act, which declares that it is unlawful for a person or firm to "monopolize . . . any part of the trade or commerce among the several States, or with foreign nations."
2. Unlawful exclusive dealing arrangements in violation of Sections 1 and 2 of the Sherman Act (this category includes Microsoft's exclusive deal with America Online).
3. Microsoft's unlawful attempt to monopolize the market for Web browsing software (in addition to using anticompetitive means to maintain its power in the market for Intel-compatible PC operating systems, Microsoft attempted to illegally amass monopoly power in the browser market) in violation of Section 2 of the Sherman Act.
4. Anticompetitive tying or bundling of Microsoft's Internet Explorer (IE) browser with its Windows operating system in violation of Section 1 of the Sherman Act (Section 1 of this act prohibits contracts, combinations, and conspiracies in restraint of trade, and this includes tying arrangements).

In order to prove the first allegation, the plaintiff in this case, the DOJ, had to demonstrate that (1) Microsoft was a monopoly and (2) Microsoft abused its monopoly power, since it is not illegal per se to be a monopoly. Most monopolies use their power to hurt consumers by charging higher prices (monopoly rents) and reducing output, but that is not the case with Microsoft, which typically sells its operating system to hardware manufacturers at a meager price of $40. Nonetheless, the DOJ set out to prove that Microsoft hurt consumer welfare in other ways.

While merely possessing monopoly power is not itself an antitrust violation, it is a necessary condition for proving a monopolization charge. The Supreme Court has defined monopoly power as "the power to control prices or exclude competition" (*United States v. E.I. du Pont*, 351 U.S. 377 [1956]). Monopoly power can therefore be inferred if a company possesses a dominant market share in the relevant market that is protected by huge entry barriers. The U.S. District Court for the District of Columbia, which first heard this case, concluded that Microsoft possessed monopoly power in the relevant market; that is, the market for Intel-compatible PC operating systems. The District Court found that Windows accounts for a 95-percent share of this market. It also concluded that Microsoft's market power derived from formidable barriers to entry. One such barrier is the "application barrier to entry," which is based on two features of the OS market: consumers want an

OS for which there is an abundance of software applications, and software developers prefer to write applications for an OS that has a large installed base. Microsoft clearly benefits from this applications entry barrier. Consumers are "locked into" Windows because it has the applications they need, and the costs of switching to a competitor are too high.

If middleware software (such as Netscape's Navigator browser) were to succeed, it would erode this barrier.[1] If applications are primarily written for the browser instead of the OS, the underlying operating system would tend to become irrelevant. Hence the threat to Microsoft's monopoly power. According to the U.S. Court of Appeals, which later affirmed the District Court's ruling on Microsoft's monopoly power,

> If a consumer could have access to the applications he desired—regardless of the operating system he uses—simply by installing a particular browser on his computer, then he would no longer feel compelled to select Windows in order to have access to those applications. . . . Therefore, Microsoft's efforts to gain market share in one market (browsers) served to meet the threat of Microsoft's monopoly in another market (operating systems) by keeping rival browsers from gaining a critical mass of users necessary to attract developer attention away from Windows as the platform for software development. (*United States v. Microsoft Corporation*, 253 F.3d 34 D.C. Cir. [2001]).

Microsoft allegedly sought to prevent Navigator from gaining market share and attracting developers by aggressively promoting its own browser. Microsoft's real troubles began when it decided to provide "built-in" access to the Internet in Windows 95. It needed to add Web browsing software to Windows to make it competitive with rival products such as IBM's OS/2 and Apple's Mac OS. Microsoft introduced Internet Explorer version 2 in November 1995. As the product steadily improved, Microsoft sought to encourage third parties to use and distribute IE (beginning with version 3), and some of these arrangements led to claims that Microsoft engaged in anticompetitive conduct.

One bone of contention under the first major allegation (that Microsoft sought to maintain its monopoly power by anticompetitive means) concerns Microsoft's dealings with its original equipment manufacturers (OEMs) regarding the inclusion of the browser. The OEM channel is one of two primary channels for the distribution of browsers. Microsoft allegedly executed deals with computer makers to exclude Netscape's browser and promote Internet Explorer. Manufacturers who refused to go along were supposedly threatened with losing access to Windows. Although there is a sworn deposition from Compaq accusing Microsoft of threatening to "terminate their agreement" for promoting Netscape and giving its icon prominence on the Presario desktop, Microsoft claims that "it has never restricted any computer manufacturer from shipping Netscape Navigator or any other computer software" (Lohr 1999).

Microsoft does admit, however, that it prevented deletion of the IE icon in favor of a competitor's browser icon, arguing that the IE browser was an essential feature of the operating system and should not be tampered with.

There is a license restriction that prohibits the removal of desktop icons, folders, and start menu entries; this restriction also forbids OEMs from allowing any user interface other than the Windows desktop to be launched when the PC system is booted. Microsoft gives OEMs limited rights under their license agreements to modify Windows. Its reasoning is that these alterations could damage the value of Windows as a "stable platform." The government held that the provisions of Microsoft's license agreement to limit the "freedom of OEM's to reconfigure or modify" Windows was anticompetitive because it prevented OEMs from altering Windows "in ways that might . . . generate usage for Navigator." In other words, "It thwarts the distribution of a rival browser by preventing OEM's from removing visible means of user access to IE" (*United States v. Microsoft Corporation*, 253 F.3d 34 D.C. Cir. [2001]).

On the other hand, Microsoft's licensing agreements have never prohibited OEMs from preinstalling programs (including Navigator) on their PCs and placing icons for those programs in the start menu. Despite this freedom of OEMs to install Netscape on their PCs, the DOJ claims that OEMs were reluctant to do so since the presence of both a Navigator and an IE icon might confuse consumers and lead to a flood of phone calls to their support lines. As a result, the government's case suggests that Microsoft succeeded in ostracizing Netscape from the OEM distribution channel, since it was impractical for the OEMs to preinstall a second browser.

The second major allegation against Microsoft is its exclusionary deals, which could potentially violate both Sections 1 and 2 of the Sherman Act. The main focus is the agreements with various online service providers or Internet access providers (IAPs). In 1996, for example, Microsoft entered into an arrangement with America Online, which agreed to incorporate IE browsing technology seamlessly into the AOL client software. AOL says that it chose IE because it was technically superior to Navigator for its purposes. In exchange for this arrangement, Microsoft agreed to place an AOL icon in its OLS folder.[2] But it is also alleged that AOL was forbidden to promote or support any non-Microsoft Web browser nor provide software using any non-Microsoft browser except at the customer's request. According to Microsoft, AOL's commitment to use IE did not prevent AOL from complying with a subscriber's request for Navigator. But according to the Justice Department, this is an unlawful exclusive dealing arrangement that excludes Netscape from efficient channels to achieve increases in market share. The burden falls on Microsoft to defend this exclusive arrangement by proving that there is some procompetitive justification.

The third allegation involves Microsoft's liability for attempted monopolization of the browser market in violation of Section 2 of the Sherman Act. According to case law, "To demonstrate attempted monopolization a plaintiff must prove (1) that the defendant has engaged in predatory or anticompetitive conduct with (2) specific intent to monopolize and (3) a dangerous probability of achieving monopoly power" (*Spectrum Sports Inc. v. McQuillan*, 506

U.S. 456 [1993]). It is alleged that Microsoft initially attempted to coerce Netscape to divide the browser market. According to this plan, Microsoft would let Netscape develop browsers for Macintosh, Unix, and 16-bit Windows systems, while it would develop browsers for the much larger market of 32-bit Windows 95 systems. According to the testimony of Jim Barksdale (the CEO of Netscape at the time), "If we refused to agree, Microsoft made it clear that they would attempt to crush us" (Wasserman 1999). Microsoft disputes this claim and says that such a "market allocation proposal" never came up in its deliberations with Netscape. But according to the DOJ, when Netscape refused to abandon the development of browsing software for 32-bit versions of Windows, Microsoft intentionally sought to expand Internet Explorer's share of browser usage and to simultaneously depress Navigator's share to an extent sufficient to demonstrate to software developers that Navigator would never emerge as the standard software to browse the Web. The government also claims that there was a "dangerous probability" that Microsoft would achieve monopoly power in the browser market.

Perhaps the most significant and contentious piece of the government's case against Microsoft was the fourth and final allegation. The DOJ contended that Microsoft was culpable for unlawful technological tying, that is, bundling its Internet Explorer browser with the Windows operating system. Initially, Microsoft relied upon contracts with its original equipment manufacturers to ensure that its browser functionality was included with Windows. For Windows 98 and beyond, however, the company modified the design of its Windows code to incorporate browser functionality. By intermingling the browser code with the code for Windows 98, Microsoft made it infeasible to disable the browser.

A tying arrangement violates the Sherman Act if "the seller has appreciable economic power in the tying product market, and if the arrangement affects a substantial volume of commerce in the tied market" (*Eastman Kodak Co. v. Image Technical Services Inc.*, 504 U.S. 451 [1992]). In the Microsoft case the Windows operating system is the tying product and the Internet Explorer browser is the tied product.

One of the more relevant cases to address this issue of tying is *Jefferson Parish Hospital District v. Hyde* (466 U.S. 21–22 [1984]). In this case the Court held that a hospital offering hospital services (i.e., surgery) and anesthesiology services as a package was guilty of tying. There was some question in this case about whether or not surgical services and anesthesiology are separate products. While the government insisted that these services were separate, the case for separability was certainly not intuitively obvious. According to the final ruling, the patients perceived the services as separate products for which they desired a choice, and the package had the effect of forcing patients to purchase an unwanted product. Thus, tying anesthesia services to surgery in *Jefferson Parish* was judged to be anticompetitive because consumers were forced to purchase products from this hospital that they would prefer to get from some other source. The Court proposed a "consumer demand" test for determining tying: In difficult cases where there is a question of the functional relation between two products, it is necessary to examine the empirical evidence of demand for the tied product separate from the tying product. The Court decreed that "no tying arrangement can exist unless there is a sufficient demand for the purchase of anesthesiological services separately from hospital service" (*Jefferson Parish v. Hyde*).

On the surface the bundling of the two products in the Microsoft case, the operating system and the Internet Explorer browser, seems to have benefited consumers, since the browser was given away for free. It was alleged, however, that unsuspecting consumers were being harmed because they were losing the ability to choose between IE and Netscape's Navigator browser. Also, this bundling is problematic because the browser is potentially a partial substitute for the monopoly product; that is, the operating system. According to the government's case, the Web browser can become an alternative platform for which applications are written, which might mean that it would one day usurp the OS's monopoly status. Navigator, for example, supports JAVA, and Microsoft supposedly feared that once introduced on users' systems, this JAVA-enabled platform would attract software developers. In the long run, then, it could displace Windows as an attractive platform for new applications and take advantage of the self-reinforcing network effect that made Windows so powerful. As a result, the DOJ concluded that Microsoft tied IE to Windows as another strategic ploy to preserve its current monopoly. Quite simply, according to the government and the Court's findings of fact, Microsoft exercised its substantial market power to preserve its "applications barrier to entry" by means of this tying arrangement. By controlling the platforms that software vendors write for, Microsoft sought to maintain the market's dependence on Windows and the applications written for Windows.

How has Microsoft sought to defend itself against this barrage of charges? With regard to the first allegation (that Microsoft is a monopoly and has maintained its power not through competition on the merits), Microsoft has steadfastly argued that it does not possess monopoly power and that it does not behave like a monopolist. It does not control output the way a traditional monopolist does. According to Microsoft, there is no evidence that it controls a significant percentage of the "productive assets" in the operating-system business, so it could not restrict total output of operating systems and thereby raise prices. Linux or IBM, for example, could easily expand their output to meet the entire consumer demand for operating systems. Microsoft further argues that the dominant market position of Windows "was created by and is dependent on consumer demand not the company's control of total output" (Microsoft's Brief on Appeal 2001). There is also some question about the relevant market: Is it the market for Intel-compatible PC operating systems (as the District Court claims), or should it also include non-Intel-compatible operating systems (such as Mac OS)? Finally, Microsoft contends that there are no structural barriers to entry that preserve its alleged monopoly power.

Some of the allegations regarding anticompetitive behavior are certainly problematic for Microsoft, but its lawyers defend Microsoft's efforts to prevent computer manufacturers from displacing the desktop icon for Microsoft's browser. Microsoft has a right under federal copyright law to prevent unauthorized alteration of its copyrighted operating system. "If intellectual property rights have been lawfully acquired, their subsequent exercise cannot give rise to antitrust liability" (Appelant's Brief 1998). Microsoft also points out that its OEMs can install a second browser in addition to IE. The company rejects the argument that two browsers will lead to "consumer confusion" and observes that some OEMs do install multiple browsers. Finally, Microsoft argues that despite the restrictions of the OEM license agreement, Netscape was not blocked from distributing its product.

Microsoft has also contended that it did not exhibit anticompetitive behavior in its struggle with Netscape, but rather procompetitive behavior. It did not prevent a competitor from reaching the marketplace (thus decreasing consumer welfare), but defeated the competitor in the marketplace through improved products, increased distribution, and lower prices (thereby increasing consumer welfare). Also, Microsoft's design of Windows did not foreclose competition from rival Web browsers. Microsoft did attempt to maximize IE's share of the browser market at Netscape's expense, but this is compatible with a procompetitive intent.

The second allegation regarding the agreements with Internet access providers can perhaps be defended on the grounds that exclusive contracts and cross-marketing agreements are commonplace in a competitive market economy and most especially in the IT industry. According to one supportive brief, "They represent vigorous competition on the merits, serving the legitimate purposes of facilitating entry into new markets and preventing IAP's from misappropriating the free advertising provided by placement on the Windows desktop" (Association for Competitive Technology and Computing Technology 2001). The bottom line is that these agreements did not deny Netscape access to the marketplace, "and AOL is again free in early 2001—as it was at the end of 1998—to replace IE with Navigator in AOL's proprietary client software, which would again make Navigator the leading Web browser software" (*Microsoft Brief on Appeal* 2001).

Microsoft's defense team attempted to refute the third allegation and the charge of attempted monopolization of the browser market with the claim that Microsoft's competition with Netscape was not anticompetitive, since it did not foreclose Navigator from the marketplace. Microsoft's lawyers also claimed that the company did not act with a "specific intent" to monopolize, but rather sought to prevent Netscape from dominating the browser market. Moreover, there is no "dangerous probability" that Microsoft will achieve domination in this market, which has not even been properly defined. "We cannot just accept the plaintiff's unproven allegation of a 'browser' market," argues the Microsoft defense team (Microsoft's Brief on Appeal 2001).

In response to the fourth and final allegation, Microsoft's lawyers pointed out that freezing the Windows operating system poses a great danger to the future of innovation in the software industry. They argue that the proposal to freeze Windows reflects a view that all beneficial product enhancements have already been developed. As Microsoft's attorneys argued in their brief to the appeals court, "Had Microsoft not added Internet technologies to its products, it would be an anachronism today" (Microsoft's Brief on Appeal 2001). Specifically, by preventing firms from integrating into their products previously provided stand-alone products the courts will chill innovation to the detriment of consumers. Thus, Microsoft contends that the government's case suggests a dangerous precedent for other software companies that produce an industry standard: Could they too be accused of leveraging their monopoly power just by adding new functionality to their products? Software products are dynamic and must be allowed to evolve; if not, consumers will suffer the consequences of outdated technologies. Moreover, does the Court's consumer demand test make sense, especially for software? As Microsoft's lawyers pointed out, word processors now include spell checkers and PCs now include modems, even though both features used to be sold separately as add-on products. Are these other examples of unlawful ties?

Microsoft further contends that it must have a right to innovate by adding new functionality to its software products. The government argues that the products are really separate and are bundled together not for the sake of efficiency but solely for an anticompetitive purpose. It maintains that Windows and IE are separate products because "consumers today perceive operating systems and browsers as separate products for which there is separate demand" (Microsoft's Brief on Appeal 2001). Microsoft, on the other hand, claims that the consumer demand test for separability is problematic and insists that the evolution of software is a process of bundling a new functionality (i.e., a new product) into an old product, even though it is still possible to provide those products separately. Without the capacity to enhance its core products in this way, they will become stagnant and ineffectual. For Microsoft there is a crucial principle at stake in this trial: Microsoft and not the government should be the final arbiter of the functionality bundled into its integrated software products.

In summary, Microsoft has consistently maintained that, far from violating the antitrust laws, its conduct was procompetitive, producing enormous consumer benefits. It cites the work of scholars like Hazlett (1999) who says, "The facts of the 'browser war' lead inexorably to one conclusion: consumers have benefited enormously from the ferocious rivalry between Netscape and Microsoft." Moreover, Microsoft claims that their actions should not be branded as anticompetitive, since they did not foreclose Netscape from the marketplace.

Despite the best efforts of its legal defense team, however, Microsoft lost the opening round of this case. Judge Jackson ruled that Microsoft violated Section 1 of the Sherman Act by tying IE to Windows. He also held that Microsoft is a monopoly in the market for "Intel-compatible PC operating systems" and that Microsoft maintained its power by anticompetitive means in violation of Section 2 of the Sherman Act. As evidence of this claim the District Court cited Microsoft's exclusion of Navigator from its OEM distribution channel. Finally, Judge Jackson held that Microsoft did attempt to monopolize the browser market, which is also in violation of Section 2. The remedy recommended by the plaintiffs and accepted by Judge Jackson was a breakup into two companies: an operating company and an applications company.

The case was promptly appealed, and in June 2001, in a stunning turn of events, a Federal Appeals Court overruled the divestiture order approved by Judge Jackson. The Appeals Court was unconvinced that this extreme remedy was warranted: "Divestiture is a remedy that is imposed only with great caution, in part because its long term efficacy is rarely certain" (Labaton 2001). Nonetheless, Microsoft was not completely exonerated, as the Appeals Court ruled that Microsoft did violate Section 2 of the Sherman Act. The judges concluded that Microsoft abused its monopoly power in order to maintain its Windows monopoly. It overturned the finding that Microsoft attempted to monopolize the browser market and said that the tying issue needed to be reconsidered, since Judge Jackson used the wrong standard. The case was sent back to District Court, and it was assigned to Judge Colleen Kollar-Kotelly. Judge Jackson was removed from the Microsoft case for granting interviews to reporters during the trial.

Judge Kollar-Kotelly immediately requested that both sides work out an agreement, and on November 1, 2001, the Justice Department announced the broad terms of a consent decree with Microsoft. According to this consent decree, PC manufacturers will have greater freedom to ship computers without Microsoft middleware (such as a browser) and to hide icons that initiate Microsoft's middleware programs. Microsoft must also disclose technical data that will help competitors make middleware programs. As this book goes to press, this consent decree awaits the court's approval.

While Judge Jackson may have gone too far in his assessment of Microsoft's culpability, the Appeals Court probably has it right. No matter how you define the market, Microsoft is a puissant monopoly and it appears to have exerted its monopoly power to suppress Netscape's Navigator, a partial substitute for Windows. Microsoft took a series of steps to prevent Navigator from maintaining its customer base so it would not be attractive to application providers. In sum, Microsoft engaged in a defensive and predatory preemption of a middleware product's interoperability with future applications. The core principle of the Sherman Act that still applies in the new economy is that a company cannot use its monopoly power to defend itself against competitors to that monopoly. The apparent outcome of this case, assuming that the Appeals Court is not overruled, preserves that critical principle, and this is obviously salient for future cases.

Some aspects of the government's case are certainly questionable, especially the claim that Microsoft tried to become a monopoly in the browser marketplace. As the Appeals Court noted, the plaintiff did not even bother to define that market, let alone make a case for monopolization. Furthermore, there may be legitimate questions about the tying allegations. The conclusion that bundling Windows and IE was illegal tying and not just product integration is surely not obvious. No company has ever been held liable for "technological tying" (i.e., integrating new functionality into an existing product). Also, as Gates himself pointed out, "The fact that our browser was integrated into Windows 95 from the outset did not in any way prevent consumers from choosing another browser" ("Bill Gates Replies" 1998).

It seems clear that we need a different standard for software, which is inherently plastic and constantly in the process of being upgraded with new features and functionality. Bundling software offers enhanced functionality and other efficiencies that can lower production costs and benefit consumers. We need much more leniency in applying the tying laws to software products. What makes this case different, however, is that Microsoft was tying a product (IE) in a bundle designed to undermine a partial substitute to its Windows monopoly. Here is where the line must be drawn with regard to bundling: When the monopolist is bundling a partial substitute, there is likely to be an anticompetitive impact. According to Hovenkamp (1999), the bundling of a partial substitute can "sabotage a nascent technology that might compete with the tying product but for its foreclosure from the market." Lessig (2000) make this same argument in his brief on the tying issue at the center of the Microsoft case. He argues in support of a "New Product Rationale," whereby "two software products combined in a new way would be considered a 'single product' for purposes of antitrust tying law," but he includes a caveat that "this conclusion would be presumptive only." That presumption would be rebutted by "the competitive threat posed by the bundling of 'partial substitutes.'" Thus, under normal circumstances bundling new software functionality is not problematic, even for a monopolist. If the software company Intuit, for example, were to bundle tax and accounting software, it would not be a case of illegal tying under this standard. But when a monopolist bundles a partial substitute, then we are likely to have anticompetitive harm and a case of tying that violates the antitrust laws.

To be sure, the Microsoft case is immensely complex and has led to strong differences of opinion in the legal and information technology communities. One reason for the divisiveness provoked by this case is that we have not really thought through the full implications of competition in the context of a network economy where network effects are predominant. Regardless of the ultimate outcome of this case, we have a long way to go if we want to better understand what constitutes the ideal of fair competition in a rapidly changing network economy.

Key Dates in Microsoft's History and Its Antitrust Trial

1975 Microsoft is founded by Bill Gates and Paul Allen.

1980 Microsoft is chosen to develop an operating system for IBM's PC; the system is called MS-DOS.

1983 Microsoft begins developing a graphical, user-friendly operating system (similar to Apple's graphical user interface), called Windows.

1985 (November) Windows 1.0 is released.

1990 (May) Windows 3.0, a much improved version of the operating system, is released, and Microsoft quickly sells over 40 million copies.

1991 The Federal Trade Commission (FTC) begins an investigation into the possibility that Microsoft's pricing policies are anticompetitive.

1993 The FTC drops the investigation, but the Department of Justice announces a new investigation into Microsoft's pricing.

1994 Microsoft signs a consent decree with the DOJ. According to the decree, Microsoft cannot force computer manufacturers licensing Windows to take its other software products. The decree does permit Microsoft to integrate other products into its operating system.

1995 Judge Stanley Sporkin (of the U.S. District Court) rejects the settlement, claiming that it does not go far enough to contain the company's anticompetitive behavior. Sporkin also attacks Microsoft for its persistent practice of promoting vaporware (his decision is reversed at a later date).

1996 (October) The DOJ first accuses Microsoft of violating the consent decree.

1997 (October 20) The Justice Department sues Microsoft for allegedly violating the consent decree by bundling the Internet Explorer browser with its Windows 95 operating system.

1997 (December 11) The U.S. District Court Judge Thomas Penfield Jackson issues a preliminary injunction barring Microsoft from requiring computer makers to install IE. Microsoft later appeals this ruling.

1998 (January 22) Because of a possible contempt citation, Microsoft permits its OEMs to install Windows 95 without an IE icon.

1998 (May 12) A federal appeals court rules that the injunction shouldn't apply to Windows 98. This enables Microsoft to proceed with the launch of Windows 98, which tightly integrates the operating system code with the code for its Internet Explorer browser.

1998 (May 18) The DOJ (along with twenty states) file antitrust charges against Microsoft, alleging that the company abused its monopoly power in the operating-system market to gain an unfair advantage in the Internet browser market.

1998 (June 23) A federal appeals court overturns the Windows 95 injunction, thereby dealing a blow to the government's case.

1998 (June) Microsoft releases its Windows 98 product.

1998 (September 1) The Justice Department revises its antitrust suit, adding allegations that Microsoft used anticompetitive practices to thwart competitors like Netscape and Sun.

1998 (September 17) Judge Jackson denies Microsoft's request to limit the scope of the upcoming trial to the narrower set of issues in the government's original complaint.

1998 (October 19) The antitrust trial commences with depositions of the major figures, such as Bill Gates.

1999 (June 24) Both sides close their arguments after seventy-six days of testimony.

1999 (November 5) In his preliminary finding of fact Judge Jackson rules that Microsoft is a monopoly. Shortly thereafter, settlement talks begin.

2000 (April 1) Judge Richard Posner announces that settlement talks between Microsoft and the federal government have ended.

2000 (April 3) Judge Thomas Penfield Jackson rules that Microsoft has abused its monopoly power and violated antitrust laws, including Sections 1 and 2 of the Sherman Antitrust Act.

2000 (April 28) As a remedy, the DOJ requests that Microsoft be dismembered into two separate companies, an applications software company and an operating-system company.

2000 (June 1) Jackson orders the breakup of Microsoft and other restrictions requested by the government.

2000 (June 20) Jackson certifies the case for immediate review by the Supreme Court and postpones the order to break up the company.

2000 (September 26) The Supreme Court says that the U.S. Court of Appeals for the District of Columbia should hear Microsoft's appeal before it takes the case.

2001 (February 26) Oral arguments begin before the U.S. Court of Appeals for the District of Columbia.

2001 (June 28) The U.S. Court of Appeals overturns Judge Jackson's breakup order, but affirms that Microsoft is a monopoly and has abused its power. The case is sent back to District Court and reassigned to Judge Colleen Kollar-Kotelly.

2001 (September 6) The Justice Department says it no longer seeks breakup of Microsoft.

2001 (October 5) Judge Kollar-Kotelly orders both sides back to the negotiating table.

2001 (October 25) Microsoft releases its new operating system, Windows XP. Critics contend that Microsoft is once again using its operating system to extend its monopoly power.

2001 (November 1) The Justice Department and Microsoft announce agreement on a settlement pact. Some Microsoft business practices, such as exclusive distribution deals, are restricted.

E-MARKETPLACES AND B2B EXCHANGES

One thing becomes clear in the wake of the landmark Microsoft trial: This is only the beginning of a long and protracted struggle between policy makers and the "winners" in the new economy, where monopoly may be becoming the rule not the exception. Business-to-business online exchanges have triggered concerns among regulators who see significant potential for abuse. There are three principal antitrust issues raised by B2B exchanges. First, the exchange itself could engage in the selective exclusion of certain competitors. Once it gains a substantial market share, an exchange could discriminate against potential market participants, and thereby hinder their competitive ability by raising their costs. Such exclusionary behavior might be counterproductive in the long run, but it cannot be ruled out. The crucial antitrust questions are whether the exclusion of a competitor from a B2B would harm competition and whether it was necessary for the effective operation of the exchange.

Second, there is the serious possibility of collusion, since the whole purpose of a B2B exchange is to facilitate information sharing. According to Labaton (2000), "The experts worry that because rival companies can see pricing information faster than in other markets, it is easier to coordinate prices without ever speaking to one another." In an open-exchange environment suppliers may be able to coordinate prices by learning ahead of time the prices of their principal rival(s). A related concern is that buyers or sellers will exploit the exchange in order to signal one another about impending price changes. The trick is to draw the line between legitimate information sharing about prices and illicit collusion or signaling.

Third, B2B exchanges may impose upon their participants an exclusivity requirement, forbidding them to participate in other B2Bs. It is possible that such a requirement could negatively impact competition among B2B exchanges. The greater the market share of the B2B imposing such a requirement directly or indirectly, the greater the likelihood of government scrutiny.

These general concerns have led to uneasiness about embryonic exchanges like Metalsite.com, an online exchange that joins together steel and aluminum companies with thousands of potential buyers. COVISINT, the exchange for automobile manufacturers' suppliers, has also been under scrutiny. According to some initial reports, the big four (Ford, General Motors, Daimler Chrysler, and Renault/Nissan) have intimated that suppliers have no choice but to sell their wares through their exchange. There were also allegations (denied by COVISINT) that suppliers had been told that they cannot work with other exchanges. If this were true, these one-sided terms could help orchestrate a shift of power to the automobile manufacturers. But some recalcitrant suppliers like Delphi and Lear agreed to join COVISINT on a non exclusive basis. Even if suppliers are free to join other exchanges, the signals of auto manufacturers couldn't be clearer: "We are not saying suppliers have to use the site, though we (the big three) will do most of our buying through it," proclaims Alice Miles, the head of Ford's COVISINT group (Weinberg 2000).

In November 2000 the Federal Trade Commission completed its antitrust review of exchanges. It concluded that B2B exchanges are not anticompetitive by nature. Hence they will be judged no differently than other businesses. According to FTC Chairman Robert Pitofsky, "The antitrust concerns B2Bs may raise are not new, and [hence] B2Bs are amenable to traditional antitrust analysis" (Moozakis 2000). With this statement the FTC clearly signaled that it will not judge an exchange until it manifests bias toward buyers or sellers, engages in collusive practices, or otherwise becomes detrimental to the free marketplace.

A strong argument can be made that if these public exchanges or consortia exhibit such bias their long-term performance will be suboptimal. Price fixing, collusion, or exclusivity requirements would defeat the whole purpose of the exchange and probably lead to its disintegration. If the dominant players in a particular exchange behave in an anticompetitive fashion, it's likely that suppliers or buyers will find other channels to exchange their products. On the other hand, if an exchange aspires to be inclusive and independent with open access to all players, it will be treated kindly by the marketplace and enjoy a high level of participation and a greater chance of long-term success.

Nonetheless, there are legitimate worries that B2B exchanges will become entangled in antitrust litigation and that this will stifle their growth. The biggest potential problem is the specter of collusion. In order to be effective, B2Bs will need a steady flow of information, and as companies in an exchange collaborate, their boundaries will begin to blur, making it all the more difficult to draw the line between efficient collaboration and collusion. As Zirin (2000) observed, "The delicate balance between the efficiency of transparency and anti-competitive conduct become seriously skewed." There are several measures that can be taken to prevent collusion, such as allowing sellers to see other sellers' prices but not their identity. B2B exchanges should seriously consider taking such steps under certain circumstances.

Given the perils of collusion, along with the possible manifestation of monopoly power, it is worth considering whether the U.S. Justice Department should adopt an agressive antitrust policy, a more anticipatory, ex ante approach rather than a reactive posture. Or should it still pursue a policy of ex post intervention? While there may be some value to an aggressive approach, this is an impractical policy that is probably not conducive to innovation in the long run.

As noted in the previous chapter, the ideal purpose of these B2B exchanges is to bring together as many buyers and sellers as possible in order to facilitate dynamic pricing and thereby lower the costs of procurement while exposing suppliers to a wider spectrum of potential buyers. The bigger the exchange, the larger the N:N community, the greater the possibility for innovative interactions. An international exchange, for example, allows sellers from all over the world to purchase products from some group of buyers, and thereby greatly expands possibilities on the demand side and the supply side. In some instances the collaboration encouraged by such an exchange will allow new markets and products to develop more quickly. Efficient exchanges will quickly realize that independence, neutrality, and openness are in their long-term vested interest. Hence, they should aspire to be open and accessible to all players in a relevant industry. Collusion, exclusivity, or other forms of egregious anticompetitive behavior defeat the purpose of the exchange. As Woods (2000) observes it would make no sense for the auto exchange COVISINT to restrict access to certain suppliers. "It would immediately be self-defeating. Initially, the auto exchange might be able to extract cost savings from those suppliers it admitted, but by limiting access to a small range of suppliers, the auto makers would actually be reducing their chances of securing parts of the right quality at a lower price."

Also, antitrust laws, designed to protect consumers against the higher prices and lower output that often accompany monopoly power, may have less relevance for B2B exchanges. Suppliers should not be protected against the buyer's capacity to find a less-expensive source of raw material through an online exchange. There is certainly nothing untoward about companies coming together in order to coax lower prices out of their suppliers. This will increase their added value and in the long run should benefit the consumer.

Exchanges, therefore, should be left alone unless it is quite obvious that there is collusion or price fixing or that competition is being inhibited through exclusionary tactics. There is a critical role for antitrust policy in the new economy, but this cumbersome "weapon" is more effective when it is used infrequently and when the monopoly abuse is unambiguous and of some duration. In most cases ex ante regulation will stifle innovation by interfering with market forces. Also, these exchanges will most likely have the capacity and the motivation to regulate themselves. It is in their best interest to eschew exclusivity and encourage participation through an open and fair marketplace. The larger the exchange community becomes, the more its "possibilities" will multiply. But if buyers or sellers believe that the exchange is "rigged," they are not likely to participate.

A much better fix, therefore, is self-regulation: Allow exchanges to regulate themselves by imposing restrictions and internal standards on their members. At the heart of this approach should be a set of rules that promote an open and fair exchange. If these exchanges fail to live up to these rules, they will most likely face the full brunt of corrective market forces. Government regulations and restraints, on the other hand, increase transaction costs and encumber the creative process with fixed rules that may interfere with the natural evolutionary process of these embryonic entities.

What would such a regulatory scheme look like? What rules might an exchange impose to ensure this fairness and neutrality? According to Sculley and Woods (1999), the key to developing such an open and competitive exchange would rest on the following conditions:

- Transparency. All transactions should be publicized with details on price and volume. Pricing transparency is essential for an efficient market with competitive process. This must include full disclosure by the sellers, who should describe their products and services so that buyers can make informed choices.
- Integrity. The exchange must ensure the integrity of the pricing mechanism. The elements of a fair pricing system include "equal access; the order with the best price has highest priority; first in, first out (FIFO); effective procedures to ensure that each seller's products are posted correctly and that buyer bids and orders are transmitted accurately; trades are consistently executed in accordance with published rules of the exchange." The bottom line is that exchanges should be as democratic as possible. Thus, every member should have equal access to the exchange, regardless of their size or the longevity of their relationship with the exchange. No one should occupy a privileged position. Also, according to the FIFO condition, if orders are received at the same price the first order received takes presence over the subsequent orders.
- Sanctions against cornering the market. The exchange must take any necessary steps to prevent domination or control by one member. One big buyer or supplier should not be able to dictate price or other terms. The more buyers and sellers actively involved in transactions, the greater the liquidity of the vitality and liquidity of the exchange.
- Standardization. Rules will regulate terms of trading, including product quality, quantities offered, acceptable price increases, transaction fees, and so forth.

At this point we have precious little experience with B2B exchanges, especially public exchanges and industrywide consortia like COVISINT. Many are still in a start-up mode and will evolve as the nature of e-commerce evolves. As these exchanges become more firmly established, they will be more apt to thrive if this self-regulatory mechanism in conjunction with market forces is given an opportunity to function. Democratic, efficient, and fluid exchanges have a much greater chance of success in the marketplace, and the chance for success will be magnified if they can be spared the heavy hand of the government's command and control regulations.

None of this implies, however, that exchanges should have free rein. They should be monitored by the FTC and disciplined if there are clear abuses. Those abuses are less likely to occur in exchanges where there are many buyers and many sellers or few buyers and many sellers. In both cases the transparency in pricing information is apt to push prices down to the benefit of customers. But where there are few sellers and many buyers it could become easier for those suppliers to coordinate their pricing by means of signals via communications on the exchange. This would have the effect of pushing up prices. Hence, exchanges of this sort must be more carefully watched. Nonetheless, it seems preferable to treat each industry exchange or marketplace independently rather than to set forth definitive rules and regulatory guidelines that all exchanges must abide by.

OPEN COMPETITION AND THE AOL–TIME WARNER MERGER

A Little Background

In the spring of 2000, millions of TV viewers in major media cities like New York were chagrined when Time Warner dropped the signal for the ABC television network from its cable system. For several days viewers could not tune into their favorite shows on ABC, such as *Who Wants to Be a Millionaire?* or *NYPD Blue*. The Walt Disney Company, ABC's owner since 1996, was locked in a bitter and prolonged contract dispute with Time Warner, but no one expected the situation to get this far out of hand. The dispute was eventually resolved and New Yorkers could once again tune into the *Millionaire* show along with their other favorite programs on ABC. But the lessons of this incident were painfully clear: Content may be king, but don't neglect the importance of content's delivery systems. According to Gruley (2000), this dispute signaled "the commanding importance of high-speed media pipelines of the future: the 'broadband' networks of cable, advanced phone lines and satellites that increasingly carry entertainment and information to consumers."

Thanks in part to its run-in with Time Warner, Disney became one of many organizations voicing some strident objections to the impending merger of America Online and Time Warner that had just been announced a few months earlier. America Online was the country's leading Internet service provider, while Time Warner was a major media and entertainment company, which owned magazine franchises such as *Time* and *Sports Illustrated*, movie studios such as Warner Brothers and New Line Cinema, and a group of record labels including Atlanta Records and Warner Bros. Records.

This $103.5-billion merger, first made public in January 2000, was finalized in January 2001, when it received the last of the necessary regulatory approvals from the Federal Communications Commission. According to Yang (2001), the merger represented "the long-awaited convergence of the analog present and the digital future." In the waning years of the analog era, content is still closely tied to its delivery systems. The owners of television stations, for example, have firm control over content and services; they produce the shows and send them over the airwaves to their viewers. But with digital technology all forms of content, including voice, data, and video, can be converted into simple bits of data (1s and 0s). Also, the digital conduits, the "pipes" that carry these data, such as optical fiber or DSL, can do so indiscriminately and independent of the particular content. The Internet, of course, greatly facilitates the global distribution of these digital data.

The combination of AOL and Time Warner comes at a propitious time, as cable companies are just beginning to offer their customers high-speed Internet access through cable lines. The AOL–Time Warner merger is expected to accelerate this trend toward broadband Internet access. Once the Internet's capacity is increased it will become the universal, low-cost delivery system for all types of digital information. With broadband, AOL and other ISPs will be able to offer real-time video streaming of motion pictures or videos of live events.

The merger's initial operational plan calls for co-COOs (Chief Operating Officers). Bob Pittman controls America Online (including Netscape), Time Warner Cable, Time Inc., HBO (Home Box Office), Turner Broadcasting System (including networks such as CNN, TBS, and TNT), and the WB television network. His counterpart, Dick Parsons, will control the content divisions that produce and sell entertainment products primarily through retail channels. This includes Warner Brothers, New Line Cinema, Warner Music Group, and Time Warner Trade Publishing. The total revenue generated by all these companies was projected to be $43 billion in 2001 (Yang 2001).

It is obvious that this marriage of entertainment and the Internet has many opportunities for synergy, such as cross-promotion and cross-marketing. In one early promotion AOL disks were included in *Sports Illustrated* magazines, while the magazine's famous swimsuit issue was heavily promoted on AOL. New Line Cinema, a smaller unit of Time Warner, has worked closely with AOL on Web-based promotions to increase sales for its films, such as *The Lord of the Rings*. Some of the more unconventional promotions have included fan chat rooms and online auctions of movie memorabilia. These arrangements point to the logic underlying this merger: Bring together different media platforms under one roof so that the same content can be delivered in different ways and be promoted in a synergistic fashion. In some respects the merger of Time Warner and Turner Broadcasting System had already demonstrated that this content-sharing principle was workable. The union of AOL and Time Warner will enable AOL to serve as another way of promoting and distributing Time Warner's diverse content.

In addition, this merger is likely to give AOL an advantage in its foray into the market for interactive TV. The company has recently begun offering set-top boxes that will allow consumers to watch regular television while they retrieve e-mail or access Web sites. A viewer could watch the evening news on part of the TV screen and pull up related articles from a Web site on another part of the screen.

Finally, AOL's instant messaging program could also be given a boost in the long run by the merger. Instant messaging, which falls somewhere between a phone call and e-mail, allows synchronous, real-time communications between open-line parties. A user keys in a message, which appears instantaneously on the recipient's screen. One popular feature of instant messaging is the "buddy list," which indicates the presence of other "chatters" online. AOL has been the undisputed leader in this area since 1996, with over 61 million users (Carroll 2001). While the telephone is not likely to become extinct anytime soon, instant messaging is becoming a credible substitute and a viable communications channel. Competitors feel that if instant messaging evolves into a platform for exchanging data such as video or music, AOL's union with Time Warner will strengthen its advantage in this nascent market.

A merger of this magnitude is not without its share of economic risks. There are the obvious risks of merging companies with such different cultures. The pace of change at AOL is alien to how things were done at Time Warner, where the organizational structure has been far more bureaucratic. Time Warner's different content units have been described as insular fiefdoms, each with a unique style and culture. More significant perhaps are the risks inherent in the strategy of vertical integration. According to *The Economist*, the principal danger is that "the content does not get the best distribution, or the distribution network does not get the best content" ("One House, Many Windows" 2000). Also, one flawed piece of content could end up damaging multiple distribution outlets. However, while this combination of content and delivery has some perils, it also has great promise and in the eyes of many economists the merger is well worth the risk.

In some respects, however, the merger seems to be going against the trend of deintegration in this industry. As the worlds of telecommunications, entertainment, and computing begin to converge, the multimedia industry is being restructured. According to Bane (1998), it is "moving from a set of three vertical businesses to a collection of five largely independent, horizontal industry segments." These segments are content, packaging (e.g., AOL or Bloomberg are both packagers or integrators of content), transmission networks (companies in this segment, like AT&T, provide the physical infrastructure that helps distribute information), manipulation infrastructure (e.g., software that performs interactive network tasks), and terminals. But this merger illustrates that conglomeration is not a dead issue as companies seek to reorganize by means of a new kind of vertical integration that brings together owners of digital conduits or pipes with content providers. At the very least this will preclude dramatic showdowns between content and distribution for companies that belong to the AOL–Time Warner network. The jury is still out on whether or not this merger will really add value for both of these companies. Will this vertically integrated Internet–media organization be nimble enough to compete with more specialized rivals? Was this merger really necessary to attain cross-promotional power? Why not a more contingent relationship, such as a partnership or a strategic alliance?

Regulatory Approval

When this merger was first proposed, the responsible U.S. regulatory agencies, both the Federal Communications Commission and the Federal Trade Commission, devoted considerable energies to studying the potential for an anticompetitive impact. Although this was not a horizontal merger, both agencies had several concerns.

There was the real possibility of *vertical foreclosure*: exploiting a vertical arrangement to diminish competition in a related vertical market (Viscusi and Harrington 1998). The new company, for example, might require Time Warner's cable customers to have AOL as their Internet service provider. Thus, the FTC had to decide whether AOL–Time Warner customers should have access to the services of their rivals (such as other ISPs) if they so desired. Should cable companies be able to leverage their control over their cable infrastructure into control over related markets such as the market for ISPs? By bundling ISP services with cable access and by refusing to allow users to select another ISP without additional fees, ISP competition could be eliminated in the residential cable market. This type of bundling could have a greater competitive impact in the future, as ISPs extend their role as gatekeepers of the Internet.

A second concern was that AOL–Time Warner would engage in *content discrimination*. The company could discriminate against content that does not originate from Time Warner, or deny its own content to other distributors. It would not be difficult for AOL–Time Warner to configure its platforms to be predisposed to Time Warner content through techniques such as preferential caching. According to *Communications Daily* (2000), "Caching technology allows popular Web sites to be stored closer to the end user, possibly at cable headend, in order to avoid Internet's backbone delays." There were also fears that AOL–Time Warner would discriminate against content in more subtle ways, perhaps through channel bias. They could, for example, rearrange channels so that a competitors' network had a higher and less-prominent number (e.g., moving MSNBC from channel 15 to 64, while leaving CNN, which is owned by Time Warner, at 14). Biased channel placement is one of several ways in which AOL–Time Warner could realize an unfair advantage by owning its own TV networks along with cable and Internet pipelines.

A final concern focused on AOL's Instant Messaging (IM) network of 61 million users, which remains closed to members of competing systems, such as those offered by Yahoo. If this market share continues to grow, opportunities for future competition may well be foreclosed. AOL has also ensured that its IM software is not interoperable with the chat software of its rivals such as iCast. Competitors such as Microsoft have repeatedly expressed concerns with this system's lack of openness and interoperability, and others worry that AOL's dominance in instant messaging could give it leverage in the competition for Internet telephony. AOL's discrimination not only suppresses innovation, but it also hurts its own customers who would undoubtedly prefer to communicate online with as many people as possible.

The Open-Access Debate

Prior to the AOL–Time Warner merger the open-access debate had already received some attention when AT&T acquired the cable company TCI, which reached 17 million customers. The TCI acquisition also gave AT&T a stake in Excite@Home, a high-speed Internet service company that connects users through cable modems. This was followed up by AT&T's acquisition of MediaOne Group, Inc., with a customer base of 8 million. The FCC declined to impose any restrictions on AT&T after this merger of MediaOne and TCI. AT&T offers high-speed Internet access over these cable lines exclusively through Excite@Home. According to Labaton (1999), the chairman of the FCC at the time, William Kennard, "in essence sided with AT&T by formulating a policy that only the Federal Government, and not local authorities, has jurisdiction, but ruling out intervention for now."

This set off a grassroots campaign to force AT&T to allow its cable customers to use Internet providers other than Excite@Home without being forced to pay large additional fees. This was a futile exercise, however, since even the courts did not seem anxious to enforce such a requirement. After AT&T assimilated TCI's cable franchise in Portland, Oregon, the city demanded that AT&T open up its cable broadband infrastructure to any Internet company on the same terms as Excite@Home. AT&T refused and in a subsequent lawsuit the Ninth Circuit Court of Appeals ruled in AT&T's favor. It held that it was a mistake to classify cable broadband access as a "cable service," and that Portland therefore had no legal basis to regulate broadband access. In Broward County, Florida, officials were persuaded to adopt an ordinance requiring AT&T to open its cable system to other Internet service providers, but the ordinance was determined to be in violation of the First Amendment since it constituted an interference in a cable broadcaster's power to set the programming for its system.

Given this string of defeats, the stakes were high in the AOL–Time Warner merger. During their deliberations both the FTC and the FCC were lobbied heavily by advocates of "open access," who believed that information or data should be able to travel from one end of the global information infrastructure to the other unimpeded. In some respects the union of AOL and Time Warner has once again brought the open-access issue directly into the spotlight. This vertical merger has linked together the three layers of the information infrastructure: The content, logical, and physical layers are combined in a fully integrated network controlled by one company. This level of vertical integration could have a profound effect on the future architecture of the Internet since it gives the physical network owner control over the logical layer (AOL–Time Warner owns the ISP, AOL, and the Netscape browser software) along with the content that flows over that network.

Open-access proponents claimed that this merger represented a potential threat to the Internet's end-to-end architecture. They stressed the need to preserve this principle of end-to-end, whereby an unintelligent, simple network processes packets of data indiscriminately; that is, without regard for their content. The Internet's simple structure has been designed for open access, and any sort of preferred access violates this basic principle. The Internet must remain, they argue, an open and neutral space that welcomes innovative content.

One danger of the AOL–Time Warner merger is that it could eliminate ISP competition in the broadband cable marketplace if Time Warner's cable customers are not given a choice of ISPs. By allowing bundling of cable and ISP services, the key architectural principle of end-to-end design could be compromised, since cable-owned ISPs would heavily influence the use of broadband technology. In all likelihood the range of services available to broadband cable users would be determined by these ISPs. Thus, an ISP such as AOL could control whether its broadband customers could be purveyors of their own Web content or whether full-length streaming video would be permitted to flow over the network. Excite@Home, for example, already makes its users sign a contract that precludes streaming video that lasts more than ten minutes. Giving the owner of the physical network the power to discriminate content is obviously in direct contradiction of the end-to-end principle. According to Lemley and Lessig (2001), "This design defeats the principle that the network remain neutral and empower users. It is the first step to a return to the architecture of the old AT&T monopoly." Moreover, it's not hard to see how control of all three layers in the hands of one integrated provider could dampen innovation. If innovators have to negotiate with AOL–Time Warner for new uses of their network, in many cases they may choose not to innovate.

Approval of the Merger

The FTC and the FCC ultimately approved this multibillion-dollar merger in January 2001, but there were some conditions imposed by both of these regulatory bodies. To some extent these restrictions amounted to a small victory for open access. The FTC insisted on a regulatory regime that would require AOL–Time Warner to open up its network to rival Internet companies. Likewise, the five-member FCC commission voted three to two (along party lines) to impose certain conditions on the merger. The two Republicans on the commission voted for the merger without conditions, but the Democrats, along with Chairman Kennard, voted to support the FTC's condition mandating that AOL–Time Warner not restrict cable subscribers from choosing an Internet service provider other than AOL. In response, the company has agreed to open up its cable lines to its rival Earthlink and two other ISPs in 70 percent of its market. In the remaining markets it must contract with three ISPs and negotiate with others "in good faith." The FCC's order also prohibited AOL–Time Warner from interfering with content transmitted along the bandwidth being used by these nonaffiliated ISPs.

The FCC did not neglect the problems associated with instant messaging. Under the FCC's order, AOL must open up its instant messaging service to competitors as it begins to provide more sophisticated services such as video streaming through Time Warner's broadband cable lines. Before offering such services, AOL "must either show that it has adopted an industry-wide standard for instant messaging or enter a contract with a competitor, such as

Microsoft Corp., that provides for network interoperability to allow communications with users of competing systems" (Carroll 2001).

A "monitor trustee" appointed by the FTC will oversee the company for the next five years. This trustee is explicitly charged with making sure that the company's cable network and interactive television allow competition. This trustee has the difficult challenge of holding in check AOL–Time Warner's dominance in line with the regulatory terms of the merger. So, for example, if an ISP wants to join the AOL–Time Warner high-speed network and is refused, the trustee will have to determine whether AOL–Time Warner has acted appropriately. This will mean that many of the company's strategic decisions will be subject to bureaucratic review, and that could hinder quick decision making in a hypercompetitive industry.

The terms of the merger are still being debated in some circles and there are many questions about the regulatory regime imposed by the FTC and the FCC. Was the FCC justified in demanding open access and in its appointment of the monitor trustee? Will the oversight lead to bureaucratic complexity and costly delays? Could this and other vertical combinations really be a threat to cyberspace through vertical foreclosure? And in the long run would the free market do a better job than regulators to ensure open access and free competition?

It is our view that this consent agreement preserving open access is at least a step in the right direction. The Internet must remain an open and neutral space, and this will be impossible if it falls victim to conduit or content discrimination. As we argued in Chapter 2, we need to preserve the principle of end-to-end so that all kinds of information can move freely and unimpeded from one end of the global network to the other. It seems likely that government regulation is necessary to sustain open access, especially since the companies involved do not have an encouraging track record. AOL, for example, once lobbied the FCC for open access when it was worried about AT&T and Excite@Home; however, it promptly changed course after the announcement of the Time Warner merger. AOL's refusal to open up its instant messaging software is another indicator of its bad faith. Excite@Home's restrictive end-user contract is also evidence of the industry's desire to avoid competition.

What is lacking so far in the ad hoc approach of policy makers, however, is consistency and regulatory parity. We need a well-conceived, national, industrywide policy that seeks to balance the need for openness with respect for commercial property rights. As Carney (2000) indicates, the openness debate triggers some tough policy issues: "If open access is mandated, how much should cable companies be compensated for sharing their private property; if they can't get an adequate return on investment, will they have the incentive to invest in new infrastructure?" A viable policy must carefully address these and other vexing questions about equal access to high-speed cable lines and openness on the Net. We have to find a way to preserve openness while also addressing this free-rider problem. The need for investment incentives is particularly acute in this capital-intensive industry. But allowing companies like AT&T or AOL–Time Warner to gain that incentive by monopolizing the market for ISPs and restricting Internet content is definitely not a welfare-enhancing solution.

POSTSCRIPT

This chapter has revolved around a careful scrutiny of three case studies that deal with the issue of fair competition on the Internet: Microsoft and the browser wars, B2B exchanges, and the access questions raised by the AOL–Time Warner merger. One common thread in all three of these case studies is the theme of innovation and the need to think about the effects of regulation on the innovation process. The Internet's current end-to-end architecture underlies the openness and availability of this free communications medium. That openness is the key to the Internet's spontaneous and rapid evolution. Therefore, responsible regulatory policies focused on preserving this design principle create value. Given the behavior of industry incumbents like AOL and Excite@Home, it seems unlikely that market forces alone can safeguard the public interests. We have also argued on behalf of the government's intervention to prevent Microsoft from leveraging Windows to the detriment of innovative software developments by potential rivals, especially when those developments might be a partial substitute for Windows. Yet it seems appropriate to give B2B exchanges some latitude, since they have an incentive to regulate themselves. In the long run it will be in the exchange's best interest to support a democratic and fair marketplace with multiple buyers and sellers. The harm associated with these exchanges is speculative, and premature regulation is apt to dampen investment incentives and thereby deter innovation. Since each exchange has an incentive toward transparency and competitiveness, self-regulation can probably be effective if it is given a reasonable chance to work.

Finally, if a B2B does cross the line, any threat to the integrity of the information infrastructure will be minimal. It is incumbent upon policy makers to develop a coherent and forward-looking competition policy for the information age that maintains a level playing field benefiting consumers. The tools and conceptual frameworks of the past do not seem to fit the fast pace or the substantive challenges of the competitive struggles taking place on the Internet. What's needed are flexible policies that can preserve important competitive values such as open access but avoid the suppression of innovation through premature intervention.

NOTES

1. Middleware refers to software like a browser that exposes its own application programming interfaces (APIs), blocks of code in an operating system that allow applications to "plug in" and function.

2. This folder appears on the Windows desktop and contains the icons of proprietary client software of online service providers. Clicking on one of these icons initiates the process of signing up for the ISP's services.

REFERENCES

Appellant's Brief. (1998). *United States of America v. Microsoft* (84 F.Supp.2d 9 D.D.C.).

Association for Competitive Technology and Computing Technology. (2001). Amicus Curiae Remedies Brief re *United States of America v. Microsoft* (97 F.Supp.2d 59 D.D.C. [2000] remedial order).

Bane, W. (1998). "The Converging Worlds of Telecommunication, Computing, and Entertainment." In *Sense and Respond*, edited by S. Bradley and R. Nolan. Boston: Harvard Business School Press.

Becker, G., and Murphy, K. (2001). "Rethinking Antitrust." *Wall Street Journal*, 26 February, A1.

"Bill Gates Replies." (1998). *The Economist*, 13 June, 19–21.

Carney, D. (2000). "Whose Net Is It, Anyway?" *Business Week*, 31 July, 99.

Carroll, J. (2001). "AOL–Time Warner Merger Clears FCC." *Wall Street Journal*, 12 January, A3.

"Communications Daily Notebook." (2000). *Communications Daily*, 11 May, 15.

Gruley, B. (2000). "Moral of Disney's War Against Time Warner: Don't Dis Distribution." *Wall Street Journal*, 3 May, A1.

Hazlett, T. (1999). "Microsoft's Internet Exploration." *Cornell Journal of Law and Public Policy* 29: 52.

Hovenkamp, H. (1999). Supplement to P. Areeda, E. Elhauge, and H. Hovenkamp, *Antitrust Law*. Boston: Little, Brown.

Khanna, T., and Yoffie, D. (1995). *Microsoft 1995*. Boston: Harvard Business School Publications.

Labaton, S. (1999). "Fight for Internet Access Creates Unusual Alliances." *New York Times*, 13 August, A1, A11.

Labaton, S. (2000). "As Competition Heats Up, So Does the Threat of Collusion." *New York Times*, 25 October, E22.

Labaton, S. (2001). "Supreme Court Voids Order for Breaking Up Microsoft." *New York Times*, 29 June, A1.

Lemley, M., and Lessig, L. (2001). "The End of End-to-End: Preserving the Architecture of the Internet in the Broadband Era." *UCLA Law Review* 48: 925.

Lessig, L. (2000). Amicus Curiae Remedies Brief re. *United States of America v. Microsoft* (97 F.Supp.2d 59 D.D.C. [remedial order]).

Liebowitz, S., and Margolis. (1999). *Winners, Losers, and Microsoft*. New York: The Independent Institute.

Lipsky, A., and Sidak, G. (1999). "Essential Facilities." *Stanford Law Review* 51: 1187.

Lohr, S. (1999). "The Justice Department v. Microsoft: The Evidence and the Answers." *New York Times,* 27 October, D5.

Mandel, M. (2000). "Antitrust for the Digital Age." *Business Week*, 15 May, 46–48.

Microsoft's Brief on Appeal. (2001). *United States v. Microsoft* (253 F.3d 34 D.C. Cir.).

Moozakis, C. (2000). "FTC Reserves Its Judgement." *Internet Week*, 6 November, 13.
Murray, A. (2000). "For Policy Makers Microsoft Suggests Need to Recast Models." *Wall Street Journal*, 9 June, A1.
"One House, Many Windows." (2000). *The Economist*, 19 August, 60–61.
Romer, P. (2000). *Amicus Curiae Remedies Brief re. United States of America v. Microsoft* (97 F.Supp.2d 59 D.D.C. [remedial order]).
Schiesel, S. (2000). "Bringing Competition into the Age of the Internet." *New York Times*, 25 December, C1.
Sculley, A., and Woods, W. (1999). *B2B Exchanges*. New York: ISI Publications.
Viscusi, W., Vernon, J., and Harrington, J. (1998). *Economics of Regulation and Antitrust*. 2d ed. Cambridge: MIT Press.
Wasserman, E. (1999). "A Defeat for Microsoft." *Industry Standard*, 15 November, 68.
Weinberg, N. (2000). "Herding Cats." *Forbes*, 24 July, 108–110.
Woods, W. (2000). "Premature Regulation." *Industry Standard*, 8 May, 214–222.
Yang, C. (2001). "Show Time for AOL Time Warner." *Business Week*, 15 January, 57.
Zirin, J. (2000). "Justice Brandeis v. B2B." *Forbes*, 17 July, 60.

6

Freedom of Expression and Content Controls

The democratization of speech and information may well be the greatest legacy of the nascent Internet era. The Internet is the newest technology of freedom, making available an abundance of ideas and a diversity of content. Thanks to its low entry barriers, this global network creates opportunities for new voices to be heard. It magnifies the power of individual citizens and it fortifies democracy by making debate on public issues more inclusive. As the Supreme Court remarked in the landmark *Reno v. ACLU* (521 U.S. 844 [1997]) decision, the Internet enables even an ordinary citizen to become "a pamphleteer, . . . a town crier with a voice that resonates farther than it could from any soapbox." According to the Court, the Internet "is a unique and wholly new medium of worldwide human communications."

There is, however, a negative dimension to the expansion of opportunities created by this new medium. There are many harmful and offensive forms of speech that tarnish the Web and make it a hostile place for some. We can easily find Web pages glorifying violence and hatred or Web pages full of explicit pornographic material. We can even find Web pages with detailed instructions on how to assemble explosive devices. Our mailboxes overflow with spam (unsolicited automated e-mail), and we sometimes feel that cheap speech will drown out the important stuff. Hence, there is an impulse to suppress certain forms of speech and to impose some limits on this technology.

This impulse has been steadfastly resisted by civil libertarians, while many policy makers have taken a more moderate approach, searching for a reasonable middle ground.

This issue of free speech in cyberspace is the most fundamental of all policy concerns. Speech is at the root of most other ethical and public policy problems in cyberspace, including privacy, intellectual property protection, and security. In the eyes of some corporations, restrictions on the free flow of information in order to protect privacy clearly amounts to a commercial free-speech issue. Intellectual property rights are also tantamount to restrictions on free speech. If someone, for example, has property rights to a trademark, others cannot freely use that form of expression.

Property rights and speech rights have become increasingly entangled, as evidenced in a case involving Terminix International Co., the largest termite and pest control company in the United States (Schmitt 1999). According to Carla Virga, in 1997 Terminix allegedly mishandled an inspection at her home. Ms.Virga responded by setting up a Web page highly critical of Terminix. The site contains details of her own negative experience with the company, along with other customer complaints that she actively solicited.

But Terminix sued Ms. Virga, alleging trademark violations. The problem is that she is using the Terminix brand name as a metatag. A metatag is a piece of HTML code, invisible to the user, that describes the Web site so that its contents can be more easily indexed by search engines. If a user were to enter the term "Teminix" as a search term on a search engine like Google, the results would return the Terminix site along with Ms. Virga's site. According to Terminix, this is simply unfair. "She is entitled to her opinion and interpretation of events," the company says, "but to the extent that she is using our trademark to bring people to a bad-mouth site, we simply want that ceased" (Schmitt 1999). As a result, the company accuses Virga of deception and claims that her activities dilute their property rights.

But what about this woman's free-speech rights? She is not seeking to make money off the Terminix brand; her Web page is noncommercial. She is only trying to express her opinion, and, in order to help disseminate that opinion, she has relied on the metatag technology to label her Web site accordingly. Isn't this what the Supreme Court had in mind when it talked about the ability of an ordinary citizen to be a virtual "town crier" with a loud and resonating voice?

This is just one of many cases where property rights and speech rights clash. Which right should take priority? Are the libertarians right to advocate for the broadest possible free-speech rights on the Net? How much protection should Net speech receive under the First Amendment? How should we deal with harmful forms of speech? Is code or law the better approach? These and other questions will form the primary axis of discussion in this chapter.

This issue is made even more complicated because of the Net's expansive global reach. Not all countries share the same attitude about democratic free speech as the United States. Countries like China have developed strategies for dealing with harmful or objectionable content on the Net, including obscenity and pornography. They also try to weed out speech that threatens national security or cultural stability. Chinese officials have consistently sought to rein in the free-wheeling Internet, even if electronic commerce is debilitated in the process. As we discussed in Chapter 1, there are sometimes significant problems when the global Internet confronts national cultures.

Finally, in this overview of speech issues we cannot neglect the topic of libelous speech and the critical issue of liability for those intermediaries who make Internet accessibility possible. To what extent should we hold Internet service provider's liable for the damage caused by defamatory statements made by their customers? On the one hand, mandating ISP liability could have an unwanted chilling effect on free expression in cyberspace, but on the other hand, failure to require ISPs to take adequate measures to curtail online defamation is not conducive to the promotion of civil discourse.

THE FIRST AMENDMENT

Before we analyze specific forms of harmful speech that plague the Internet, some discussion of the First Amendment is essential. The amendment itself is straightforward enough: "Congress shall make no law respecting the establishment of religion, or the free exercise thereof; or abridging the freedom of speech or of the press; or the right of the people peaceably to assemble, and to petition the Government for a redress of grievances." The purpose of this amendment is to protect freedom of individual thought and expression. Although the right to free speech is strong, it is not absolute. But how far should this right extend? What is the scope of this civil right to freedom of expression?

Over the years several free-speech principles have emerged from the remarkable number of cases that have dealt with First Amendment issues. These principles articulate when the government can intervene in speech issues and what the limits are of protected free speech. Here is a concise overview of the more salient principles:

If a law restricting speech "burdens" more speech than is necessary in order to serve a compelling government interest, it will be considered unconstitutionally "overbroad."

The government cannot compel anyone to endorse a "symbol, slogan, or pledge."

Government restrictions on the "time, place, and manner" in which speech is allowed are constitutional only if they meet these three conditions:

- they must be "content neutral."
- they must leave other opportunities for speech to occur.
- they must "narrowly serve a significant state interest."

Content-based government restrictions on speech are regarded as unconstitutional unless they serve a "compelling state interest"; there are, however, six general exceptions, that is, six forms of speech that are not protected by the First Amendment:

- Speech that will likely induce "imminent lawless action."
- "Fighting words," i.e., insulting words apt to start a fight or a conflict of some sort.
- Obscenity: "patently offensive" speech that lacks "serious literary, artistic, political, or scientific value."
- Child pornography.
- Defamatory statements, defined as "communication that tends to harm the reputation of another so as to lower his esteem in the eyes of the community."
- Certain forms of commercial speech that are deceptive or pertain to illegal products. (Fisher 2001)

It is important to note that the First Amendment protects citizens from the government's attempts at prior restraint that impose restrictions on free-speech rights. Private parties, however, have much more latitude in restricting speech. An online service provider, for example, may use a filter to screen out Web sites with hate speech, but if such a policy were mandated by the government it would most likely constitute "state action" and trigger First Amendment issues. Berman (2000), among others, believes that the Internet should lead us to reconsider this "state action" doctrine, since online service providers and others have extraordinary power to place restrictions on speech through technical means, and yet the First Amendment would not apply to their restrictive activities. He calls for a revision of the "state action" doctrine in order to better safeguard free-speech rights. Fried (2000), however, points out the downside of initiating such a revision despite the influence of the Internet:

> By limiting the First Amendment to protecting citizens from government (and not from each other), the state action doctrine enlarges the sphere of unregulated discretion that individuals may exercise in what they think and say. In the name of First Amendment "values," courts could perhaps inquire whether I must grant access to my newspaper to opinions I abhor, must allow persons whose moral standards I deplore to join my expressive association, or must remain silent so that someone else gets a chance to reach my audience with a less appealing but unfamiliar message. . . . I am not convinced that whatever changes the Internet has wrought in our environment require courts to mount this particular tiger.

As we take our bearings before we analyze specific free-speech cases it is important to keep in mind that basic constitutional principles, such as those embodied in the First Amendment, are not affected by the development of new technologies. The right to free speech within the parameters established through elaborate case law is not altered in this radically new context of the digital network. According to Tribe (1999), "Even though the Internet allows nearly anyone to obtain or transmit information instantaneously to and from anywhere on the planet, it does not deserve more—or less—free speech protection than older media."

THE PROBLEM OF CYBERPORN

When *Time* magazine published its famous cover story on Internet pornography in July 1995, it had no idea that this story would have such a huge impact, albeit for the wrong reasons. The cover was grotesque: There was an image of a very young child shocked by lurid images on a computer screen. Underneath the photo there was a simple question: "Can we protect our kids and free speech?" Those who took the time to read the story by Philip Elmer-DeWitt (1995) discovered the apparent pervasiveness of pornography in cyberspace. Elmer-DeWitt based his article on a study of online porn entitled "Marketing Pornography on the Information Superhighway" (Rimm 1995). The purpose of this Carnegie Mellon study, which was later published in the prestigious *Georgetown University Law Journal*, was to measure the amount of pornography available online. According to *Time*, the Carnegie Mellon researchers found 917,410 sexually explicit images, descriptions, stories, and film clips. Also, "On those Usenet newsgroups where digitized images are stored, 83.5% of the pictures were pornographic." Based on this and other disturbing data about porn's ubiquity in cyberspace, the *Time* article concluded that "parents have legitimate concerns about what their kids are being exposed to."

We later learned that the Carnegie Mellon study was deeply flawed, full of misleading statements that exaggerated the cyberporn problem. Nonetheless, even though it was based on faulty data, the *Time* article had sounded the alarm about pornography. Thanks to this cover story and many other similar stories, there was a mild hysteria sweeping the United States, an apprehension that the Net would be swallowed up by porn sites. This publicity helped to secure the passage of the Communications Decency Act in 1996. This was the first policy initiative in what has been a protracted and formidable struggle against cyberporn. The CDA made it a crime to knowingly transmit over the Internet "indecent" or "obscene" material to anyone under eighteen years of age. It also criminalized the display or transmitting of any message "that, in context, depicts or describes, in terms patently offensive as measured by contemporary community standards, sexual or excretory activities or organs."

But this federal law was immediately challenged by the ACLU and fifty-six other groups and corporations, including Microsoft (*ACLU v. Reno*, 929 E.D. PA [1996]). The basis of the challenge was that this law was both too broad and too vague. The act covered obscene material, which is no problem since it is illegal no matter where it is disseminated, but it also extended to a category of "indecent" or "patently offensive" material, which was never carefully defined. The law's vagueness and apparent broad scope could mean that respected literary works or explicit sexual material of scientific value might be affected. These arguments struck a chord with the federal district court in Pennsylvania that ruled in favor of the ACLU.

The government appealed and the case, *Reno v. ACLU* (521 U.S. [1997]), quickly ended up in the Supreme Court. During oral arguments both sides grappled with a proper analogy for the Internet. As Greenhouse (1997) points out, "Analogy is the only real road map for courts when technological change leaves them in unknown legal territory." If the Court accepted the analogy of radio or television, the CDA might be acceptable. Legislators have been given more latitude in regulating these media because of their "uniquely pervasive presence"; that is, the ease with which young children can tune in and be exposed to salacious material. On the other hand, if the Supreme Court relied on the analogies of the telephone or the newspaper, there would be little hope for the CDA, since the Court has ruled that private telephone conversations are not subject to the "pervasive presence" danger of radio and television.

In June 1997, in a unanimous decision, the Supreme Court ruled, as expected, that the CDA was unconstitutional. The opinion, written by Justice Stevens, held that Internet speech was entitled to the highest level of First Amendment protection. This is the same level of protection afforded to newspapers and books. Unlike radio and television, this new medium was to be given a place on the highest level of the First Amendment hierarchy. Here is a brief excerpt from Justice Steven's opinion:

> The vagueness of the CDA is a matter of special concern for two reasons. First, the CDA is a content-based regulation of speech. The vagueness of such a regulation raises special First Amendment concerns because of its obvious chilling effect on free speech. Second, the CDA is a criminal statute. In addition to the opprobrium and stigma of a criminal conviction, the CDA threatens violators with penalties including up to two years in prison for each act of violation. The severity of criminal sanctions may well cause speakers to remain silent rather than communicate even arguably unlawful words, ideas, images. . . .
>
> We are persuaded that the CDA lacks the precision that the First Amendment requires when a statute regulates the content of speech. In order to deny minors access to potentially harmful speech, the CDA effectively suppresses a large amount of speech that adults have a constitutional right to receive and to address to one another. That burden on adult speech is unacceptable if less restrictive alternatives would be at least as effective in achieving the legitimate purpose that the statute was enacted to serve.

Despite this unequivocal defeat, members of Congress did not relinquish their efforts to devise an appropriate antipornography law. In 1998 Congress passed the Child Online Protection Act (COPA), which was signed by President Clinton in October of that year. This law sought to force commercial Web sites to collect some type of identification (such as a credit card number) before making available material that is judged "harmful to minors." The penalty for violating the COPA was $50,000 or six months in prison. Unlike its predecessor, this law tried to define much more carefully what constitutes objectionable sexual content that is "harmful to minors." According to COPA, "The average person, applying contemporary community standards would find [that] this material taken as a whole and with respect to minors is designed to appeal to, or is designed to pander to, the prurient interest." Also, the material "depicts, describes or represents in a manner patently offensive with respect to minors an actual or simulated sexual act or sexual conduct [and] lacks serious literary, artistic, political, or scientific value for minors."

Despite this more careful wording and its narrower focus, COPA ran into the same constitutional problems as the CDA. A lawsuit was quickly filed by the ACLU and several other groups, including the Internet Content Coalition, which represented publishers such as MSNBC and the *New York Times*. In February 1999 the Third Circuit Court of Appeals issued a preliminary injunction blocking this law, declaring that it violated the First Amendment. The primary problem was the reference to "contemporary community standards" as a basis for determining speech that would be allowable on the Internet. The government appealed this ruling to the Supreme Court which heard oral arguments in November 2001. Most legal experts concur that COPA will probably meet the same fate as its predecessor.

Truly obscene material, like child pornography, is illegal in real space as well as cyberspace, so there is no need for new cyberlaws to outlaw this particular obscenity. Nonetheless, cyberspace presents some new challenges, such as simulated digital representations of children involved in sexual activity. To deal with this problem, Congress in 1996 passed the Child Pornography Prevention Act (CPPA), which never received the same attention and notoriety as the CDA. This federal law criminalizes the possession and creation of fake child pornography, computer-generated images of children in sexual situations. The argument for this law is that these simulated but authentic images help support the market for child pornography, while it desensitizes those who might be inclined to view this material. The act makes it a crime to create, distribute, or possess an image "that appears to be of a minor engaging in sexually explicit conduct." However, in a case brought by the Free Speech Coalition, a federal appeals court in San Francisco found that the language of the bill (phrases such as "appears to be") was too vague, and it ruled that the CPPA is unconstitutional. The government has also appealed that decision to the Supreme Court.

Critics of Congress's legislation say that this law constitutes a thought crime and that the suppression of ideas, no matter how repugnant, violates the First Amendment. The CPPA seems to punish someone for the creative act, an act that does not involve any real children. "The fundamental problem," according to Eric Freedman of Hofstra Law School, "is that the statute goes beyond regulating the use of real children in the production of pornography and attempts to suppress the idea of juvenile sexuality. It proceeds on the premise that the underlying idea is so pathological that it should be banned from public discourse" (Liptak 2001)

It is difficult to dismiss the argument, however, that the availability of child pornography based on digital imagery will encourage real pornography and ultimately the abuse of real children. Also, if the possession of "virtual" images is lawful, it would make enforcement of laws against real images much more difficult, since it is not so easy to distinguish between the two. Anyone who was apprehended for possession of child pornography could just argue that they believed that the alleged pornography was a lawful virtual image. While we would contend that the CPPA, perhaps with some modifications, should be upheld for the sake of the common good, this case provokes troubling questions about the verisimilitude of the virtual and its impact on the very real world of child pornography and the sexual abuse of children.

This succinct review of policy initiatives, especially the CDA and COPA, shows that law so far has been ineffectual in dealing with pornography in cyberspace. Laws appear to impose burdens that cannot be tolerated by the First Amendment. If we think of this issue in terms of Lessig's framework, we realize that we need another constraint if we want to deal more effectively with the problem of pornography. Code seems to be the most likely candidate, but can code be a worthy surrogate for the law?

CODE AND CONTENT CONTROLS

At the core of the debate about the CDA, COPA, and other forms of content regulation is the fundamental question of how the Net should be governed. Were the courts mistaken in striking down these laws? Do we need top-down controls to handle cyberporn and protect children? The *Time* article may have contained a big dose of hyperbole and the Georgetown study may have been flawed, but the ubiquity of pornography in cyberspace is a serious problem that will not vanish on its own.

Even if one could formulate a more precise law that was consistent with the First Amendment, it is insuperably difficult to deal with pornography through laws imposed by a national sovereignty. The opportunity for regulatory arbitrage is just too great. The United States might have ironclad antiporn laws, but what's to stop the purveyors of pornography from setting up their Web servers in the Cayman Islands or in Jamaica, where the United States has no jurisdiction?

Given the burdens imposed by laws on free speech and the threat of regulatory arbitrage, a more decentralized approach may be feasible. Let the onus of regulation or control fall on parents, schools, libraries, and other organizations. Of course, reliance on such a decentralized solution is not without opposition and controversy. But before we consider the roots of any opposition, let us review the code that can make content control possible.

There are any number of filtering software programs that have been designed to protect children. The first type include content filters. CyberPatrol, CyberSitter, Net Nanny, N2H2 Internet Filtering, and X-Stop are popular and reasonably effective products. These programs categorize Web sites based on their content. The vendors first classify Web sites into a variety of self-defined categories (for example, "Nudity" or "Obscene") and then develop a list of specific Web sites that fall within these categories. Automated systems are heavily involved in combing the Web for questionable sites, but usually the final decision about classification is made through human review. When a user requests a certain site the program checks to see if that site is on a category list of unacceptable locations, and if the site is on that list, access is denied. This process is known as "list-based blocking." For the most part, users must rely on the software vendor's judgment about restricted sites, but some systems are more flexible, allowing users to add and remove sites.

There are two obstacles to effective list-based filtering. The first is a reflection of the inherent volatility of the Web. Lists are doomed to be incomplete: Pornographic Web sites come and go, so it is difficult for even the most scrupulous software vendor to identify all objectionable sites. Also, most vendors do not release information about which sites they block and some are not even forthcoming about which criteria or categories they use. How do they define what constitutes "objectionable material"? How can parents or schools be sure that vendors are not casting too wide a net; that is, filtering out controversial forms of political speech or valid forums for sexual education?

Platform for Internet Content Selection (PICS) is another architecture that filters speech. PICS is a protocol for rating and filtering content on the Net. It divides the task of filtering into two activities: labeling, which involves rating the content of a site, and then filtering the content based on those labels. PICS provides a standard format and supports multiple labeling schemes or rating services. Internet content providers can embed a label within their own Web site (this is called self-rating), or third parties could rate Web sites independently and post labels about them. In either case, a common labeling vocabulary is available for use. Once the content is rated, users must have software that can read those labels in order to determine which sites are to be blocked. Both the Netscape and Internet Explorer browsers support PICS, and the popular search engine Alta Vista has the capability to restrict search results to acceptable sites based on PICS ratings. Thus, if parents were concerned about protecting their children from pornography, they might choose the third party rating system of the Christian Coalition and purchase a browser such as Netscape, which incorporates a PICS-compatible filter.

PICS has provoked the ire of many legal scholars. For Lessig (1997), among others, PICS epitomizes all that is wrong with the constraints imposed by code: "Blocking software is bad enough—but in my view, PICS is the devil," he says. Hyperbole aside, there are some potential problems with the use of PICS. First, it is a universal censorship system that could be used to censor any kind of material, not just pornography and hate speech. As a result, PICS can be adopted to block access to unpopular political speech or dissenting viewpoints as well as to pornographic material. Also, PICS cannot aspire to neutrality or pure impartiality: To some degree a rating scheme will always reflect the bias and subjectivity of its authors. Finally, rating systems of third parties will need constant updating and revision, and hence they will have a difficult time keeping up with the rapid pace of change on the Net.

But the fundamental problem from Lessig's viewpoint is that we are ceding to those who rate content (private industry, public interest groups, etc.) the government's or the court's role as an arbiter of speech rights. Companies and computer programmers are making decisions about what Web sites children should see or not see. In addition, filtering, especially when it happens upstream at the level of an ISP, is often untransparent to the end user.

There is one more potential problem with filtering architectures: Sometimes they work too thoroughly and too perfectly. Thanks to PICS, users can filter out vast amounts of online speech and tailor content to their own liking. But, as Lessig (1999) remarks, "There is also value in confronting the unfiltered." Broad exposure to the reality around us makes us well-rounded individuals and more informed citizens. Excessive content filtering is also incompatible with the rich and diverse intellectual culture that most countries seek to foster. These same arguments are echoed in Shapiro (1999), who describes the "ignorance and narrow-mindedness" of the control revolution manifest in activities like filtering.

While these objections to PICS should not be casually dismissed, none of them suggest that there is something fatally wrong with this protocol. There is a case to be made for voluntary rating, especially for the purpose of controlling the access of children to questionable content. Good faith, voluntary rating of Internet content, may well be the least restrictive means of controlling speech while protecting the public interest.

The use of filters and blocking software in libraries has been an especially nettlesome issue. Some libraries have opted for unfettered Internet access for all their patrons (even minors), and this is consistent with the American Library Association's (ALA) position. The ALA has based its position on the Library Bill of Rights, which stipulates that "a person's right to use a library should not be denied or abridged because of origin, age, background, or views."

But the public library in Loudon County, Virginia, found it difficult to fully accept the ALA's philosophy. It installed a popular filtering software, X-Stop, on its nine computers in order to filter out pornographic Web sites, which, in its view, should not be available to library patrons. As a result, users, including adults, who attempted to access a pornographic Web site were confronted instead with the following message flashing on their screen: "Violation!! Violation!!" While some users applauded the Library's action, others vigorously complained. Soon, the Loudon County Public Library found itself embroiled in a nasty lawsuit brought by Mainstream Loudon, a local Civil Liberties Union organization, representing Loudon County residents who claimed that the library's policy infringed upon their right to free speech under the First Amendment.

During the course of the trial it became apparent that X-Stop blocked certain sites that did not contain pornographic material. For example, it blocked the "Safer Sex" Web page and the "Books for Gay and Lesbian Teens/Youth" Web page. The defense argued that the library's policy should be interpreted as an acquisition decision to which the First Amendment does not apply. It should not be construed as a decision to remove library materials, but as a decision about what sort of content the library should select for its patrons. The plaintiff, on the other hand, contended that the library's action must be seen as a removal decision: It was as if the Loudon library system had purchased an encyclopedia and had removed any unsavory content by cutting out selected pages. The court appeared to lean to the plaintiff's side on the issue, and in a dramatic moment one of the defendant's own expert witnesses admitted that "filtering cannot be rightly compared to 'selection' since it involves an active, rather then passive exclusion of certain types of content" (*Mainstream Loudon v. Loudon County Library*, 24 F. Supp. 552 E.D. VA. [1998]). This was damaging testimony that shifted the preponderance of evidence to the plaintiff.

A second set of arguments involved the nature and role of the public library. Loudon County Library argued that the library is a nonpublic forum, so state action is not appropriate in this case. But the plaintiff argued that "the Loudon County government, through defendant library board, intended to create a public forum when it authorized its public library system" (*Mainstream Loudon v. Loudon County Library* 1998). This assertion is consistent with previous cases, such as *Kraemer v. Bureau of Police* (1992), which ruled that the library is a limited public forum.

Finally, the Loudon County library contended that its policy was constitutional since it was the least restrictive means of achieving two key objectives: "1. minimizing access to illegal pornography, and 2. avoidance of the creation of a reasonably hostile environment." In its rebuttal to this argument the plaintiff pointed out that the Loudon board could not cite any situation where content on a computer terminal was harassing or contributed in any way to a hostile environment. It also listed a litany of less-restrictive means: using filters that could be switched off for adults, educating patrons on proper Internet use, and so forth.

In the end the U.S. District Court for Eastern Virginia sided with the plaintiff. It found that the library's policy was overinclusive, limiting access of all patrons to material that was unfit for juveniles but suitable for adults. The library's policy was also impugned for lacking standards, for entrusting blocking decisions to Log-On Data Corp (X-Stop's producer), and for failing to include adequate procedural safeguards. Judge Brinkema's conclusion in this case is quite emphatic:

> Although defendant is under no obligation to provide Internet access to its patrons, it has chosen to do so and is therefore restricted by the First Amendment in the limitations it is allowed to place on patron access. Defendant has asserted a broad right to censor the expressive activity of the receipt and communication of information through the Internet with a Policy that (1) is not necessary to further any compelling government interest; (2) is not narrowly tailored; (3) restricts access of adult patrons to

protected material just because the material is unfit for minors; (4) provides inadequate standards for restricting access; and (5) provides inadequate procedural safeguards to ensure prompt judicial review. Such a Policy offends the guarantee of free speech in the First Amendment and is, therefore, unconstitutional. (*Mainstream Loudon v. Loudon County Library* 1998)

Despite the ruling in this lawsuit and other concerns about filtering, in late 2000 Congress passed a bill requiring schools and libraries to install filtering technology as a condition for receiving federal funds. This legislation is the Children's Internet Protection Act (CHIPA). This law, signed reluctantly by President Clinton, is linked to the federal government's e-rate program, which provides an opportunity for schools and libraries to be reimbursed for the costs of connecting to the Internet or subsidized for other telecommunications expenses. The law requires that computer terminals used by adults must have filters that block Internet access to visual images that are obscene or involve any sort of child pornography. According to Kaplan (2001), "For library computer terminals used by children under 17, libraries have to screen out these two categories of material plus a third one: visual material that is 'harmful to minors,' such as sexually-explicit images without social or educational value that are obscene for children but legally protected for adults." Public schools seeking e-funds must implement the same type of filtering scheme.

Congress did not specify criteria for which types of content should be prohibited or for the exact methods to be used. Thus, the law leaves these decisions to the discretion of local officials. According to Senator John McCain, the bill's cosponsor, CHIPA "allows local communities to decide what technology they want to use and what to filter out so our children's minds aren't polluted" (Schwartz 2001).

A diverse group of public libraries and library associations has filed a lawsuit against this new filtering law, attacking its constitutionality (*Multnomah Public Library et al. v. U.S.*, 402 E.D. PA [2001]). The lawsuit claims that CHIPA violates the First Amendment: "by forcing public libraries to install such technology, CHIPA will suppress ideas and viewpoints that are constitutionally protected from reaching willing patrons."

Much of the opposition to CHIPA is premised on the overinclusive nature of imprecise filters and the fact that censorship decisions are being made by code writers at filtering companies rather than by a judge. In the past it has been the courts that declare some work as obscene, but is it legitimate to delegate that responsibility to a software company? CHIPA has many defenders, but both sides have agreed that the controversial elements of this legislation will probably not be resolved until it too is reviewed by the Supreme Court.

The following is a review of the U.S. Policy initiatives to combat Internet pornography:

- Communications Decency Act, 1996: Makes transmission of indecent material to minors illegal; ruled unconstitutional by the U.S. Supreme Court.
- Child Pornography Prevention Act, 1996: Makes it a crime to distribute, receive, or possess an image that "appears to be of a minor engaging in sexually explicit conduct."
- Children's Online Protection Act, 1998: Compels commercial Web sites to restrict access to material considered "harmful to minors"; unconstitutional according to the Third Circuit Court of Appeals; under Supreme Court review.
- Children's Internet Protection Act, 2000: Requires schools and libraries to use filtering devices as a condition for receiving e-rate funds; currently being challenged by civil-rights groups.

POLICY ASSESSMENT OF ANTIPORNOGRAPHY LEGISLATION

We have argued with some insistence in previous chapters on behalf of self-regulation and self-ordering in cyberspace whenever it is possible and realistic. Given the likelihood of conflicts with the First Amendment and the unavoidable threat of regulatory arbitrage, federally mandated speech controls are not a fitting solution for dealing with harmful speech. A more decentralized approach seems appropriate: Let parents, local schools, and local communities make their own decisions about controlling Internet content. Filtering or blocking software implemented by the end user represents a more viable resolution to the problem of cyberporn. We recognize that filters or rating schemes are imperfect and that there are many documented incongruities in filtering software. This is due to the fact that filters block some sites erroneously because they cannot understand the context in which certain language is used. We presume, however, that filtering devices and labeling schemes such as PICS will have greater proficiency in the future, so that legitimate information is inadvertently censored as little as possible. Whether systems can acquire the contextual expertise necessary for optimum precision is a matter of some debate.

We have also argued that because of the potential for collateral damage, self-regulation through filtering mechanisms must be executed in a careful and responsible manner. Software vendors, of course, must behave responsibly in the way they develop this code, which has the same impact as the law, and users must be conscientious in how they deploy these systems.

Let us review some of the conditions of responsible development and use of these automated content controls. We alluded to this topic in Chapter 3, and we can now expand on the criteria suggested there. Above all, the principle of end-user autonomy should be respected. Thus, the use of PICS or other automated content controls should be strictly voluntary: Parents or schools should be allowed to choose whether to restrict Web content, while Web site developers can choose whether to label their sites. In contrast, hierarchical filtering by the government or a mandatory rating system sponsored by the government would be inappropriate and imprudent. It would impose a uniform solution to what has always been regarded as a local problem. At the same time, ISPs and other intermediaries should also refrain from filtering the Internet for cyberporn, though they can make it possible for parents to shield their children from objectionable content. Second, a Web site that does choose to label itself must have the integrity to label that site accurately; this so-called first-party rating is preferable to third-party rating, since it allows content providers the chance to classify their own sites. Third, third parties that do rate Web sites must strive to provide fair, accurate, and consistent ratings that are subject to reasonable external scrutiny. They must also be flexible enough to judiciously handle appeals from Web sites that maintain that they have been mislabeled. Fourth, there should be an adequate transparency level in blocking software or rating schemes. What does transparency mean in this context? At a minimum, blocking software vendors should reveal their categories (e.g., "Adults Only, Nudity") with ample examples, along with their methodology for classifying Web sites in the appropriate categories (e.g., are sites added to the list subject to human review?). In the past, filters have blocked the Web site of the National Organization for Women and other sites that espouse feminist themes. Such blocking based on ideological grounds is inappropriate under any circumstances, but it is especially irresponsible unless the rating service has adopted a certain political agenda that it explicitly reveals to its patrons. Fifth, since this code functions as the law of cyberspace, it should be subjected to objective external audits and "peer review." Filtering companies argue that their categorization lists of blocked sites are proprietary information, but disinterested third parties could be employed to review and certify those lists.

We conclude this discussion on pornography with a summary that takes the form of several propositions about free speech in cyberspace. These are by no means a priori principles, but we should begin by stating something that is a priori. There is no right more vital to a democratic society than freedom of expression, and *everyone* should have the right to speak out about public affairs. Such expression promotes the truth, permits political and social participation, and contributes to the self-fulfillment of a human person. These values lie at the core of free-speech rights. The right to free speech, however, is not absolute, legally or morally; we all know that obscenity, libel, and so on are not protected by the First Amendment. In general, the closer speech is to these core values, the more odious are attempts to suppress it. That is why the suppression of political dissent in China is far worse than attempts to limit the availability of indecent material to children.

Given that assumption, we propose the following principles, which become progressively more controversial. We realize that not everyone will agree with these propositions, but hope that they will stimulate further debate and reflection about these complex issues.

Proposition 1

Direct or indirect government censorship of the Internet is ill-advised and unworkable. The federal government is better off allowing local communities to solve this problem with the help of technology; this is in keeping with the decentralized structure of the Internet. Even CHIPA is a bad idea: If some communities deploy these controls only for the reward of e-rate funds, they might be inclined to use them in a careless or haphazard way without careful selection of the right systems. On the other hand, if these communities are motivated to do this because of their own value structures, they are apt to be much more scrupulous and conscientious in the implementation process.

Proposition 2

Computer-mediated communications should allow for more freedom than broadcast media. Communication on the Internet has certain asymmetries when compared to communication on radio and television: With radio and television, the number of speakers is limited by the high cost of speaking and by the available spectrum and the listeners are merely passive recipients of communications. With the Internet, the number of speakers is boundless and listeners are much more active. Also, unlike television and radio, Internet users generally receive only the communications they affirmatively request, and are not a passive or "captive" audience. Thus, the Internet is not yet as pervasive a presence as radio and TV, and the dangers of encountering obscenities or other unwholesome speech do not call for strict government regulation at this point.

Proposition 3

Responsible private choices about free speech should be respected. This is an argument for the prerogative of parents and private institutions such as private schools and libraries to engage in limited and well-informed content control (such as the filtering of pornographic Web sites) in order to uphold their unique and discrete value systems.

Proposition 4

Schools that function in loco parentis *should not abdicate their duty to responsibly restrict Internet content.* Both parents and teachers have a duty to help shape the education of young children. This means assisting them in determining what books they will read, which TV programs they will watch, and which Web sites they will access. Without this guidance children will not be able to develop the moral and intellectual faculties (summed up so well in

Aristotle's notion of *phronesis* or practical wisdom) that will enable them to make responsible and rational choices as adults. What makes restrictions on Web content responsible would be the following conditions: Limits are carefully placed only on speech considered "harmful to minors" that is found to subvert community values; forms of speech that are at the core of this basic right to free expression are untouched; users, including children, are informed of the rationale behind the access limits that have been imposed; and the content controls do not interfere with the broader free-speech rights of adults.

Proposition 5

Local communities and their representative institutions, such as public libraries, should also be allowed to make responsible choices about free speech, even if they are envisaged in the eyes of the law as limited public forums. In 1973, when the Supreme Court reaffirmed that obscenity was not protected by the First Amendment, it also underlined the "right of the nation and the states to maintain a decent society." At the very least, then, public institutions should have the flexibility to filter the Internet in order to protect young children from pornographic speech, obscenity, and indecent speech judged to be harmful to minors, as long as they do so according to the conditions of responsibility articulated in Proposition 4. This proposition supports the efforts of local public libraries to curb pornographic forms of speech by segregating terminals and using filtering only for children's terminals, making sure that adults remain unaffected by these measures.

One last word about automated content controls and decentralized regulations: We realize there is conflicting evidence about the effectiveness of filters and blocking programs. There is evidence of both overblocking (blocking Web sites that do not fit within the category definitions) and underblocking (failing to block content that does fit within those category definitions). While the scope of the problem is in dispute, there is probably a consensus that filtering programs need to do a better job. This may mean a heavier dependence on human review and the need to conduct periodic quality control studies to verify the accuracy of decisions made about particular Web sites. These programs should also make end-user customization simpler and more convenient so that decisions about blocked sites can be overridden by parents or other authorized users. We must also understand that filtering architectures will never be infallible, but if they can suppress 80 to 90 percent of the Web sites that meet their category definitions with minimal overblocking, they will have achieved an enviable success rate. In addition, there may be other architectures that enable decentralized regulation without the shortcomings of filters. Lessig and Resnick (1999), for example, propose zoning architectures that deserve consideration. Zoning solutions have variations but in essence they would require the end user to forward information about his or her age (or about other relevant characteristics) to the content provider so that the content provider can make a decision about whether to provide its content. Regardless of which architecture is used, we maintain that in the long run the problem of unwanted speech can be handled more expeditiously by technology than by government intervention.

HATE SPEECH

At first glance, the Web site for the World Church of the Creator looks innocent enough. It is welcoming and vividly presented in bright crayon colors. But one soon learns that this is the site of a neo-Nazi group located in East Peoria, Illinois. Like most anti-Semitic hate sites, there is polemical material laced with vicious ethnic slurs. At one time the site had a section called Creativity for Children. This was linked to a Nazi propaganda children's book that refers to Jews as "poisonous mushrooms."

In the United States, this site, however offensive is perfectly legal. The First Amendment protects most forms of hate speech as long as it does not incite others to violence. In Europe, however, such sites are not tolerated. Germany, for example, has stringent laws that expressly forbid certain material and criminalize anti-Semitic hate sites. French laws forbid material that incites racial enmity.

But just like purveyors of pornography, hate site operators can play the game of regulatory arbitrage, and indeed have demonstrated remarkable resiliency. The Web site of the Charlemagne Hammerskins, which menacingly warns that there are still "one way tickets to Auschwitz," was shut down in France but soon came back online by way of an Internet server in Canada. Repugnant racist rhetoric, like pornography, is immensely difficult to contain on an open and free medium such as the Net.

It is no surprise that after September 11, 2001, there has been an increase in anti-Islamic hate speech. Web sites critical of Islam have sprouted up on the Web. In addition, anti-Islamic postings have multiplied and some have been especially vicious. One of the messages posted on an AOL bulletin board said "Kill all of those who worship Allah." ISPs have been especially sensitive to such postings and have hired more screeners to search for inflammatory material.

But just how extensive are these reprehensible hate speech sites? Certainly, hate is not as pervasive a problem as pornography. According to Perine (2000), the Simon Wiesanthal Center "estimates there are more than 2,300 problematic Web sites, including more than 500 extremist sites authored by Europeans, but hosted on American servers to avoid the stringent anti-hate laws in Europe." Other estimates are more conservative, but everyone agrees that the Internet gives a new forum to this virulent form of expression.

This proliferation of hate speech has caused major headaches for Internet service providers, which sometimes are accused of giving hate mongers a forum. Auction sites such as eBay and Yahoo have come under fire for permitting the sale of items such as Nazi memorabilia and Klan hoods. Yahoo also hosts many online clubs, such as the "White Knights of the K.K.K." After criticism from organizations like the Simon Wiesenthal Center, Yahoo removed some of these clubs form its portal service.

Even when portals like Yahoo seek to balance the value of free speech and civil discourse, they encounter intractable problems. Consider Yahoo's recent run-in with a French court, which occurred when two French antiracist groups filed suit against Yahoo, demanding that they remove swastika flags and other Nazi memorabilia from their auctions on the American Web site. French law expressly prohibits the display or sale of objects that incite racial hatred, and this includes any World War II Nazi memorabilia. Judge Jean-Jacques Gomez ruled in favor of these two groups, concluding that Yahoo had violated French law and offended the "collected memory" of France. He ordered Yahoo to make it impossible for French users to access any auction site that contained illegal Nazi items.

Despite its objections, Yahoo was ordered to install filtering technology that would block this questionable material for all French users. If it failed to comply, Yahoo would face a steep fine of $13,000 a day. The court dismissed Yahoo's claims that preventing access would be technically impossible after an independent panel reported that a filtering system based on geographical origin would be effective in preventing 90 percent of French citizens from viewing auctions of the Nazi memorabilia.

Legal experts are skeptical that the French legal order could ever be enforced. Yahoo is an American company, and it's likely that only an American court could have jurisdiction. But the implications of this ruling are portentous. What is especially worrisome is that this decision would inspire other countries to impose restrictive rules or laws on ISPs or other Web services. If every country or local sovereignty tries to enforce its particular laws on the Net, cyberspace will begin to look like real space; that is, characterized by borders and regional regulations. It will lose its global reach and the valuable quality of universality. Cyberspace was surely not designed to work this way. "The Internet was designed without any contemplation of national boundaries," said Vincent Cerf, who designed much of the Internet's initial structure. "The actual traffic in the Net is totally unbound with respect to geography" (Guernsey 2001). The French court's decision sets a terrible precedent that must be resisted before other sovereignties follow suit.

Like pornography, hate speech is best dealt with at the end points (i.e., at the level of the end user), rather than through legislation or through hierarchical filtering. Decentralized code-based solutions, such as PICS geared for anti-Semitic or other hate-oriented sites, are workable and responsible solutions. But the labeling issues are complex, since there can be a subtle distinction between hate speech and legitimate political expression. There is sometimes considerable subjectivity involved in classifying speech as "hate speech." For many years the Simon Wiesanthal Center has monitored hate speech on the Web and fought bravely against the growing number of anti-Semitic sites. On occasion, however, their classification of what constitutes hate speech is highly debatable. In 1990, for example, they criticized the online service provider Prodigy for allowing these messages to be posted on one of its bulletin boards:

> Did it ever occur to you that Israel might be the cause of most of the terrible trouble in the Middle East? Israel is the Bad Guy in the Middle East. Without Israel most of the problems would go away.
>
> I wonder if some Israelis ended up with J. Edgar [Hoover's] secret files. They seem to have a strong hold on OUR officials. (Paine 1993)

While this is indisputably biased political expression that would be offensive to some, it is also political commentary that in the opinion of most people would not rise to the level of true hate speech. Similarly, the current barrage of inflammatory anti-Islamic speech creates big headaches for ISPs who are seeking to curtail the most offensive Web sites without stifling the online debate about Islamic fundamentalism. Any effort to eradicate hate speech, no matter how well-intentioned, runs the risk of expunging legitimate political expression as well. This makes hate speech much more difficult to deal with than pornography for cultures like the United States, which place such a strong emphasis on free political expression and speech about public affairs.

ONLINE THREATS

Speech that incites violence or that is likely to cause imminent lawless action is not protected by the First Amendment. But when does threatening speech or hate speech rise to this level? There have been several high-profile cases involving such speech, but by far the most provocative one is the case of the Nuremberg Files. The Nuremberg Files Web site is the product of the American Coalition of Life Activists (ACLA), a fringe antiabortion group that advocates violence against abortion providers. The Web site consisted of graphic imagery of aborted fetuses along with a list of doctors who provided abortions and the location of their clinics. But that list had a ghoulish twist: The names of murdered doctors were crossed out, and the names of those doctors who had been wounded were printed in gray. In 1998 several hours after Dr. Barnett Slepian was murdered by a sniper in his home in Amherst, New York, his name was crossed off the Web page.

Understandably, many of the doctors on this list felt threatened and with the help of Planned Parenthood they filed suit against the ACLA. The suit alleged a direct connection between the ACLA's activities and the attacks on those doctors who provided abortions, and it contended that the site was organized to promote violence and harassment. In its defense the ACLA argued that this speech was protected under the First Amendment since it was not a direct threat but merely a list of doctors and clinics. The Web site's author, Neal Horsley, stated that his intention was to provide information but not to cause harm. Horsley believes that abortion will be a crime and he wants to preserve a public record of abortion providers so that they can be brought to justice. The jury in the case concluded that the statements were "true threats," and it awarded the plaintiffs $109 million. The judge also issued an injunction forbidding the further display of the threatening speech on the Nuremberg Web page.

However, in March 2001, the Ninth Circuit Court of Appeals overturned this decision on the basis that this speech was protected by the First Amendment. According to the opinion rendered by the appeals court,

> Defendants can be held liable if they "authorized, ratified or directly threatened" violence. If defendants threatened to commit violent acts, by working alone or with others, then their statements could properly support the verdict. But if their statements merely encouraged unrelated terrorists, then their words are protected by the First Amendment. (*Planned Parenthood v. American Coalition of Life Activists*, 41 F. Supp. 2d 1130 [9th Cir.] [2001])

The thrust of the appeal's opinion was that the courts must be careful to distinguish between strongly worded or harsh speech and statements that are explicitly threatening. The court alluded to the relevance of the fact that this speech was public discourse, which deserves a higher level of protection than "privately communicated threats."

The Nuremburg Files case defies a simple analysis. On one side, a reasonable argument can be put forth that the site incites imminent violence. In particular, the act of crossing out names seems to put this form of expression beyond the ambit of protected speech, since it implicitly encourages that other names be crossed out for the sake of the antiabortion cause. Also, one could claim that those responsible for this site should be prosecuted for cyberstalking, a new cybercrime that is not yet very well defined.

On the other side, the site's defenders argue that there is no credible threat here. In the trial Horsley's lawyers argued that the Web site's authors did not intend to provoke violence but to provide factual data, even if those data are provided in a provocative manner. Proof of willful intent is surely difficult to establish in this case. There is no explicit advocacy of violence against these doctors, and speech of this nature may be a necessary social cost for an Internet that allows such a broad "marketplace of ideas." Moreover, it would be quite difficult to legislate or develop policies against this type of inflammatory speech, which seems to incorporate veiled threats. Some have argued for a broadening of state stalking statutes to include harassing online behavior that doesn't necessarily involve direct conduct or direct threats, but any changes along these lines might raise constitutional questions.

THE WAR AGAINST SPAM

The war against spam has been relentless but futile. Opponents have tried many weapons, including restrictive legislation, blocking devices, and even "black holes." But spam is a persistent force in cyberspace and has not yet succumbed to these innovative defensive mechanisms. Spammers still employ many clever tricks to cloak their identities or dupe ISPs to forward their mail. According to Armstrong (2000), "The number of mass e-mailings has grown 400% over the past year to nearly 5,000 a day . . . [and] within the next five years, 40% of incoming e-mail is going to be spam, up from 10% today."

What is spam? Actually defining and categorizing spam is no easy matter. Spam is usually defined as unsolicited commercial e-mail, but this assumes that it must be "commercial"; that is, it must emanate from an organization advertising or pedaling products or services. Perhaps a better and more inclusive definition is "automated unsolicited bulk e-mail." But should all unsolicited bulk e-mail be considered nuisance spam mail? Given the need to respect and protect speech of public concern, this would depend on the nature of the speech, the volume of the mailings, and frequency of transmission. Regardless of how we define it, the economics of spam are irresistible, since the marginal cost of sending another electronic message is virtually zero.

The primary problem with spam is that it shifts costs from the advertiser to the recipient of the e-mail and to the ISPs that must deliver the messages. Spam has been aptly described as "postage due marketing" (Rausch 1995). The biggest cost associated with spam is the consumption of computer resources. For example, when someone sends out spam the messages must sit on a disk somewhere, and this means that valuable disk space is being filled with unwanted mail. Also, many users must pay for each message received or for each disk block used. As the volume of spam grows and commercial use of the Internet expands, these costs will continue their steady increase.

Further, when spam is sent through Internet service providers they must bear the costs of delivery. This amounts to wasted network bandwidth and the utilization of system resources such as disk storage space along with the servers and transfer networks involved in the transmission process. Despite its efforts to control junk e-mail, AOL and other ISPs report that millions of pieces of spam still engulf their systems each day. Spam is a negative externality, since it clogs the pipes through which all Internet communications must flow and slows down the entire system.

Despite the undeniable social costs of spam, the notoriety of certain spammers, and the fact that spam is often associated with fraudulent merchandise, unsolicited automated e-mail triggers difficult moral and legal issues. As we have intimated, spam is not always easy to identify, and attempts to draw the line between spam and more important forms of free expression can be difficult. Should all bulk unsolicited e-mail, even noncommercial communications, be classified as spam? If the Internet is to realize its full potential as a "democratizing force," shouldn't some forms of unsolicited automated e-mail be permitted? Some of this unsolicited e-mail may include speech of public concern, which is of central importance for First Amendment protection.

These concerns come to the fore in the case of *Intel Corporation v. Hamidi*, (Permanent Injunction; Sup. Ct. of Calif. 98ASO5067 [1999]). On six occasions during a three-year period (1996 to 1998) Hamidi sent e-mail messages complaining about Intel's discriminatory employment practices to over 30,000 Intel employees at their e-mail addresses on Intel's system. One message, for example, accused Intel of grossly underestimating the size of impending layoffs. Hamidi also originated a Web site known as "FACE INTEL," where he propagated his message about the irregularities in Intel's employment polices and practices.

Intel contended that Hamidi's e-mails were intrusive and constituted a form of spam. Hamidi refused Intel's request to desist from sending the messages. Intel then attempted to filter out Hamidi's messages, but he was able to bypass Intel's blocking mechanism. Intel felt that it had little recourse, and in October 1998 it sued Hamidi. The company requested an injunction to stop him from sending these e-mail messages to its employees. Hamidi lost the first round of this legal struggle when Judge John Lewis of the California Supreme Court issued a summary judgment in favor of Intel and enjoined Hamidi from sending unsolicited e-mail to any of the e-mail addresses on Intel's corporate system.

Hamidi's lawyers had argued that these e-mail messages did not disrupt Intel's system. But according to the judge, "The evidence establishes (without dispute) that Intel has been injured by diminished employee productivity, and in devoting company resources to blocking efforts and to addressing employees about Hamidi's e-mail. These injuries, which impair the value to Intel of its e-mail system, are sufficient to support a cause of action for trespass to chattels" (*Intel Corp. v. Hamidi*). The court also rejected Hamidi's contention that his messages were protected by the constitutional guarantee of free speech. Hamidi's speech was invasive and tantamount to harmful trespass.

But what about Hamidi's free-speech rights? Is there any validity to the claim that those rights had been violated? What separates Hamidi's communication from the most pernicious form of spam is its noncommercial status. His speech dealt with issues of public concern—that is, the unfair human resources policies of Intel—and hence it is quite different from commercial advertising. This is precisely the type of speech that the First Amendment is designed to protect. One could argue that Hamidi is one of those "town criers" in cyberspace who were praised by the Supreme Court in *Reno v. ACLU*. To be sure, the e-mails are a nuisance for Intel, but five or six mailings over a three-year period does not impose a terrible burden on the company. Perhaps if Hamidi were sending a message every week to 30,000 employees there would be a stronger case for intrusion and diminished employee productivity, but in this case the burden does not seem to outweigh the intended benefits to society. This may be the price Intel has to pay for connecting to a quasi-public forum like the Internet. Do we really want to stifle all forms of unsolicited speech of a political nature in cyberspace, even if it is being directed at a few thousand people? According to Hamidi himself, "The Internet . . . means that for the first time someone like me can communicate en masse instantaneously. I want to support that freedom" (Kaplan 1999). Admittedly, this is a tough case where speech rights and property rights conflict, but in those situations where the magnitude of disruption is slight, benefit of the doubt should be given to free-speech rights

The Hamidi case is a troubling one, but it is not representative of most incidents involving the transmission of spam. Most would agree that undisputed cases of spam, unsolicited commercial speech, should be prevented or at least discouraged. But what is the right remedy for spam? One possibility, of course, is to look for a public policy solution. This could take the form of an outright ban on spam or a labeling requirement. The first option could be implemented by amending the Telephone Consumer Protection Act (TCPA) of 1991, which makes it illegal to transmit unsolicited commercial advertisements over a facsimile machine. The TCPA could be modified to include unsolicited bulk commercial e-mail as well as "junk" faxes. But the costs imposed on the recipient of junk faxes is much higher than the costs imposed on the recipient of junk e-mail: There is the costs of paper and the fact that the phone line is being tied up. Message preclusion is therefore a bigger factor for fax communications than it is for e-mail. In addition, there is something different about spam, which, unlike a fax, is a one-to-many communication. Also, as we have argued, it would be hard for the law to define "spam" with the necessary precision. A law against spam could end up creating an undue burden for free speech.

A labeling requirement has also been proposed so that spam could be more easily identified and deleted by unwilling recipients. There are two problems with this. A label might actually have the unintended effect of serving to legitimize spam. A requirement that spam have a label might be seen as the government's approval of this communication, and this could bestow upon spam the respectability that it currently lacks. Also, a government-imposed labeling requirement could bump up against the First Amendment. According to Carroll (1996), "The First Amendment places limitations on the government's ability to require that labels be put on unsolicited commercial solicitations."

Some states like Washington have tried to regulate spam. Its 1998 antispam law, considered the most restrictive in the United States, bans spam that is sent to Washington state residents with a misleading subject line and an invalid return e-mail address. However, a recent Superior Court ruling in Seattle found that this statute violated the interstate commerce clause of the U.S. Constitution. Judge Robinson "found that the Internet differs significantly from fax, postal mail or other forms of communication because of the difficulty in determining someone's state residence from an e-mail address" (Lewis 2000). The case has been appealed to the state Supreme Court.

There are also more "bottom-up" approaches to the problem of spam. Junk e-mail may be yet another area where self-regulation and self-ordering through code work better than laws and policies. ISPs and large corporations rely on a multitiered system of filters. There are numerous filters and programs for individuals, such as Mail Essentials (www.gficomms.com), with efficacious antispam capabilities. This particular program blocks messages based on the originating domain, and it also scans for keywords that indicate the potential for spam. Even popular e-mail programs such as Microsoft Outlook come with sophisticated filters that allow users to create rules that will screen their messages.

In addition to these fairly reliable filters, there are also "black holes," such as Paul Vixie's Realtime Blackhole List, which is managed by a nonprofit organization known as the Mail Abuse Prevention System (MAPS). The RBL is a list of Internet service providers or other network providers (such as MIT or IBM, which connect to the network directly) who send spam or are determined to be "spam friendly"; that is, they allow known spammers to use their service for relaying messages. Those ISPs and network providers that are blacklisted will have all of their e-mail bounced, not just the e-mail of the spammer. Thus, if ISP X is blacklisted, other ISPs that subscribe to the RBL list will boycott *all* of the e-mail from X's service. E-mail sent to nonsubscribing network providers is not affected. A third party must nominate a company for the blackhole list, but any RBL board member can remove someone from the list.

Reliance on the use of black holes to curb spam has created a major controversy, especially for ISPs and organizations that have been blacklisted. In the summer of 2000 Harris Interactive, an online market research company, filed a lawsuit against MAPS. It alleged that MAPS placed Harris on its blackhole list and that this prevented the company from sending polls to about 2.7 million users who agreed to participate in an online survey. The company's president, Gordon Black, called the whole process an "abomination" (Wingfield 2000). In its defense, MAPS contends that Harris lets participants "opt out" but it should only send poll data to someone who has voluntarily "opted in." In fact, MAPS's standard is even higher than opt in. Businesses conducting commerce via e-mail must get two levels of confirmation: The user must voluntarily opt in by providing their e-mail address to an online marketer, and once a message or a marketing pitch has been sent by the vendor, the user must verify his or her interest by responding or visiting the Web site. Only then can the vendor continue to send promotional e-mail. Companies that do not abide by this "double opt-in" system risk being blacklisted.

A *Wall Street Journal* article on MAPS poses the fundamental question in this debate: "Should one organization hold the power to determine whether millions of Internet messages get through to their destinations?" (Wingfield

2000). Lessig would undoubtedly give a negative answer to this question. The problem is that vigilantes like Vixie and compliant network service providers are deciding policy questions about spam and the Net outside of the democratic process. According to Lessig (1999), "This is policy making by the 'invisible hand'. It's not that policy is not being made but that those making the policy are unaccountable." In his view, of course, this is a perfect illustration of how policy should not be made.

The RBL debate is a classic example of the conflict between the bottom-up versus top-down approach to policy making: Should we just let the spam wars rage on and allow vigilantes, ISPs, and beleaguered corporations to chose their best weapons? Or is a more efficacious approach one that is based on a centralized policy and unambiguous laws that limit or even prohibit the transmission of spam?

Can a case be made for this sort of vigilantism and other bottom-up antispam efforts? According to Post (2001), one huge obstacle to resolving spam by legislation is cyberspace's "jurisdictional conundrum . . . the difficulties inherent in mapping territorial legal regimes on to a medium in which physical location is of virtually no significance." States like Virginia and Washington have found that their antispam laws are ineffectual because spam originating outside their territorial borders are immune to their laws. The same will apply for federal antispam legislation: It cannot apply to spam originating in Canada or Europe.

There are other reasons why centralized antispam policies may not be the ideal solution. Post (2001) argues that what the RBL is doing amounts to old-fashioned "shunning," which gets the spammer's attention even better than the law. Also, ISPs are better equipped and more knowledgeable than Congress to deal with spam, and RBLs are less likely to be "captured" by fickle policy makers.

To be sure, there are problems with MAPS–RBL. It may try to be conscientious about who ends up upon its list, but mistakes get made and that can cause serious financial damage, as alleged by Harris Interactive in its lawsuit. Also, is MAPS the proper organization to set the standard for what constitutes spam, demanding two levels of confirmation? What right should a private company have to establish and enforce such a standard? Also, ISPs that subscribe to RBL are imposing these rules on its customers and potentially depriving them of considerable e-mail originating from online service providers who are judged to be "spam friendly." The problem is that all of the mail from this ISP is blocked, not just the spam. Unless end users are pretty sophisticated and choose ISPs on the basis of whether or not they subscribe to RBL, it seems as if their autonomy is being compromised by this hierarchical approach to the suppression of spam.

In my view, reliance on antispam filters is a preferable solution. It will minimize collateral damage and avoid the problems associated with MAPS. These filters can be installed by ISPs as a protective mechanism against known spammers that overwhelm their networks, or they can be activated at the end points, downstream in the information flow, by organizations and individuals. This will ensure that all nonspam mail gets through to its destination, and this is not the case with RBL. It will come as no surprise that we do not agree with Lessig's objection to privatized solutions to the problem of spam. We do, however, share his concerns about MAPS. If filtering programs are implemented responsibly and diligently by online service providers and by end users, they can amount to a more effective solution to the problems of spam than a policy approach, which will inevitably suffer from the jurisdictional conundrum of cyberspace.

DEFAMATION AND ISP LIABILITY

In the last few years defamation on the Internet has emerged as a controversial topic of Internet law. As in real space, so in cyberspace, defamation is not a protected form of speech. But there are questions about the scope of an Internet service provider's liability for defamation in the realm of cyberspace. More precisely, to what degree, if any, should Internet service providers be held accountable for preventing or limiting the damage of defamatory statements made by individual users? On the one hand, mandating ISP liability could have an unwanted chilling effect on free expression in cyberspace, but on the other hand, failure to require ISPs to take adequate measures that will curtail libel is not conducive to civil discourse or the protection of private reputations. The broader issue of ISP liability for other forms of content is also important, but we wll confine our remarks here to the problem of defamation, recognizing that some of the same principles would apply to disputes about online threats or perhaps even some extreme forms of hate speech.

Defamation is defined as communication that harms the reputation of another and lowers that person's esteem in the eyes of the community. It can take two forms: libel refers to written or printed defamation, and slander refers to oral defamation. When a victim alleges defamation he or she must prove that the publication of the defamatory statement refers to the victim and that it is a "false statement to a person's discredit" (Cavazos 1997). It is obvious that the primary liability for libel lies with the original defamer, since that individual is the direct cause of the defamation and should be held directly accountable and blameworthy. However, other parties, or intermediaries, that give the defamer a forum may also be held vicariously liable for the defamation. This might include, for example, a newspaper that carelessly allowed libelous comments to be made by one of its columnists or a television station that aired defamatory remarks.

There are different standards of liability for distributing defamatory information depending upon the role one plays in the process. Under the standard of publisher liability, "One who repeats or otherwise republishes defamatory material is subject to liability as if he had originally published it"(*Restatement of Torts*, §580B [1976]). Thus, publishers such as newspapers and magazines are held liable and accountable for the defamation that appears on their pages, since they exercise editorial control over these publications. According to the standard of distributor liability, a distributor (such as a bookstore) is not liable unless it knows or has reason to know of the defamatory content. Distributors clearly do not exercise editorial control over the materials that they sell and therefore cannot be held to the same standard as a publisher. Under the standard of common carrier liability a common carrier such as the telephone company has "qualified immunity": Unless it knows or has reason to know that defamation is occurring, it has no liability for defamatory remarks made by its customers. Given the volume of communication that occur over the phone lines, it would be ludicrous to hold a common carrier liable for slanderous speech in the vast majority of cases.

Our primary concern is the vicarious liability of the Internet service providers that give most individuals access to the Internet. If an individual defames someone else through online communications, does the ISP have any liability in these situations? The category of Internet service providers includes companies such as Prodigy, America Online, EarthLink, and many others who provide their customers with access to the Internet for a monthly fee or an hourly rate. Although not formally classified as ISPs, there are also many commercial and noncommercial hosts (such as universities and corporations) with dedicated Internet links. They typically provide students, faculty, and employees with Internet access free of charge. These hosts would face the same liability issues of commercial ISPs.

Some of the confusion surrounding cyberspace defamation is the legal system's inability to fit an Internet service provider neatly into one of the categories already listed. Is an ISP best categorized as a publisher, a distributor, or perhaps even a common carrier? If an ISP were considered to be a publisher, it would be liable for defamatory content in the same way that newspapers and other media are held liable for the content of the stories they publish. If an ISP were classified as a distributor, there would be some liability, but only if it were informed of defamatory material and failed to remove it in a timely manner. Finally, if an ISP were to be held to the standard of a common carrier, it would not be liable unless it knew of the defamatory message before it was transmitted and did nothing to stop that transmission.

Judges have handed down different rulings regarding ISP liability depending upon the level of editorial control an ISP has exercised. In the first such case, *Cubby, Inc. v. CompuServe* (776 F. Supp. S.D.N.Y. [1991]), the court ruled that CompuServe was not liable for disseminating an electronic newsletter with libelous content. According to the U.S. District Court of New York, CompuServe was acting as a distributor (and not as a publisher), since it did not exercise editorial control over the contents of its bulletin boards or other online publications. CompuServe was regarded as a conduit for unfiltered information, just as a bookstore or a library. This case seemed to affirm that if ISPs made no effort to monitor content they would not be liable for that content.

But in 1995 a New York judge ruled in *Stratton Oakmont, Inc. v. Prodigy* (WL 323710 N.Y. Sup. Ct. [1995]) that Prodigy was liable for libelous messages posted on its bulletin boards since it acted as a publisher by screening content. Prodigy had positioned itself as a family-oriented, electronic network that screened out objectionable messages, thereby making the network more suitable for children. According to Anthes (1995), Prodigy sought "to find a middle ground between assuming the mantle of publisher and having an 'anything goes' approach to content." Members signed a contract and agreed not to display any "defamatory, inaccurate, abusive, obscene, profane, sexually explicit, threatening, ethnically offensive, or illegal material" (Spinello 1997). The company prescreened postings using a keyword system to catch obscenities, solicitations, or blatant hate speech.

However, with such a crude filtering system it would be difficult to screen out most libelous statements, since they often consist of ordinary language. In October 1994 a message was anonymously posted on Prodigy's "Money Talk" bulletin board alleging that the president and others at the Stratton brokerage firm had committed criminal and fraudulent acts in connection with the public offering of a stock for a company known as Salomon Page, Ltd. The message claimed that the offering was a "major criminal fraud" and that Stratton was a "cult of brokers who either lie for a living or get fired" (Spinello 1997). Despite Prodigy's argument that it was not technically feasible to screen all messages, the New York court decided that an ISP exercising any form of control over its content was in fact a publisher and not a distributor and should be held legally liable as a publisher. Prodigy appealed the ruling, but the case was eventually settled out of court.

Both the CompuServe and Prodigy cases provide some insight into the different roles that ISPs can play and the different degrees of liability that can be associated with those roles. According to the logic of these cases, the more editorial control the ISP exercises, the greater its exposure to liability for users' defamatory comments. On the other hand, if the ISP adheres to a more hands-off editorial approach, it will be more insulated from liability.

In 1996 Congress entered the fray and promulgated a new policy on ISP liability, partly as a response to the controversial Prodigy ruling. The ill-fated Communications Decency Act contains Section 230(c), which grants broad immunity from liability to ISPs that carry content generated by its subscribers. While most of the CDA was found to be unconstitutional, Section 230, known as the "Good Samaritan" exemption, was left intact. Congress sought to neutralize the Court's decision in the Prodigy case, since that decision effectively created a powerful disincentive for filtering. According to the CDA, "No provider or user of an interactive computer service shall be treated as the publisher or speaker of any information provided by another information content provider."

The broad scope of Section 230 was confirmed in the case of *Zeran v. America Online* (129 F. 3d 327 4th Cir. [1997]). This suit was brought by Kenneth Zeran, who alleged that AOL was negligent in not removing postings indicating that he sold T-shirts glorifying the Oklahoma City bombing. Zeran was the subject of many threatening phone calls and he immediately called America Online to remove the libelous posting and issue a retraction. An AOL representative informed Zeran that the posting would be removed, but then refused to remove a second posting as a matter of AOL policy. Zeran appealed and was told that the posting would be removed, but such postings kept appearing for several weeks.

In the lawsuit, the Fourth Circuit court rejected this challenge to ISP immunity and ruled in favor of AOL. It cited Congress's rationale for granting this immunity: "To maintain the robust nature of Internet communications," and to prevent ISP's from "severely restrict[ing] the number and type of messages posted" out of constant fear of liability. The court ruled that Section 230 exempts ISPs even from distributor liability (as well as publisher liability); that is, there is no obligation to take affirmative action even when notified. Although it is true that Congress says nothing about distributor liability and perhaps intended to leave it in force, the Fourth Circuit court reasoned that "distributor" is a subset of the word "publisher" and as a result ruled that ISPs are exempt from both distributor and publisher liability.

While ISPs applauded this ruling, it has also had many detractors, who claimed that the court overstepped its bounds in this case. According to Sheridan (1998), "When Congress said 'publisher', it meant 'publisher', not 'distributor.'" In his view, ISPs should be immunized from publisher liability, but not from some form of distributor liability. Sheridan argues that this interpretation is more consistent with the actual text of the CDA. Under distributor liability AOL would only be liable if it were unreasonably slow in removing the messages upon notification or negligent in trying to track down the perpetrator. As it stands, Zeran was left in a defenseless position, since he could not remedy the damage inflicted upon him without AOL's help: He had no ability to post a retraction, track down the culprit, or remove the defamatory statements. Thanks to this broad ruling he had no legal recourse and was forced to rely on the goodwill of AOL.

A second case that confirmed the scope and import of CDA's Section 230 is *Blumenthal v. Drudge* (992 F. Supp. 44 D.D.C. [1998]). In this well-known case White House aide Sidney Blumenthal filed suit against AOL for defamatory material written by Drudge. Drudge was commissioned and paid by AOL to publish his Drudge Report on the AOL network. AOL had the prerogative to exercise editorial control over the contents of this report and heavily promoted its association with Drudge. One could plausibly argue, therefore, that AOL was not functioning as a passive conduit for "another information content provider." Nonetheless, a court determined that AOL was not liable in any way for Drudge's remarks. The court's reasoning here was consistent with the relevant CDA provision and its decision in *Zeran v. AOL*, which interpret that statute in the broadest possible way: ISPs are immune from both publisher and distributor liability, even if they sponsor the source of that information and have the right to control its content.

Thus, while the judgment in the Prodigy case appeared to hold ISPs to a higher standard of liability if they operated as publisher, this precedent was negated in the latter two cases, where the court declared that ISPs had absolute immunity in the area of defamation liability based on this controversial interpretation of Section 230 of the Communications Decency Act.

Assuming the continued relevance of libel law in cyberspace and the need to allocate responsibility, should ISPs have such broad immunity? Does this policy articulated in the CDA maximize social welfare? Or should ISPs, like other publishers and even distributors, be held accountable in some fashion for libelous remarks? As we have seen, the basic reasoning for immunizing ISPs is predicated on the assumption that it is unfair and burdensome to hold an ISP liable for the illegal conduct of its customers.

While such reasoning is quite sensible, the rulings in the *Zeran* and *Blumenthal* cases, based on interpretations of the CDA, are extreme and disappointing. As more and more users frequent cyberspace, the challenge to maintain civil discourse will be greatly magnified. This formidable challenge will not be made easier by a blanket rule of ISP immunity from liability in defamation cases. Failure to hold ISPs liable even in some limited fashion could lead to an escalation in incidents of libel on the Internet, leaving victims without much recourse in some cases. This is especially problematic in cyberspace, where potential defamers have a better opportunity to act anonymously and to keep their identities concealed.

On the other hand, the ruling in the *Stratton* case was also misguided. Treating the ISP as a publisher of content that is not its own because it has attempted to filter out objectionable material seems unfair. Can we locate some middle ground in this debate? While the polar extreme positions of strict liability and absolute immunity defy moral common sense, is it possible to define reasonable parameters of liability for an ISP that will protect defamation victims without burdening the ISP?

Before proceeding here we must clarify precisely what is meant by responsibility or accountability. In this context we consider holding ISPs liable or accountable since they provide a forum for the defamatory statements. They do not directly or intentionally cause the dissemination of those remarks, but in facilitating Internet accessibility they provide the occasion for those remarks. However, just because an ISP provides a broad forum for defamation does not necessarily imply accountability. Accountability must be grounded in some standard that considers what ISPs can reasonably do to prevent defamation or at least limit its damage. There should be some proportionality between one's ability to avoid harmful conduct (or prevent another's harmful conduct) and a corresponding duty to do so. The apposite principle is that "ought implies can." For the most part, we should only hold someone accountable for actions over which they can exercise some measure of "regulative control" (Fischer 1991).

Also, in this context, economic feasibility must factor into this analysis. It would be unfair and counterproductive to insist on control at any cost, so the issue of economic feasibility must become part of the moral calculus. If we ignore economic concerns we run the risk of demanding a level of control that is prohibitively expensive and may end up forcing some ISPs out of business. This is obviously not a prudent policy from a social-welfare perspective.

The upshot of this is simple enough: We should not hold ISPs accountable or blameworthy for failing to do what is virtually impossible or insuperably difficult. One argument put forth in the *Zeran* case that has some merit is the contention that it would be impossible for America Online to monitor 10 million e-mail messages and 250,000 message postings each day. Moreover, there may be other reasons why such monitoring is socially unacceptable: As Carome (1997) and AOL's other lawyers pointed out, it would "cast a pall of censorship" over the Internet. Therefore, in the vast majority of cases it is unrealistic to expect that an ISP will have the capacity to prevent the initial occurrence of defamation given the sheer volume of communications they must deal with and the likelihood that the damaging statements will not contain any easily recognizable keywords that could be selectively detected by electronic filters.

This does not necessarily mean, however, that ISPs are helpless in the face of defamation. What type of regulative control over libelous statements can an ISP reasonably exercise? Once put on notice that a defamatory statement has been posted, an ISP clearly has the control to prevent any further damage by quickly removing that statement. It can also assist the victim in issuing a retraction. Moreover, it may be able to prevent its reoccurrence by taking certain actions against the defamer, assuming that the defamer can be tracked down without the need to take extraordinary measures. Although the ISP will need to investigate in order to confirm the victim's accusation, the economic feasibility of taking these postscreening steps should not be a terrible hardship. Indeed, while ISPs have rightfully asserted that prescreening would be especially burdensome, they have not made the same argument that postscreening would impose similar economic or administrative burdens.

ISPs sometimes act like publishers when they sponsor or operate newsletters or other online publications over which they exercise editorial control. At other times, when they are simply functioning as a conduit for other information content providers, their role is equivalent to a distributor. Clearly there must be a higher standard of liability when they assume a publisherlike role. Yet in *Blumenthal v. Drudge* America Online was immunized from liability for alleged defamatory remarks in the Drudge Report, despite the fact that AOL operated this online gossip column, aggressively promoted the column to its customers, and explicitly reserved the right to exercise control over its contents. If an ISP functions as a publisher it must be held to a higher standard of liability; that is, it must be held accountable for defamatory remarks in the same way that the *New York Times* or other media would be held accountable.

In most situations, however, ISPs will not be acting as publishers but as distributors, passive conduits for the exchange of information by their legions of subscribers. In this context, ISPs should assume responsibility for postscreening even if the law allows them to do otherwise. They should not take refuge in misguided policies and questionable legal precedents. But the policy should also be changed so that no one is victimized by an intransigent ISP that fails to live up to its moral obligations. Congress needs to amend Section 230 of the CDA so that an ISP has the liability commensurate with its role either as publisher or as distributor. Unless we abandon blanket immunity for ISPs and reach the type of compromise sketched out here, it is likely that ISPs will become the unwitting accomplices of many Internet defamers, who are often hiding behind the cloak of anonymity.

Libelous speech is different from pornography and hate speech; it cannot be regulated from the bottom up through code. It requires some regulation from the top down through carefully crafted statutes. Unfortunately, the current statute is inimical to the interests of the Internet community.

CONCLUSIONS

As we bring this chapter to a close, it is worth emphasizing that the First Amendment is not responsible for the abuses and social ills associated with the Internet. But some of these problems have caused profound desolation, and they cannot be simply ignored. The government still has the power to enforce the laws against some forms of harmful speech in cyberspace, such as child pornography, since this is speech that no one has a right to. But what can be done about speech that is legally acceptable for adults but harmful to minors? The dangers in cyberspace are real and palpable, and the law can only go so far. Pornography is more accessible for minors and malicious purveyors of hateful discourse seem to be expanding their reach. Impassivity is not an acceptable option. This is why code is so crucial. The circumspect and responsible deployment of that simple code, such as filters and labels, can protect vulnerable segments of the population while not burdening the free-speech rights of others.

As we have discovered, there is a policy chasm in many areas: Laws against cyberporn have been struck down, hate speech remains permissible in most countries, and spam has not yet been subjected to systematic legal restrictions. The debate about how to fill that chasm is lively and vociferous. Should American policy makers find a way to formulate more precise antipornography laws that will pass "constitutional muster"? Is the Children's Internet Protection Act that relies on private surrogates to do the government's work on the right track? Should there finally be some laws and policies that curb the spread of the virulent hate speech and ugly racist rhetoric that invades the Web? Should countries like France enforce their laws against hate speech on the global Internet? Should we make spam illegal or at least try to prevent further escalation of the chaotic spam wars through responsible policies?

We have argued here that most of these policy initiatives would be damaging and ineffective, though we surely realize the noble motivations of those who take the other side in this debate. Our preference is to avoid centralized hierarchical restrictions on speech and to preserve end-user choice through technology. We have also demonstrated the problems precipitated by the enforcement of particular laws pertaining to speech on a universal network. The legal reasoning used by a French court to stop Yahoo may be abused by authoritarian governments anxious to deprive their citizens of their ability to speak out about issues of public concern.

One thing seems certain. How we address these issues will have a lot to do with the evolution of the architectures of cyberspace. Right now the Internet is a permissive environment with corrupting influences, but it is also a liberating place without boundaries and without fences. The Net's global reach and universality is one of its most attractive features. But it becomes swiftly apparent that imposing restrictive policies and enforcing local laws could make the Net an unfamiliar terrain, with the same borders and territorial disputes that we find in the physical world. This is not an appealing notion for those who have become accustomed to a free-wheeling and open Internet with few controls on the distribution and redistribution of information.

REFERENCES

Anthes, G. (1995). "On-Line Boundaries Unclear." *Computerworld*, 5 June, 16.

Armstrong, L. (2000). "Making Mincemeat Out of Unwanted E-Mail." *Business Week*, 18 December, 234–235.

Berman, P. (2000). "How (If At All) to Regulate the Internet: Cyberspace and the State Action Debate." *University of Colorado Law Review* 71: 1263.

Carome, P. (1997). "Intellectual Property: Don't Shoot the Messenger." Available: http://www.jpmag.com/carome.html

Carroll, M. (1996). "Garbage In: Emerging Media and Regulation of Unsolicited Commercial Solicitations." *Berkeley Technology Law Journal* 11: 2.

Cavazos, E. (1997). "The Legal Risks of Setting Up Shop in Cyberspace." Available: http://www.cism.bus.utexas.edu/ravi/ed_paper.html

Elmer-DeWitt, P. (1995). "Cyberporn." *Time*, 3 July, 38–45.

Fischer, M. (1991). "Responsibility and Failure." In *The Spectrum of Responsibility*, edited by P. French. New York: St. Martin's Press.

Fisher, W. (2001). "Freedom of Expression on the Internet." Available: http://eon.law.harvard.edu/ilaw/speech

Fried, C. (2000). "Perfect Freedom or Perfect Control." *Harvard Law Review* 114: 606.

Greenhouse, L. (1997). "What Level of Protection for Internet Speech?" *New York Times*, 24 March, D5.

Guernsey, L. (2001). "Welcome to the Web. Passport, Please?" *New York Times*, 15 March, E1.

Kaplan, C. (1999). "In Intel Case, Property Rights vs. Free Speech." *CyberLaw Journal*, 28 May.

Kaplan, C. (2001). "Free-Speech Advocates Fight Filtering Software in Public Schools." Available: www.nytimes.com/jan19

Lessig, L. (1997). "Tyranny in the Infrastructure." *Wired*, July, 96.

Lessig, L. (1999). "The Spam Wars." *Industry Standard*, 11 January, 16.

Lessig, L., and Resnick, P. (1999). "Zoning Speech on the Internet: A Legal and Technical Model." *Michigan Law Review* 98: 395.

Lewis, P. (2000). "State Asks Supreme Court to Uphold Anti-Spam Law." *Seattle Times*, 7 April, 43.

Liptak, A. (2001). "When Is a Fake Too Real? It's Virtually Uncertain." *New York Times*, 28 January, F3.

Paine, L. (1993). *Prodigy Services Company (A)*. Boston: Harvard Business School Publications.

Perine, K. (2000). "The Trouble with Regulating Hate." *Industry Standard*, 31 July, 94.

Post, D. (2001). "Of Black Holes, and Decentralized Law-Making in Cyberspace." In *Readings in CyberEthics*, edited by R. Spinello and H. Tavani. Sudbury, Mass.: Jones and Bartlett.

Rausch, R. (1995). "Postage Due Marketing: An Internet Company White Paper." Available: http://www.Internet.com:2010/marketing/postage.html

Rimm, M. (1995). "Marketing Pornography on the Information Superhighway." *Georgetown University Law Journal* 83: 1849.

Schmitt, R. (1999). "Terminix Suit Aims to Mute a Web Critic." *Wall Street Journal*, 3 December, B1.

Schwartz, J. (2001). "Internet Filters Used to Shield Minors Censor Speech, Critics Say." *New York Times*, 19 March, A15.

Shapiro, A. (1999). *The Control Revolution*. New York: Century Foundation.

Sheridan, D. (1998). "*Zeran v. AOL* and the Effect of Section 230 of the Communications Decency Act upon Liability for Defamation on the Internet." *Albany Law Review* 61: 147.

Spinello, R. (1997). *Case Studies in Information and Computer Ethics*. Upper Saddle River, N.J.: Prentice-Hall.

Tribe, L. (1999). "The Internet vs. the First Amendment." *New York Times*, 28 April, A32.

Wingfield, N. (2000). "MAPS Can Be a Roadblock to E-Mail Access." *Wall Street Journal*, 3 August, B5.

7

Intellectual Property Wars and Knowledge Monopolies

There are probably many tales in the Internet's brief history that conjure up the epic biblical battle between David and Goliath, but none are more extraordinary than the stories behind two trials that dominated the news in the summer of 2000. To be sure, the major story that summer was the upcoming presidential election, but nonetheless everyone was talking about Napster, a software program created in 1999 by Shawn Fanning, then a nineteen-year-old college student, that enabled him to trade music files with his friends. Fewer people were talking about the DeCSS trial, but it too was turning out to be quite significant. This trial was necessitated by the actions of a precocious Norwegian high school student, Jan Johansen, who wrote a program that cracked the encryption code for DVD (Digital Versatile Disc) movie files. In both cases the U.S. legal system had taken swift action to protect the beleaguered music and movie industries. But no court injunction can stop the spread of these technologies, which threaten to undermine the online distribution of movies and music.

John Perry Barlow (1994), among others, predicted a transformation in society's understanding of intellectual property. But he also understood the complexity of the issue. According to Barlow,

> The riddle is this: if our property can be infinitely reproduced and instantaneously distributed all over the planet without cost, without our knowledge, how can we pro-

tect it? How are we going to get paid for the work we do with our minds? And, if we can't get paid, what will assure the continued creation and distribution of such work? Since we don't have a solution to what is a profoundly new kind of challenge, and are apparently unable to delay the galloping digitization of everything not obstinately physical, we are sailing into the future on a sinking ship. This vessel, the accumulated canon of copyright and patent law, was developed to convey forms and methods of expression entirely different from the vaporous cargo it is now being asked to carry. It is leaking as much from within as from without.

While some struggle to keep this vessel afloat, others proclaim that it's time to face reality and let information be "free." But despite the apparent emergence of a "free information" ecology movement in cyberspace, the debate about information policy and the scope of intellectual property protection has never been more intense. As commerce moves online the pressure to protect commercial property has directly interfered with that ecology. Rather than abandon copyright law, pragmatic policy makers have sought to mold this law so it fits the reality of digital networks. Hence the genesis of new laws like the Digital Millennium Copyright Act (DMCA).

This chapter will be devoted to these intellectual property issues, which have been cast into high relief by these well-publicized trials. It begins with an overview of the various rationales for these intellectual property laws. This includes some discussion of the law itself. The first specific issue for consideration is cyberpatents; that is, the granting of patents for business methods. From any angle it is hard to argue that these patents promote innovation. We then turn to a discussion of how information in a digital format has posed such a formidable challenge for content creators and providers. The right to control reproduction of creative works has been the essence of copyright protection, but how can the swapping of digital music and DVD files really be controlled? In this context we will look at whether code-based solutions, such as digital rights-management systems, are technologically feasible and ethically suitable.

The chapter will also focus on the scope of trademark protection. What is entailed in the ownership of a domain name? Does it preclude the usage of derivative names? As we shall see, the potential for direct collision with free-speech rights raises troubling concerns. The final theme is the issue of trespass, which arises in light of activities like deep linking and "spidering." If these activities constitute "trespass," the implication is that a Web site is a form of property. But is that really so? Also, is the listing of auctions on eBay's Web site a mere compilation of data or is it entitled to some type of property protection?

Our purpose in this elaborate discussion will be to attempt to appreciate the shifting regulatory landscape that has come about thanks to the changing economics of reproducing, distributing, and accessing information. We will also try to assess the ability of technology itself to handle some of these problems. Code, of course, will never be able to replace the law, which must strive to maintain that precarious balance between protections that are too strong and those that are too weak.

INTELLECTUAL PROPERTY: A THEORETICAL PERSPECTIVE

There are three prominent theories that attempt to justify the ownership of intellectual property from a philosophical or normative perspective:

1. Utilitarianism.
2. The Lockean or labor-desert theory.
3. The personality theory.

We cannot concern ourselves here with the viability of these theories, though we acknowledge that each has certain deficiencies. As Fisher (1998) has observed, none of these theories can provide a determinate means for resolving questions of legal entitlements or complicated ownership issues, "rather, each is best understood and employed as a language, a paradigm helpful in identifying considerations that ought to be taken into account when determining who should own what." They are, therefore, simply fruitful avenues of reflection for helping us think critically about intellectual property and ownership questions. Despite their ultimate indeterminacy, these theories enable us to make more nuanced and reasoned judgments about intellectual property issues, especially when the law is inchoate.

The utilitarian approach assumes that the utility principle, sometimes expressed as "the greatest good of the greatest number," should be the basis for determining property entitlements. It has several variations, but the main argument is based on the premise that people need to acquire, possess, and use things in order to achieve some degree of happiness and fulfillment. Since insecurity in one's possessions does not provide such happiness, security in possession, use, and control of things is necessary. Furthermore, security of possession can only be accomplished by a system of property rights. Also, utilitarian philosophers such as Bentham justified the institution of private property by the related argument that knowledge of future ownership is an incentive that encourages people to behave in certain ways that will increase socially valuable goods. It would certainly appear that the basic utilitarian argument can be easily extended to intellectual property. According to the Landes–Posner model, since intellectual products can often be easily replicated due to low "costs of production," there is a danger that creators will not be able to cover their "costs of expression" (e.g., the time and effort involved in writing a novel or producing a music album). Creators cognizant of this danger are reluctant to produce socially valuable works unless they have ownership or the exclusive prerogative to make copies of their productions. Thus, intellectual property rights induce creators to develop works they would not otherwise produce without this protection, and this contributes to the general good of society (Fisher 1998).

The second approach, sometimes referred to as the labor-desert theory, is based on the premise that the person who works upon common or unowned resources has a right to the fruits of his or her labor. John Locke (1952) stated this simple thesis in the fifth chapter of his *Second Treatise on Government*, where he brings property to the center of political philosophy. According to Locke, people have a natural right or entitlement to the fruits of their labor. Thus, if someone takes common, unusable land and through the sweat of his brow transforms it into valuable farmland, that person deserves to own that land. Locke's basic argument is that labor is an unpleasant and onerous activity and hence people do it only to reap its benefits; as a result, it would be unjust not to let people have these benefits they take such pains to procure. In short, property rights are required as a return and suitable reward for laborers' painful and strenuous work. Locke, however, stipulates a proviso that one can acquire such a property right only as long as one leaves "enough and good enough" for others.

Although Locke had in mind physical property such as land, it would seem that this theory is naturally applicable to intellectual property as well. In this case the relevant resource is common knowledge (i.e., unowned facts, ideas, algorithms, etc.), and one's intellectual labor that contributes value to this common pool of knowledge should entitle one to have a natural property right in the finished product, such as a novel, a computer program, or a musical composition. Even if this sort of labor is not so unpleasant and difficult, Hughes (1997) argues that a property right is still deserved, since that labor creates something of social value. Further, the granting of most intellectual property rights will satisfy the Lockean sufficiency proviso. Nozick (1974) contends that the proper interpretation of this proviso is that ownership of intellectual property through labor is acceptable if others do not suffer any net harm. He argues that patents, for example, satisfy this proviso, since without this incentive—that is, without the prospect of a long and strongly protected monopoly for one's innovation—there would probably be no innovation and everyone would be worse off.

However, whether an intellectual property claim meets this proviso depends on what we mean by the intellectual resources, which belong to the commons. If we follow Hughes's (1997) interpretation (which is slightly different from Nozick), it refers to the set of all "reachable" ideas; that is, ideas that are available to us or within our grasp. According to Hughes, the development and expression of most ideas inspires people to reach new ones and thus expands the commons rather than depletes it. For instance, by granting eBay a property right in its Web site, we do nothing that will impede others from developing their own novel ideas (based perhaps on what they see at the eBay site) that will in turn result in new and unique Web sites. Also, the raw materials (such as graphics, text, standard musical harmonies, algorithms, etc.) that are woven together into a multimedia Web site remain (or should remain) part of the commons and available for other Web site creators. As a consequence, as long as the property right is properly implemented, it should not yield any net harm, since the resources available for other creators will not be constricted in any meaningful way when that property right is bestowed.

The basis of the third and final approach is that property rights are essential for proper personal expression. This theory has its roots in Hegel's philosophy. Hegel argued that property was necessary for the realization of freedom, as individuals put their personality into the world by producing things and engaging in craftsmanship. According to Reeve (1986), "Property enables an individual to put his will into a thing." Property then is an expression of personality, a mechanism for self-actualization. This theory seems particularly apt for intellectual property. As human beings freely externalize their will in various things, such as novels, works of art, or poetry, they create property to which they are entitled because those intellectual products are a manifestation of their personality or selfhood. It is an extension of their being and as such belongs to them. While not all types of intellectual property entail a great deal of personality, the more creative and individualistic one's intellectual works, the greater one's "personality stake" in that particular object and the more important the need for some type of ownership rights (Hughes 1997). This theory has much more currency in Europe than it does in the United States.

As we move on to discuss various intellectual property policies, these theories can serve as a guide, some basis for a critical and objective evaluation of those policies. Is a particular policy a response to economic pressures or does it promote utility and reward a heavy investment of labor?

CYBERPATENTS

Priceline has been one of many small companies to take on Microsoft in a competitive turf war. According to the company's founder Jay Walker, Microsoft is the "biggest bully" in cyberspace. What has Microsoft done this time? Priceline alleged in late 1998 that Microsoft's Expedia travel service violated its patent by allowing consumers to indicate what they are willing to pay for a hotel room or an airline ticket. Like Priceline, Expedia's Web site enabled customers to engage in C2B commerce by naming their own prices.

This may seem like a trivial allegation, especially in the wake of Microsoft's other problems at that time, but Priceline.com received a patent for its now famous "name your price" service. There is no doubt that this innovative pricing mechanism transforms the buying experience for the consumer, and price-sensitive Internet shoppers have helped to make Priceline.com a commercial success. But does this simple business model deserve the proprietary rights and exclusivity provided by a patent?

To answer this question we must review some background on patent protection. A patent is a government-issued grant that gives an inventor the right to exclude others from making and using or selling the patented item for a period of twenty years, measured from the filing date of the patent application. For a U.S. patent, protection applies only in the United States, so a patent application must be filed in each country in which protection is required. The U.S. patent system is essentially designed to create a "race to invent"; its purpose is to create incentives for big breakthroughs by providing strongly protected monopoly rights for the production and sale of the invention.

The requirements for patent protection are simple enough. The patented entity must have utility and it must be novel and nonobvious. It may be a process, machine, product by-process, or composition of matter (e.g., a drug). Abstract ideas, laws of nature, algorithms, and naturally occurring substances are not suitable candidates for patent protection. Over the years the scope of patent protection has expanded. For example, one still cannot get a patent for a naturally occurring substance, but it's now possible to get a patent if one develops a new plant variety exhibiting new qualities. And patents are granted for surgical procedures and for software products.

For decades patents were unavailable for business methods because they were considered to be abstract ideas. But in the 1990s the Patent and Trademark Office began granting patents for some business methods, treating them as process patents. In 1998 the U.S. Court of Appeals for the Federal Circuit seems to have ratified business method patents in the *State Street Bank and Trust Co. v. Signature Financial Group, Inc.* case (149 F. 3d 1372 [1998]). This case upheld a controversial patent granted to Signature Financial Group for a data-processing system that was designed to churn out mutual fund asset-allocation calculations. A lower court had found the patent to be invalid because patent law bars granting patents to a mathematical algorithm and to a business method. But the appeals court held that the transformation of data by a machine into a final share price was a practical application of an algorithm (and not an abstract idea), since it produced "useful, concrete, and tangible results." The court also held that the "business method" exception was "ill-conceived" and a "no longer applicable legal principal." The court stated that business methods were not different from other methods or processes, and that "patentability does not turn on whether the claimed method does 'business' instead of something else, but on whether the method, viewed as a whole, meets the requirements of patentability as set forth in Sections 102, 103 and 112 of the Patent Act."

This ruling led to a flood of applications for business-method patents. In 1998, 420 business-method patents were issued based on 1,300 applications, and in 2000, 1,000 patents were issued out of 7,500 applications (Fisher 2001). Since many of these patents were for online business methods, they became known as "cyberpatents." Some examples of such patents include Priceline.com's "name your price" model; Amazon.com's single-click method, which allows qualified customers to make their purchase with one click of a mouse; and a model for building online customer profiles and using them to recommend products and services (see Chartrand 2001).

What is especially unsettling about this flood of Internet patents is the discontinuity with how innovations were previously handled in the Internet's brief history. The basic protocols of the Internet, such as TCP/IP, were not patented, nor was their original software. Tim Berners-Lee never sought a patent for the hyperlinking technology that is the basis of the World Wide Web. This open approach stimulated rather than impeded Web innovation. In his critique of Internet patents, publisher Tim O'Reilly pointed out that the "Web is a gift" without which companies like Priceline would not exist (Levy 2000).

Nonetheless, supporters of Internet patents argue that patents in cyberspace are just as important for innovation as patents in real space. Jeffrey Bezos, chief executive officer of Amazon.com, contends that these patents are necessary to protect innovation, but he concedes that they should be of shorter duration, perhaps only three to five years. According to Angwin (2000), proponents of business-method patents "argue that such intellectual property is the fuel of the New Economy—that without these patents, inventors would be too afraid of copycats to go forward with their creations."

But arguments on the other side of this issue seem more convincing. Many of these cyberpatents have been awarded for conventional ideas that have been applied in a new way. Does an online version of an old concept or method really represent an "innovation" that deserves patent protection? Thus, a significant objection to most business-method patents is that they do not meet the criterion of "nonobviousness." An obvious invention is defined as one whose subject matter would have been obvious to a person who possessed "ordinary skill in the art" at the time the invention was created (*Graham v. John Deere*, 383 U.S. 1 [1966]). Isn't there something rather obvious about Amazon.com's one-click method? Wouldn't a skilled programmer consider the one-click method to be "obvious"? Isn't there also something obvious about Priceline's reverse auction, which mimics the way dutch auctions work in the real world?

In order to make a judgment about a patent's validity, the patent examiner must identify relevant "prior art." Investigating the prior art of business methods, however, is difficult, because these methods are sometimes kept secret so that they will not be imitated by competitors. Also, the investigation would require that patent officers have a strong background in business, which is often not the case.

The U.S. Patent and Trademark Office has become more sensitive to the issue and has promised to review its procedures for awarding patents for online practices. Of course, thanks to the *State Street* decision its discretion is limited. Nonetheless, the patent office has taken steps to improve its patent-application process by requiring broader searches of past inventions. This will at least help insure that an idea is truly innovative. However, any real changes in patent protection, such as a reduction in scope or duration, would require congressional action or a new court decision reinterpreting the precedent-setting *State Street* case.

Unless Congress takes action, the Internet "patent wars" are likely to get much worse. As many new e-commerce patents are granted, they will be used as weapons to gain market control of important e-commerce sectors. Patents have played a crucial role in the history of America's economy, and they did stimulate innovation in the industrial age. In that period, however, developing and marketing innovative products was a capital-intensive effort. Most innovations qualifying for cyberpatents, however, do not entail major capital investment. Instead of spurring innovation, business-method patents could have the reverse effect, since they might preclude incremental improvements on basic business models if companies are compelled to negotiate a licensing arrangement every time they want to make one of those improvements. There is also apt to be some unintentional infringement of these patents, which can only be avoided with more frequent searches of voluminous patent records.

Moreover, if we consider online patents from the vantage point of intellectual property theory, their justification seems thin. Most of the Web business models that have been patented do not entail substantial investments of time and money. It is difficult to imagine that the formulation of these basic ideas (like one-click shopping), along with their incorporation into software, required a significant investment of human capital. The work is not commensurate to the value of a long, heavily protected monopoly. It would be difficult, therefore, to invoke the labor-desert theory of Locke as a justification. Also, a utilitarian justification is highly questionable, since these patents tend to dampen innovation and limit competition on the Web. Priceline's lawsuit against Expedia was a major factor in delaying Expedia's entry into the name-your-price segment of the travel business. Expedia or other companies might have been able to add some incremental improvements to this method, but if the patent prevails, it will not be able to do so without the expensive proposition of licensing this technology from Priceline. These and other social costs (such as legal expenses) of online patents seem surely to outweigh the limited benefits. Therefore, it is difficult to make the case that cyberpatents increase aggregate social welfare. True intellectual capital deserves protection from the grasp of free riders, but simple and obvious ideas like one-click shopping do not seem to fit this category.

TRADEMARKS AND DOMAIN NAMES

The protection of trademarks has been a challenge for almost every major corporation doing business on the Web. They have had to fight off tenacious cybersquatters and others determined to encroach on expensive property rights or sully a well-respected brand name. Prior to the dot-com frenzy a California man bought up domain names of investment banks like goldmansachs.com and msdw.com (Morgan Stanley Dean Witter). When questioned by these investment banks about his intentions, he offered to sell them the names for a "modest" fee of $75,000.

Domain-name speculators like this individual, usually called "cybersquatters," have been a nuisance, but the issue is not as simple as trademark owners might suggest. What we have also witnessed is a conflict between Internet domain-name registration policy, which has operated on a first-come, first-serve basis, and trademark law. The issue is also complicated by the fact that at present a domain name for a commercial Web site is unique. In real space, for example, there are numerous registrations for the "Acme" trademark, but on the Web only one company can own the "acme.com" domain name. Furthermore, Internet users routinely guess at domain names. I may not know Disney's exact domain name, but disney.com is a pretty good guess. This means that easily recognizable, intuitive domain names are valuable corporate assets. And the more common the name, the more valuable the asset becomes. Who deserves these valuable names like disney.com? Is it the first person to apply for disney.com even if that person has no connection to Disney Corporation? Or is it the Disney Corporation, the owner of the Disney trademark in real space?

Hasbro Toys sought the domain name www.clue.com for an online version of its "Clue" board game, but it was preempted by Clue Computing. Does Hasbro have any legitimate claim to this domain name based on trademark law? Does Clue Computing's claim have standing, especially since it applied for the domain name before Hasbro? Before we consider how these questions get resolved, we must turn to a rudimentary analysis of trademark law theory.

A trademark is a word, phrase, or symbol that concisely identifies a product or service. Typical trademarks include the Nike "swoosh" symbol, names like "Pepsi" and "Dr. Pepper," and logos such as the famous bitten-apple image crafted by Apple Computer. To qualify as a trademark the mark or name must be truly distinctive. In legal terms distinctiveness is determined by several factors, including the following: Is the trademark "arbitrary or fanciful," that is, not logically connected to the product (e.g., the Apple Computer logo has no connection to a computer), and is the trademark powerfully descriptive or suggestive in some way?

According to the terms of the Federal Trademark Act of 1946 (the Lanham Act), trademarks are generally violated in one of three ways: infringement, unfair competition, or dilution. Infringement occurs when a registered trademark is used by someone else in connection with the sale of its goods or services. If an upstart athletic-shoe company tried to sell its products with the aid of the "swoosh" symbol it would be violating Nike's trademark. The general standard for infringement is the likelihood of consumer confusion. If a trademark has not been registered, the owner can still claim unfair competition if it is copied by someone else. Finally, trademark owners can also bring forth legal claims if their trademarks are diluted. Dilution is applicable only to famous trademarks that are distinctive, of long duration, and usually known to the public through extensive advertising and publicity. Dilution is the result of either "blurring" or "tarnishment." Blurring occurs when the trademark is associated with dissimilar products, for example, using the Jaguar trademark name to sell suits for men. Tarnishment occurs when the mark is portrayed in a negative or compromising way or associated with products or services of questionable value or reputation.

Trademark law does allow for fair use of trademarks and also use for purposes of parody. In fair-use situations the trademark name normally assumes its primary (versus commercial) meaning; for example, describing a cereal as comprised of "all bran" is different from infringing on the Kellogg's brand name "All Bran." Parody of trademarks is permitted as long as it is not closely connected with commercial use. Making fun of a well-known brand in a Hollywood skit is probably acceptable, but parodying that brand in order to sell a competing product would most likely not be allowed.

Domain-name disputes can involve trademark law in one of two ways. First, there is trademark infringement, which requires that the alleged infringement cause a likelihood of consumer confusion. The second potential problem with a domain name is the possibility of dilution (i.e., that a domain name dilutes or diminishes the value of an established trademark). Consider, for example, the Nike trademark. If someone develops Nike-brand DVD players there is not a great likelihood of confusion. However, if consumers begin to think of Nike as a trademark either for athletic shoes (and apparel) or DVD players, then Nike's trademark is no longer distinctive. Despite the claims of some trademark owners, however, noncommercial use and criticism generally do not represent trademark dilution.

Both trademark infringement and dilution are in violation of the Lanham Act (Sections 1114 and 1125 [c]). In November 1999 Congress passed the Anti-Cybersquatting Consumer Protection Act as an amendment to the Lanham Act (Section 1125d). This amendment created a new cause of action or new form of trademark violation.

The act expressly prohibits cybersquatting or other forms of domain-name speculation. It is now against the law to purchase unclaimed but commercially valuable domain names and sell them off at a high profit. Trademark holders can file suit against domain-name registrants who have allegedly misappropriated their trade name or a name that is "confusingly similar" to their mark. This legislation clearly broadens the application of trademark infringement, but there are legitimate questions about whether this expansion is justified. The problem is that this new law makes it easier for trademark owners to go after domain names that are similar to or dilutive of their trademarks. This concerns legal scholars like Jessica Litman (2000), because "it threatens to reinforce the assumption that domain name space is and should be an extension of trademark space." And, according to Litman, "it also may take us further down the road toward making commercial speech the favored flavor of discourse on the Internet."

Domain-name disputes used to be handled exclusively through the court system, but thanks to ICANN there is another venue available for dispute resolution. ICANN has developed a uniform mandatory dispute policy that will settle domain-name disputes. It is called the Uniform Dispute Resolution Procedure (UDRP). The UDRP has established certain criteria to determine whether an organization has the right to a domain name. The complainant must prove that "the domain name is identical to or confusingly similar to a trademark or service mark to which has rights" (ICANN 1999). It must also show that the domain name has been registered by another and is being used in bad faith. Paragraph 4(b) of the UDRP (ICANN 1999) lists four circumstances as evidence of bad faith:

(i) the domain name was registered primarily for the purpose of selling it to the complainant or a competitor for more than the documented out-of-pocket expenses related to the name; or

(ii) the domain name was registered in order to prevent the mark owner from using it, provided that the registrant has engaged in a pattern of such registration; or

(iii) the domain was registered primarily to disrupt the business of a competitor; or

(iv) by using the domain, the registrant has intentionally attempted to attract users for commercial gain by creating a likelihood of confusion as to source or affiliation.

The UDRP seems like a reasonable response to the cybersquatting problem as long as the definition of "bad faith" is not interpreted in such a way that free-speech rights are adversely affected. The anticybersquatting legislation, on the other hand, was probably premature. U.S. lawmakers should have given the UDRP a chance to work before developing this legislation, which introduces unnecessary complications and possible conflicts. Also, other countries may respond with their own legislation, and this will further undermine the UDRP and generate even more confusion.

One potential problem, alluded to by Litman (2000), is that the claim of "bad faith" could become a pretext for stifling free speech. The larger question concerns the extent to which a domain name should be a vehicle of digital expression. For example, a Web site critical of the Scientology movement calls itself www.scientology-kills.net. It was promptly sued by Scientology, which alleged tarnishing of its reputation. But this Web site was not being used for commercial purposes and was not interested in selling the name to Scientology, so it seems unfair to argue "bad faith." Should we allow domain names like this one to express an editorial comment? The use of domain names in this way makes trademark owners uneasy, but it is hard to argue that this does not constitute a valid form of expression.

It is also important that domain names for Web sites devoted to product criticism not fall in the "bad faith" category. The tire manufacturer Bridgestone–Firestone filed a "bad faith" claim through the UDRP against the domain name www.bridgestone-firestone.net. This Web site was established by a former employee and it is used as a forum for posting product and company criticisms. The UDRP panel upheld the employee's claim to this domain name and his right to maintain this Web site.

Although the arbitration panel made the right choice in this case, there is some preliminary evidence that the deck is stacked in favor of the trademark owners who file these claims. A study concluded in July 2001 found that 81 percent of cases have been decided in favor of the trademark holders (Angwin 2001). Of course, the reason behind this high rate is that those complainants may have a legitimate case most of the time, so we will need more evidence before reaching any firm conclusions about the equity of this process.

COPYRIGHT PROTECTION AND THE DIGITAL DILEMMA

Digital technology has made it much easier and cost effective to reproduce, distribute, and republish all sorts of information in a digital format. This includes books, articles, movies, and music. To compound the problem, each digital copy is a perfect replica. At the same time, computer networks have altered the economics of distribution, making it trivially easy to transfer this information instantaneously. It seems virtually impossible to control the distribution of digital information in cyberspace, and herein lies the difficulty of enforcing traditional copyright laws.

How can content creators distribute their work to paying customers while protecting it from "free riders"? Also, how can we protect content creators without overprotecting intellectual property and tilting the balance in favor of producers rather than users? Copyright protection is a delicate balancing act, and that balance can be easily threatened by aggressive policies designed to protect content providers.

Copyright Law: An Overview

Some recent changes in copyright protection seem to have shifted the balance that was first articulated in the U.S. Constitution. The Constitution recognizes the propriety of government-sponsored monopolies for "author" and "inventor" in order to "promote the Progress of Science and Useful Arts." Copyright was seen as grounded in common law and based on a natural right, and hence it was given important constitutional status. A copyright differs from a patent, since it represents a right to make copies, whereas a patent is a right to control the royalties to a novel product or an invention. According to Goldstein (1994), "Copyright is the law of authorship and patent is the law of invention." The Constitution, however, does strike a balance between author's rights and the public good, since it demands that a copyright be granted for a limited term, so that after a certain period copyrighted works will become part of the public domain. A copyright, therefore, has never been conceived as an absolute or unlimited right.

Copyright law has obviously come a long way since the Constitution was crafted. Copyright law now protects a literary, musical, dramatic, artistic, architectural, audio, audiovisual, or visual work from being reproduced without the permission of the copyright holder. To be eligible for copyright protection, the work in question must be original; that is, independently created by its author. The work must also be "fixed in a tangible medium or expression." A dance itself (such as a waltz) cannot be copyrighted, but a visual recording of that dance could be eligible for copyright protection. Copyright protection extends to the concrete expression of an idea, but not to the idea itself. Thus, copyright laws cannot be used to protect ideas, concepts, principles, algorithms, or other such intellectual objects. Whatever idea or concept the author has must be uniquely embodied in a particular form in order to be copyrighted. An idea that takes the form of a movie plot, for example, is not subject to copyright protection, but the actual script is eligible for such protection.

The framers of the Constitution never intended to give copyright holders complete control over their works, and hence copyright protection has limitations. One such limitation or "safety valve" (Goldstein 1994) is the "fair use" provision. Copyright laws permit "fair use" of these creative works, which can be cited or displayed for educational or critical purposes. Copyrighted literary works can be quoted and a small segment of a video work can be displayed for limited purposes, including criticism, research, classroom instruction, or news reporting. Commentary, criticism, and parody may not be in the best interests of copyright holders, but they are in the public's best interest. Also, making private copies of certain material is considered fair use. For example, in *Sony v. Universal* (659 F. 2d 963 9th Cir. [1981]) the U.S. Supreme Court affirmed that consumers can make a video copy of a television program for their own private use.

Also, copyright protection does not extend ad infinitum. Originally, a copyright only lasted for fourteen years. For many years the term of a copyright was the life of the author plus fifty years for an individual author (such as J. D. Salinger), and seventy-five years for a corporate author (such as Disney). However, thanks to the controversial Sonny Bono Copyright Term Extension Act (CTEA), those terms were recently extended to the life of the author plus seventy years and ninety-five years, respectively.

Still another "safety valve" is the first-sale doctrine. This permits consumers who have purchased a copyrighted work such as a book or music CD to lend or sell that work to someone else without permission of the copyright holder. The purpose of this provision is to further the public exchange and dissemination of ideas.

The sphere of copyright law and policy today seems rife with paradoxes and contradictions. On the one hand, laws like the Sonny Bono Copyright Extension Act are strengthening the power of copyright holders. At the same time, we continue to hear dire predictions that digital technologies will pose an unprecedented threat to the future of copyright law. Copyright law, however, has never been static and it has demonstrated remarkable resiliency to handle new technologies like photography and the VCR. Does this bode well for digital technology? Are predictions of copyright's extinction premature? To some extent this depends on the nature of this technology: Is it so qualitatively different from previous technologies that it will completely undermine copyright protection? It also depends on how far lawmakers are willing to go to protect digital copyrights. Will digital music and movies render copyright obsolete, or will it lead to draconian measures that threaten those critically important "safety valves"?

Digital Music: MP3 and Napster

The digital distribution of music has become a reality thanks to a format called MP3 (Motion Picture Experts Group—Layer 3). MP3 is an audio compression format that creates near-CD-quality files that are as much as twenty times smaller than the files on a standard music CD. While standard music files require 10 megabytes for each minute of music, MP3-formatted files require only 1 megabyte. It has become the standard for storing, accessing, and distributing music on the Web. Digital music can now be transmitted as a "containerless" file over the Internet and subsequently stored on the user's computer system.

While this novel distribution method has thrown the music industry into some degree of chaos, it does have certain advantages. Direct distribution of music files is a prime example of the disintermediation promised by Internet technology. Authors, composers, and performers can publish and distribute their music online without the assistance of recording companies. This low-cost distribution method creates benefits for both the creators of music and their customers. Downloading digital music is certainly more convenient for customers than purchasing it in retail stores or through mail order, and, as Fisher (2000) points out, this mode of music distribution tends to promote "semiotic democracy." The "power to make meaning, to shape culture" will no longer be so concentrated. Rather, it will be more dispersed among a broader range of musicians and artists, who do not need to sign big contracts in order to produce and distribute their music.

The downside of this system, of course, is the potential for piracy. Since MP3 files are unsecured, they can be effortlessly distributed and redistributed in cyberspace. The music industry's response to this problem has been predictable. They have doggedly pursued the operators of Web sites that promote digital music sales, like MP3.com, along with intermediaries like Napster. Consider the case of MP3.com, which "allows users to store music in virtual lockers on its site, dream up their own play lists, and tap in instantly from any Web-connected device" (Weintraub 2000). MP3.com enabled customers to assemble databases of their favorite music, but those customers had to prove that they had purchased a "hard copy" of the CD from one of MP3.com's partners. The main database of MP3 files, from which users assembled their personal list, consisted of copyrighted songs off 40,000 CDs that MP3.com had copied without permission.

The idea attracted many young customers, and MP3.com's revenues, originating primarily from advertising, reached over $80 million in fiscal 2000. But the company has subsequently been sued by the Recording Industry Association of America (RIAA) for violating copyright laws (*RIAA v. MP3.com*, 00 Cir. 0472 JSR S.D.N.Y. [2000]). In April 2000 Judge Rakoff sided with the music industry and ruled that MP3.com had clearly violated Section 106 of the copyright law and that its copying of copyrighted musical material did not constitute "fair use." Fair use did not apply, according to Judge Rakoff, because MP3.com copied music in its entirety and its actions were "commercial" and "nontransformative." The company reached a settlement with the record companies, agreeing to pay them $80 million in damages along with future royalties. In September 2000 the same judge ordered MP3.com to pay Universal Music (which was not part of the original suit) $25,000 per CD. This payment would have forced the company into bankruptcy, but a more moderate settlement was reached shortly after that ruling.

Intermediaries such as Napster have not fared much better. Napster is the creation of Shawn Fanning, a Northeastern University student, who left after his freshman year to write this celebrated piece of software. Napster operates by allowing a Napster user to access the systems of other Napster users for a particular piece of music. Once that music is located, it can be downloaded in MP3 format and stored on the user's hard drive. Napster had hoped that its status as an intermediary would give it immunity from the legal problems associated with the breaking of copyright laws. Napster does not store or "cache" any digital music files on its own servers. Napster also has a copyright policy in which it disavows any responsibility for the illicit activities of its subscribers.

These precautions, however, did not help Napster, and in December 1999 A&M Records and the RIAA sued the company for vicarious copyright infringement, demanding $100,000 each time a song was copied by a Napster user. Several months later the rock band Metallica also sued Napster for copyright infringement. The company's legal troubles culminated in the summer of 2000, when the RIAA filed a motion for a preliminary injunction to block the recordings of all the major labels from being swapped through Napster. The RIAA was worried about the precedence of allowing copyrighted music to be exchanged so freely and openly. In its main brief the RIAA summed up the problem quite clearly: "If the perception of music as a free good becomes pervasive, it may be difficult to reverse" (RIAA 2000).

On July 26, 2000, District Judge Marilyn Patel ruled in the RIAA's favor. She ordered Napster to stop allowing copyrighted material to be traded through its system. According to Gomes (2000), in her ruling, "Judge Patel harshly reprimanded Napster for being little more than a giant music-piracy operation and rejected out of hand the company's central legal claim—that people have a right to put digital copies of music on the Internet." Despite the harsh ruling, two days later Napster won a reprieve as the Ninth Circuit County of Appeals stayed Judge Patel's injunction pending an appeal. This allowed Napster to continue its normal operations.

However, this was not the end of Napster's legal confrontation with the RIAA and other aggrieved parties. Although it had initially stayed Judge Patel's injunction, in February 2001 a three-judge panel of the U.S. Court of Appeals for the Ninth Circuit issued a ruling that supported Judge Patel's original order. The appeals court ruled that Napster's music-sharing site facilitated copyright infringement on a massive scale. The court required Judge Patel to narrow the scope of her injunction so that it would require both Napster and the record companies to identify the copyrighted music shared by Napster users. The substance of the injunction remained unaltered: It was Napster's responsibility to prevent the exchange of any copyrighted music.

Despite Napster's apparent defeat, it is worth reviewing the legal arguments that have been marshaled in its defense. For its main defense the company's lawyers invoked Section 512 of the Digital Millennium Copyright Act. This section of the DMCA provides the operators of "transitory digital network connections" with a safe harbor against any liability for copyright infringement. Napster also contended that the exchange of these music files by its members constituted "fair use" of that music and that it was not copyright infringement.

Is there any validity to these arguments? Can Napster's business possibly be justified on legal or even on moral grounds? Are Napster users infringing the law when they download music for their own "personal use"? Or should this activity be considered as "fair use"? We cannot answer all of these questions in depth, but a good place to begin is an evaluation of the Ninth Circuit Court's decision, which stands out as a well-reasoned and balanced analysis of the Napster problem.

One of the precedents cited in Napster's defense was *Sony v. Universal Studios* (659 F. 2d 963 9th Cir. [1981]). In this case the court ruled that VCR manufacturers were not liable for the copyright infringement engaged in by any VCR users. The reasoning behind this decision was that "contributing infringement would be found only if the product in issue had no substantial non-infringing use" (Goldstein 1994). The VCR could be used for both lawful and unlawful copying, and VCR manufacturers should not be held accountable for the latter, since the bulk of VCR tapings were lawful and noninfringing. Napster argued that they were no different from the VCR manufacturers. Its service too is typified by "substantial non-infringing uses," since some of the music copied by its members was not protected by a copyright.

Hence, it should not be held liable for any unlawful copyright infringement initiated by its users.

Judge Patel strongly disagreed with this particular argument. She opined that in Napster's situation there was substantial infringing use, so *Sony v. Universal Studios* did not apply. The Ninth Circuit Court, however, delivered a much more nuanced judgment about this question. It concluded that while there may be "substantial noninfringing uses" of the Napster system, Napster is in a different position from the VCR manufactures since it has proximity and capability. It has "actual knowledge that specific infringing material is available using its system." It also has the ability to block access to those supplying the infringing material. Napster's "knowledge" had come from the record companies, which presented to the company the names of over 12,000 copyrighted music files whose exchange was being facilitated through the Napster system. The burden is on the record companies to inform Napster that a copyrighted file is being shared, but once Napster is so informed, it must assume the burden of removing or filtering that file.

This seems to be a reasonable and fair solution, grounded in sound theory about the scope of liability. When there is proximity (knowledge) and capability, there is usually accountability. If one knows that a harm such as copyright infringement is occurring and has the capability to stop that harm, there is a moral obligation to do so.

Despite its apparent defeat, Napster has many defenders who continue to argue that our anachronistic copyright laws have no place on the Net. Shouldn't this be a copyright-free zone? But the protection afforded by copyright laws remains central to the vitality of a free and creative society. The purpose of copyright law is to protect creative expression in order to induce creative activity. If implemented correctly, copyright law is welfare enhancing, since it provides a stimulus for future creativity. Will a good novelist invest the time and money to write a quality work if free riders can copy and sell the novel without compensating the author? Will movie studios invest $150 million in production expenses unless the end product has some copyright protection so they can recoup their investment? The higher the cost of expression, the greater the incentive effects of copyright protection.

One might argue, however, that while we need these laws in real space we can do without them in cyberspace. But this is a naïve idea. The boundaries separating these two spaces are too porous. As a result, whatever is created in real space will most likely migrate to cyberspace. Hence, at the present time it seems unfair and unrealistic to designate cyberspace as a copyright-free zone where anything goes.

Others critical of the Napster ruling argue that the court may have been too presumptuous in taking such definitive action against Napster. Perhaps it would have been better to let digital music models evolve and work out some type of compensation scheme. The issues in the Napster case are ambiguous, they argue, and the court's intervention may represent hasty and officious judicial regulation. This is not an unreasonable argument, but the RIAA's perspective is also valid: The perception of music as a free good fostered by sites like Napster may be too difficult to reverse and one way to help change that perception is through judicial action.

The DeCSS Trial and the Anticircumvention Act

In 1998 the Digital Millenium Copyright Act was signed into law by President Clinton. The complex regulations incorporated into this act ban circumvention technologies in order to help make available digital works on the Internet. The DMCA forbids the manufacture and distribution of technologies designed to bypass technical protection systems (such as an encryption system) typically used to protect the digital works of copyright holders.

There are two types of anticircumvention rules in the DMCA. First, it outlaws the act of circumventing "a technical measure that effectively controls access to a [copyrighted] work." If I purchase a CD ROM video game, it could require me to register with the manufacturer (via modem) so that the CD ROM will only recognize the password forwarded to me by the manufacturer and will only work in this one machine. If I were to use this CD ROM in a friend's computer I would be violating the DMCA by circumventing technical measures that control access to the work. It may be legal under the first-sale doctrine of the Copyright Act to lend this CD ROM to a friend, but this once benign action is now effectively barred by the DMCA.

The DMCA also makes it illegal to manufacture or distribute technologies that enable circumvention. According to Ginsburg (1999), "If users may not directly defeat access controls, it follows that third parties should not enable users to gain unauthorized access to copyrighted works by providing devices or services (etc.) that are designed to circumvent access controls." There are exceptions to this statute, including a general exception for interoperability: Companies can circumvent technical measures if it is necessary to develop an interoperable computer program (see Section 1201f).

A highly controversial legal challenge to the DMCA was presented in the case of *Universal Studios v. Remeirdes* (111 F. Supp. 2d 294 S.D.N.Y. [2000]). This case is about a software program known as DeCSS, which decrypts DVD files. DVDs are small discs that can hold a full-length motion picture. These discs can be played on free-standing DVD players or on personal computers equipped with DVD drives.

DVD files, like digital music files, are insecure. Use of the DVD format brought "an increased risk of piracy by virtue of the fact that digital files, unlike the material on video cassettes, can be copied without degradation from generation to generation" (*Universal v. Remeirdes*). Given the vulnerability of DVDs to illicit copying, they have been protected with an access-control system that encrypts the contents. This system, known as the Content

Scramble System (CSS), was developed by Matshusita Electric Industrial Company and Toshiba Corporation. The entire DVD industry has adopted this standard. Consequently, all movies in digital format distributed on DVDs are protected with CSS.

If computer users want to watch DVD movies on their personal computers instead of dedicated DVD players, those computers must be using Mac or Windows, since they are the only CSS-compatible operating systems. But in the fall of 1999 Jan Johansen of Larvik, Norway, decided that he wanted to watch DVD movies on a computer that ran the Linux operating system. He set out to create a software program that would play DVDs on Linux, and this meant that it would be necessary to crack the CSS encryption code. Johansen cracked CSS with ease in a program he called DeCSS. He posted the DeCSS source code on the Web in order to ensure its widespread distribution. Soon many other Web sites began posting DeCSS source code and the program quickly proliferated through cyberspace.

In January 2000, eight major Hollywood studios, including Paramount Pictures, Universal Studios, and MGM Studios, filed a lawsuit against three New York men who operated a Web site distributing DeCSS. These defendants publish a magazine for hackers called *2600: The Hacker Quarterly*, and in November 1999 they posted DeCSS on their magazine's Internet Web site. The suit contended that DeCSS was little more than a "piracy tool" that would be used to produce decrypted copies of DVD movies for distribution over the Internet. The lawsuit also alleged that DeCSS violated Section 1201 of the DMCA, which makes it illegal for anyone to provide technology that is intended to circumvent access controls (such as encryption) that protect literary or creative works. The defendants contended that DeCSS is form of protected expression and that Section 1201 of the DMCA discriminated against DeCSS because of its content.

In February 2000 Judge Lewis Kaplan issued a preliminary injunction prohibiting the defendants from posting DeCSS on their respective Web sites pending the trial. Following this court order two of the defendants settled with the movie studios. But the third defendant, Eric Corley, refused to settle, and the case continued. Mr. Corley removed the DeCSS code from his Web site, www.2600.com; however, he added links from his site to a number of other target sites that contained the DeCSS software. In April 2000 lawyers for the movie studios filed a petition with Judge Kaplan urging him to amend his previous order and to prohibit Corley from linking to Web sites with the DeCSS code. It claimed that "the appearance of these hyperlinks is not an inadvertent act but, instead, part of a deliberate effort to proliferate DeCSS as widely as possible" (Schumann 2000).

The actual trial began in the summer of 2000. Corley's defense team challenged the absolute right of the movie industry to control how DVD discs are played. It argued that DeCSS simply preserves "fair use" in digital media by allowing DVDs to work on computer systems that are not running Mac or

Windows operating systems. Consumers should have the right to use these disks on a Linux system, and this required the development of a program such as DeCSS. Fair use is a First Amendment "safety valve" that prevents the DMCA from a collision with the First Amendment. Further, Section 1201(c) of the DMCA expressly preserves fair use: "Nothing in this section shall affect rights, limitations, or defenses to copyright infringement including fair use."

In addition, the defense argued that the ban on linking was tantamount to suppressing an important form of First Amendment expression. Links, despite their functionality, are a vital part of the expressiveness of a Web page and therefore their curtailment violates the First Amendment. Finally, the defense team argued that computer code itself is a form of expressive free speech that deserves full First Amendment protection. This includes both source code and object code. A computer scientist appearing as an expert witness proclaimed that an injunction against the use of code would adversely affect his ability to express himself.

On August 17, 2000, Judge Kaplan ruled in favor of the movie industry, concluding that DeCSS clearly violated the DMCA. He ordered Eric Corley to remove the DeCSS software from his Web site, along with any links to sites containing that program. In his ruling Judge Kaplan rejected the notion that the DMCA curtailed the "fair use" right of consumers. He did agree that source code is a form of expressive speech and that First Amendment issues are germane, but the judge concluded that DeCSS "does more . . . than convey a message. . . . It has a distinctly functional non-speech aspect in addition to reflecting the thoughts of programmers. Consequently, because of its functional nature this category of speech does not deserve full First Amendment protection" (*Universal v. Remeirdes*).

The case was appealed to the U.S. Court of Appeals for the Second Circuit. A three-judge panel heard oral arguments in May 2001. At the end of those arguments the judges invited both sides to answer eleven questions that attempted to determine how to apply the First Amendment to computer code (e.g., "Does DeCSS have both speech and non-speech elements?"). These and other questions suggested to some observers that this panel was looking at this case from a First Amendment perspective, but that is by no means assured.

Beyond the narrow legal question addressed in this case there are obviously much larger issues pertaining to the First Amendment and its apparent conflict with property rights. To what extent should the First Amendment protect computer code that is considered a form of speech? Does the First Amendment also support a basic "freedom to link" to other Web sites?

This case also raises questions about the DMCA law itself. How can "fair use" be preserved if copyrighted material is in encrypted form and programs like DeCSS are outlawed? Has Congress gone too far with this piece of legislation? For good reason the DMCA has provoked a widespread sense of unease, except for those in Hollywood who lobbied for this legislation. The chief problem with the DMCA is its complexity and ambiguity. For example, it is unclear under its anticircumvention regulations "whether fair use can be raised as a defense . . . if the circumventor's use of a copyright tool thereafter is fair and noninfringing, and whether if so, it is lawful to make a tool to accomplish a fair use circumvention" (Samuelson 2000). The law also makes it illegal for individuals to use an anticircumvention tool to make a backup copy of a book or movie, although it is perfectly permissible to make such a copy under copyright law. The law is confusing, but it seems to forbid breaking through the protection measures in order to make the legal copy. The DMCA, therefore, needs revision so that it does not preclude, even inadvertently, what is allowable under copyright law: fair use, making a legal backup copy, and so forth. The thrust of a revised DMCA should be to make circumvention tools illegal if their principal purpose is to violate copyright protection.

Copyright Term Extension

The DMCA was not the only piece of copyright legislation passed in 1998. In October of that year the House and Senate also passed the Sonny Bono Copyright Term Extension Act. It was signed into law by President Clinton on October 27, 1998. This legislation extends the term of copyright protection by twenty years: For individual authors the term is now life of the author plus seventy years (instead of fifty years), and for corporations the term is now ninety-five years (instead of seventy-five years).

The law met with a strong reaction by those who saw this as a prime example of how policy makers could be captured by corporations and persuaded to develop laws not in the public interest. For the most part the stimulus for copyright term extension emanated from the entertainment industry, especially the Disney Corporation, which was concerned about the imminent loss of Mickey Mouse to the public domain in 2004. There was no shortage of other advocates for term extension, including descendants of the prolific song writer George Gershwin.

While supporters have claimed that this term extension will have no cost for the general public, opponents argue that those costs could be quite substantial. For one thing, no creative works or objects will enter the public domain until at least 2019. Also, the CTEA seems to absolutize a right that had always been conceived as limited and balanced by the public interest. The initial term of copyright protection was a mere fourteen years. As Lessig (2000) writes, "Copyright . . . has morphed from a short, relatively insignificant regulation of publishers to a restriction that is effectively perpetual."

What Congress failed to realize in its zeal to pass the CTEA is the extent to which creative activity depends upon a robust and self-renewing public domain. The public domain allows cultural resources to be freely available so that others can build upon those resources, thus shedding new light on cultural traditions. Disney itself has relied heavily on the resources of that public domain. Consider its adaptation of Victor Hugo's *The Hunchback of Notre Dame* or its use of classical music in the movie *Fantasia*. Many writers and composers base their creations on preexisting works: *Mourning Becomes Electra* could not have been written without inspiration from the *Oresteia* and *West Side Story* could not have been composed without *Romeo and Juliet*.

As Nietzsche (1962) reminds us in *Also Sprach Zarathustra*, all creation (*schaffen)* is really a renewal or re-creation (*umschaffen*) of what others have done in the past. Creators find their inspiration in the past. They are constantly retrieving past works or cultural accomplishments and projecting a new interpretation upon them. If we go too far in protecting our intellectual property we run the risk of erecting a formidable fortress around creative works that will deplete the intellectual commons, which contains the building blocks for the creators of tomorrow. Hence, copyright laws should not blithely dismiss the importance of the public domain, which is so crucial for the purpose of creative recycling.

The CTEA seems particularly difficult to justify when viewed through the lens of intellectual property theory. It is hard to argue that this retrospective expansion of copyright will create an extra incentive for creators, who have been amply rewarded for their labors with a lifetime of protection. And fifty years after one's death seemed plenty of time to allow one's heirs to enjoy some of those rewards. But what purpose is served by a twenty-year extension? The authors will not be around to enjoy any of the royalties from an extension, and in most cases those royalties will be rather small when reduced to their present value. According to Nimmer (1970), "It can hardly be argued that an author's creativity is encouraged by such an extension, since the work for which the term is extended has already been created." Thus, from a utilitarian or labor-desert point of view one would be hard pressed to defend the moral or social propriety of this legislation.

Deep Linking and Related Controversies

Another property dispute which deserves some attention involves the practice of "deep linking." A link is a connection within the same Web site or between two different Web sites. For example, a hyperlink within a Web page may contain the URL for another Web site that is activated with the click of the mouse. While most links take the user to the other Web site's home page, it is possible to bring the user directly to subordinate pages within that Web site. This practice has become known as "deep linking."

The controversy over deep linking is epitomized in the case of *Ticketmaster Corp. v. Microsoft Corp* (CV97-3055 RAP C.D. Cal. [1997]). In 1997 Ticketmaster Group Inc. filed suit against Microsoft for federal trademark infringement and unfair competition. Microsoft operates a Web site called Seattle Sidewalk, which functions as a guide to recreational and cultural activities in the Seattle metropolitan area. Seattle Sidewalk provided abundant links to related Web sites, including a link to Ticketmaster, which operates a popular ticket-selling Web site. That link, however, bypassed the Ticketmaster home page and went directly to the respective pages for purchases to events listed in the Seattle Sidewalk page. For instance, a listing on the Seattle Sidewalk page for the Seattle Symphony would include a direct link to a Ticketmaster subpage that would allow users to purchase their symphony tickets.

According to Ticketmaster, by bypassing its home page Seattle Sidewalk users were not being exposed to the extensive advertising and promotional announcements that were posted there. This diminished the value of that advertising and ultimately lowered the rates that could be charged to future advertisers. A second problem with this mode of linking concerned Ticketmaster's relationship with MasterCard, which was promised to receive greater prominence than other payment methods. Unless Ticketmaster could control how users navigated the site it could not keep its commitment to MasterCard. Ticketmaster also complained that Microsoft was able to generate advertising revenues on the basis of this link because Microsoft posted a banner advertisement on the same page on which it displayed the Ticketmaster name and link. This case certainly raised the fundamental problem with deep linking from the target site's perspective: It not only reduces the value of the target site's advertising, but deprives that Web site of its proper exposure and recognition.

In its defense Microsoft argued that "Ticketmaster breached an unwritten Internet code in which any Web site operator has the right to link to anyone else's site" (Tedeschi 1999). There was an out-of-court settlement of this lawsuit in February 1999. Although the terms of that settlement were not disclosed, Microsoft did agree to link to Ticketmaster's home page instead of to its subpages.

In order to analyze this case we must first consider whether a Web site is property and, if so, what specific property rights are implied by ownership. It seems plausible that by relying on the theoretical frameworks suggested above, a convincing case can be put forward that a Web site should be considered as the property of its creator(s). From a Lockean perspective, one could argue that the production of a Web site is most often a labor-intensive activity, and hence this effort deserves the reward of a property right.

Likewise, the utilitarian argument that ownership rights are justified because they maximize social utility and provide an incentive to build future Web sites is also valid. It surely seems reasonable to conclude that the prospect of future ownership and all that it entails is an incentive for the creation and embellishment of Web sites, many of which require a high cost of expression. While it may be too much to say that no Web site would ever be created without the prospect of ownership, it seems obvious that without such an incentive the rate of creation would be reduced, especially for commercial Web sites, where there is an expectation of ownership and control in order to generate the revenues that will pay for this investment. Also, the quality of Web sites would be diminished, since there is generally a strong correlation between quality and a high cost of expression, and the higher the cost, the more Web authors look to ownership rights to help ensure a return on their investment. Without the protection of ownership there would likely be a preponderance of "cheap" Web sites; that is, sites where the cost of expression is low.

But even if a Web site is a form of intellectual property, what does it mean to say that one "exercises control" over this property? What is included in the bundle of property rights that derive from one's "ownership" of a Web site? In order to answer this question we must consider what is implied by the "ownership" of property. According to Honore (1961), ownership is defined as "the greatest possible interest in a thing which a mature system of law recognizes." This definition acknowledges that property ownership is not absolute, but it also suggests that there is a set of powers, rights, and privileges that constitute ownership. Along these lines, Honore argues that the liberal notion of ownership (as opposed to absolute ownership) includes the following elements: the right to possess, the right to use, the right to manage, the right to income, the right to capital, the right to security, the right of transmissibility, the absence of term, the prohibition of harmful use, liability to execution, and residuary character. A full treatment of each of these elements is well beyond the scope of this discussion, but two elements seem especially pertinent for our analysis, especially in light of the Ticketmaster case: the right to manage and the right to income. The right to manage is the right to decide how and by whom a thing shall be used, while the right to income means the right to appropriate the value generated by allowing others to use one's property.

If the principles of utility and labor-desert have engendered a property right in a Web site, it follows that one should have one of the most basic rights of ownership; that is, the right to derive income from that site, especially since that income is the primary reward for that labor and an incentive for future creations. By making the investment of labor, energy, and capital the owner is surely entitled to maximize the return on that investment, which is realized by the right to earn income by allowing others to use that site. Any restrictions on that particular right would be tantamount to a disincentive for investing heavily in the socially valuable activity of new Web site creation. It seems evident then that a property right based on the labor-desert rationale would surely be hollow unless the property owner can get a return on his or her investment as enabled by the right or "power" to earn income.

If this is so, what does it imply about the activity of deep linking? The Ticketmaster case presented the general problem. Web site X derives revenues from advertisements, which appear primarily on its home page, but Web site Y links to a subordinate page and completely bypasses those ads. Consequently, many users who visit site X do not see these ads. This has the effect of reducing the eyeball contact with the advertising and this will negatively affect the rates that can be charged to advertisers. Therefore, deep linking to site X undercuts its revenues and thereby interferes with its right to earn income from that site. In summary, Y's activities or liberties with respect to site X impede X's efforts to derive a material benefit from allowing others to use its property, and this is inconsistent with its right to earn income.

In summary, then, if ownership is to have any real meaning for the Web site author, it must include these basic elements cited by Honore, including the rights to manage and to derive income. The bottom line is that if a Web site is to be regarded as property with a legitimate owner, that owner has the right to control his or her intellectual product; that is, to set the rules and conditions for how that Web site will be accessed and used by others.

But there is another side to the equation when intellectual property issues are concerned. The Web site author as property owner should not completely neglect or ignore the interests of other stakeholders. There is always a danger that when one focuses exclusively on his or her individual property rights the needs and interests of other parties will be shortchanged. This is incompatible with a moral point of view, which requires respect for the perspective and legitimate interests of others. Further, too narrow a focus on the individual's rights ignores the social role of creative activity. There is a need, therefore, to balance the Web site property rights that we have identified with proper respect for the common good of the Web, the sharing and dissemination of information.

What implications does all of this have for routine activities such as linking? As we have already intimated, there must be some recognition that linking is a vital and expressive activity that furthers the goal of open communication; that is, the free flow of ideas and information. Given a moral obligation to respect the common good and the social nature of information, some reasonable limits should be self-imposed on the property rights enjoyed by Web site developers. One way of achieving this balance is to assume that there is an implied license to link to any target site's home page, since this sort of linking has not been the source of much contention. The target site should prevent such links or demand permission only under unusual circumstances. Deep linking should also be permitted and encouraged in cases where there is no harm that accrues to the target Web site, such as a loss of revenues or a threat to the site's integrity. Web sites that suffer no such appreciable harm should allow deep linking out of regard for the free flow of information. Deep linking should not be blocked for arbitrary or trivial reasons. But there should not be a presumptive right to engage in deep linking under any set of circumstances, given the potential harms that can occur, and users must bear this in mind as they add hyperlinks to their Web sites.

SPIDERS AND TRESPASS

Web site property rights issues also surface in the ongoing legal dispute between eBay and Bidder's Edge (BE). Bidder's Edge, a small company founded in 1997, functions as an auction aggregation site. It offers its users the ability to search for auction items across multiple online auction sites (such as eBay, Yahoo, etc.) without the need to search each site individually. BE maintains a database of comprehensive auction information assembled by scanning online auction sites. The BE site contained information on more than 5 million items that were being auctioned at 100 auction sites. Approximately 70 percent of the auction items in the BE database were from eBay auctions. Bidder's Edge uses a software robot that operates across the Internet to compile auction listings for its database. Let's assume that a particular user is interested in bidding on Roman coins. The user can enter "Roman coins" as a search criterion at BE's site, and in response he or she will receive a list of all related items, sorted by auction closing date and time.

The eBay site uses "robot exclusion headers" to inform searching robots that its site does not permit unauthorized robotic activity. BE, however, ignored this robot exclusion message and continued to search through eBay's site without permission. eBay officials told BE to cease its robotic operations; the company refused but it did agree to attempt to work out a licensing arrangement, though to no avail. After eBay and Bidder's Edge failed to reach a licensing agreement for BE's searches, eBay sued the auction aggregating site for trespass.

According to court documents, BE accessed the eBay site about 100,000 times each day in order to keep its system current, and "eBay alleges that BE activity constituted up to 1.53% of the number of requests received by eBay, and up to 1.10% of the total data transferred by eBay" (*eBay v. Bidder's Edge*, 100 F. Supp. 2d 1058 C.D. Cal. [2000]). The eBay lawsuit requested preliminary injunctive relief preventing BE from accessing the eBay system. This was based on several causes of action such as trespass, unfair competition, and unjust enrichment. eBay claimed that it was being harmed by the "lost capacity of its computer systems resulting from BE's use of automated agents."

In May 2000 District Judge Ronald M. Whyte issued the preliminary injunction sought by eBay, which banned BE from using its software robots to scan eBay's site without permission. In his decision Judge Whyte concluded that BE had engaged in "trespass to chattels"; that is, an unauthorized interference with another's personal property that causes some harm. The judge was clearly sympathetic with the claim that BE's robotic activity was causing injury and potential economic loss to eBay. He also worried that failure to grant the injunction would be a green light for other aggregators to follow suit: "If BE's activity is allowed to continue unchecked, it would encourage other auction aggregators in similar recursive searching of the eBay system such that eBay would suffer irreparable harm from reduced system performance, system unavailability, or data losses" (*eBay v. Bidder's Edge*). The case is now being considered by the Ninth Circuit Court of Appeals.

According to Kaplan (2000), this dispute is significant because it suggests competing visions of the Internet. Bidder's Edge sees the Net as "a vast library, full of information that should be openly available to Web users." It regards eBay's auction listings as public information, since for the most part it has been generated by the sellers and not by eBay itself. On the other hand, a lawyer for eBay has suggested that the Internet is more like "Main Street," with many stores and establishments open to the public. But while retail stores on Main Street are open to the public, the store owner can control his or her property and determine the conditions of access.

One could also argue that what's at stake here is the property right to control access juxtaposed to the public's interest in having comparative pricing. One of the virtues of electronic commerce is the capacity to make pricing information much more transparent, but if sites like eBay can stop robots and spiders or block the efforts of price-comparison sites, the public's interest in acquiring comparative data will be compromised.

From a purely legal perspective, eBay would appear to be on shaky ground in asserting any intellectual property right in its data. Until 1991, data compilations were protected under a "sweat of the brow" or Lockean rationale, but that changed in *Feist Publications v. Rural Telephone Service* (499 U.S. 340 [1991]) when the Supreme Court ruled that telephone white pages or other uncreative collections of data were not eligible for copyright protection.

On the other hand, eBay does appear to have an intellectual property interest here, at least from a social and moral perspective, that should not be casually dismissed. As we argued in the deep linking discussion, there is a compelling case to be made that the logical Web site is a form of intellectual property. Also, the eBay server that is allegedly burdened by BE is eBay's personal property. Thus there is something to be said for the argument of trespass, especially given the heavy reliance on the eBay site, the burden of 100,000 visits a day, and the fact that BE's activities are compromising eBay's ability to use its bandwidth and system capacity for its own purposes. Unlike the *Hamidi* case, the magnitude of the nonpermissive activity is a material factor in this case along with the probability that BE will be mimicked by other aggregators. If eBay were a physical auction house like Southeby's it would have the right to control access and to refuse to allow onto its premises anyone who might disrupt the proceedings. Why should we treat a virtual auction house as if it were a public entity, at the mercy of aggregators and others who want to use that auction house's assets for their own vested interest?

On the other hand, eBay should not discount the common good and the benefits of having aggregate information about auction prices compiled from different sites. Hence, it should strive to work out a fair licensing agreement with sites like BE, since such an arrangement will promote consumer welfare. But it does not seem fair to regard eBay's listings as common property. Given its investment in the physical and logical infrastructure, isn't eBay entitled to some proprietary interest in these auction listings? While it may not be in the public interest for policy makers to grant copyright or patent protection for database listings such as eBay's, it is not fair to ignore valid property claims in a logical Web site and in the physical servers used to operate that site.

RIGHTS-MANAGEMENT SYSTEMS

Is code a viable alternative or a supplement to the regime of regulations that now offer extensive protection for intellectual property? Code-based protections for content can take several forms. The most basic is the simple username–password access system. A digital rights-management (DRM) system is a more secure and thorough way to provide protection through technology instead of law. According to McSwain (1999), rights-management systems perform two basic functions: First, these systems make sure that the content is maintained "in a secure 'container,' either hardware or software, which performs encryption and decryption on the digital software." Second, this container "stores precise instructions detailing which uses to permit, which uses to deny, and how much to charge for each, thereby 'managing' the rights relationship between the user and content provider." Stefik (1997) describes these systems as "trusted systems" and explains how they can take many forms: a trusted reader for viewing digital books or a trusted player for listening to music, trusted printers for making copies, and so forth.

DRM has great appeal for content owners, since it can precisely restrict access according to a set of conditions or "business rules." According to Howe (2001), "Files can be programmed to allow—or disallow—anything from copying and sharing to playback on various devices, depending on the user's license."

From a broader economic perspective these systems also have appreciable benefits, since they can protect intellectual property and handle potential free riders without the high transaction costs of traditional structures. Physical distribution entails tremendous inefficiencies, but if DRM can replace physical content-distribution systems without the worry of unauthorized access, content providers will be able to drastically lower their distribution costs. Delivery over the Net will also make possible major economies of scale.

Furthermore, the government's costs for enforcing intellectual property laws will be reduced. These systems may even preclude the need for additional regulations: If we have strong containers to protect digital content the law's role in the property wars of the future could be scaled back. Stefik (1997) also argues that trusted systems will benefit consumers, since they will induce more confident content providers to make their content available over the Internet.

The DRM industry is still in its infancy. Its total revenues in 2000 were only $100 million, but market researchers, such as IDC, project revenues of $3.5 billion by the year 2006 (Howe 2001). DRM providers, such as Real Networks, are preparing for explosive growth in digital music distribution, while niche players like InterTrust are making deals to handle online book distribution.

So why not move ahead with rights-management systems? While this approach may seem like a logical solution to the problem of intellectual property protection on the Internet, it also poses some unique challenges. How would fair use or the first-sale doctrine with DRM coexist? Would critics, scholars, and teachers need to go through elaborate mechanisms to access their material? Moreover, if DRM forbids any sharing of a book or movie with someone else, it will preclude the first-sale option. These systems also enable content providers to choose who will access their material, and it's possible that certain groups might be excluded from viewing or listening to certain material. If trusted systems are not constructed properly, they could eviscerate the fair use and first-sale provisions of copyright laws and make creative works less accessible to the general public.

Critics of DRM also assail its infringement of privacy rights. Content providers will be able to know who is reading their books or listening to their recordings. DRM permits unprecedented monitoring and metering of those who have licensed these digital works. This is an unsettling development, especially if this information ends up in a dossier that is sold to third parties.

Rights-management systems provide yet another vivid example of Lessig's (1999) point that code can be more powerful and comprehensive than law in regulating the Internet. Code allows for almost perfect and foolproof control that is beyond the capability of a more fallible but flexible legal system. In effect, the code threatens to privatize copyright law without the appropriate checks and balances we find in public copyright law. Consider Lessig's admonition about these systems:

> What happens when code protects the interests now protected by copyright law? . . . Should we expect that any of the limits [now provided by copyright law] will remain? Should we expect code to mirror the limits that the law imposes? Fair use? Limited term? . . . The point should be obvious: when intellectual property is protected by code, nothing requires that the same balance be struck. Nothing requires the owner to grant the right of fair use.

Lessig (1999) is arguing that both fair use and the entry of works into the public domain will be jeopardized by these systems, since nothing requires that the balance now provided by copyright law be preserved. The problem is that those writing the rights-management code can embed their own intellectual property regulations into that code: They can program the system to charge a fee for any use and ignore any fair use or first-sale considerations by anchoring the content to a specific user. It is possible, of course, that rights-management systems will be constructed that will at least try to strike the right balance. Lessig seems to deny this, but some developers of DRM may realize that there are moral and social issues at stake here and will work to preserve fair use or its equivalent in their systems.

We argue that it would be irresponsible and imprudent to design these rights-management systems without allowing for fair use and without respecting other safety values such as first-sale. There is a lively debate about the technological feasibility of developing a system that would include a realistic provision for fair use, but that discussion is beyond the scope of this analysis. Suffice it to say that doing so will be a challenge, since system developers will need to anticipate the myriad array of fair use requests without being duped by those trying to manipulate the system. But according to industry analysts such as Ashish Singh, "Fair use algorithms could be written into the code, and that would become the hook, the attractiveness of the product" (Howe 2001).

Thus, rights-management systems should be given a chance, but they should be constructed with sensitivity to traditional values such as fair use and privacy. If this code can be developed responsibly by avoiding the excesses of overprotection and by safeguarding some degree of anonymity, it could yield economic efficiencies while easing the burden on policy development and enforcement. This may involve reliance on trusted third parties to safeguard the public interest. Rights-management systems could be versatile tools that facilitate self-regulation, but only if they are developed in a morally competent fashion.

CONCLUSIONS AND RECOMMENDATIONS

The perceptive reader will notice an alarming trend in the pattern of recent intellectual property legislation. The trend toward stronger protection in the DMCA, the CTEA, and in the granting of business-methods patents is quite evident. Excessive intellectual property protection has unmistakable negative consequences. It tends to contract the public domain and to concentrate production in the hands of those who own the protected content. Policy makers must take steps to reverse this momentum.

At the risk of oversimplification, let us suggest that the problems of intellectual property in the digital age can be reduced to one overriding question: How do we provide the right level of intellectual property protection, just enough to induce innovation and creativity? The assault on the intellectual property system comes from both the right and the left. Those on the right are part of a copyright-centric culture that wants an ultraconservative approach that will enclose as much content as possible for as long as possible. Hollywood and much of the entertainment industry subscribes to this philosophy. On the left we find those who embrace a philosophy of "information socialism." They believe intellectual property rights are outmoded. At its deepest level we find this viewpoint coupled with postmodern questions about the nature of authorship and original creativity. But we have embraced and defended an intermediate position: Let's provide just enough protection to reward creative workers for their labor and to spur future innovation, but avoid overly strong protection that will deplete the intellectual commons and fail to promote the social welfare.

With these ideas in mind, we offer a few specific recommendations:

- Lawmakers must look closely at business-methods patents that will discourage incremental innovation in cyberspace. If necessary, patent law needs to be adjusted to prevent obvious business methods like one-click shopping or customer profiles from being eligible for patent protection.
- Policy makers must avoid "capture" by content providers so that mistakes like the misguided CTEA are not repeated. This act does little to encourage innovation, and it should be repealed.
- The DMCA needs revision and clarification so that exceptions for fair use are fully respected. Samuelson (2000) also advocates "clarifying and broadening the encryption research and computer security exceptions and adopting a general or other 'legitimate purpose' exception to the statute to make the law more balanced and effective."
- Copyright law requires an amendment to clarify digital music rights. There must be clarity on what copyright owners should be paid when their songs are put on the Internet. In some cases the music companies have asked for multiple royalty payments, and new rules are needed to specify whether such payments are justified.
- Corporations must exercise restraint and avoid extending their property rights too far. There are legitimate free-speech concerns about their dubious legal efforts to prevent use of their trademarks in domain names for the sake of parody or criticism.

Finally, intellectual property rights should be managed through the careful interaction of law and code. Architectures such as rights-management systems can achieve certain policy goals with greater efficiency than the law. However, these systems should not interfere with widely recognized liberties (such as the right of fair use) and they should not undermine public purpose.

REFERENCES

Angwin, J. (2000). "'Business Method' Patents Draw Growing Protest." *Wall Street Journal*, 3 October, B1, B4.

Angwin, J. (2001). "Are Domain Panels the Hanging Judges of Cyberspace Court?" *Wall Street Journal*, 20 August, B1.

Barlow, J. (1994). "Selling Wine without Bottles: The Economy of Mind on the Global Net." Available: http://www.eff.org/pub/Publications/John_Perry_Barlow/HTML/idea_economy_article.html

Chartrand, S. (2001). "Patents." *New York Times*, 30 July, C2.

Fisher, W. (1998). "Property and Contract on the Internet." Available: http://cyber.law.harvard.edu/ipcoop/98fish.html

Fisher, W. (2000). "Digital Music: Problems and Possibilities." Available: http://www.law.harvard.edu/Academic_Affairs/coursepages/tfisher/Music.

Fisher, W. (2001). "Business Method Patents." Available: http://eon.law.harvard.edu/ilaw/Presentations

Ginsburg, J. (1999). "Copyright Legislation for the 'Digital Millennium.'" *Columbia–VLA Journal of Law and the Arts* 23: 137.
Goldstein, P. (1994) *Copyright's Highway*. New York: Hill and Wang.
Gomes, L. (2000). "Napster Ruling May Be Just the Overture." *Wall Street Journal*, 28 July, B1.
Honore, A. M. (1961). "Ownership." In *Oxford Essays in Jurisprudence*, edited by A. Guest. New York: Oxford University Press.
Howe, J. (2001). "You're Gonna Pay for This." *Wired*, October, 140–149.
Hughes, J. (1997). "The Philosophy of Intellectual Property." In *Intellectual Property*, edited by A. Moore. Lanham, Md.: Rowman and Littlefield.
ICANN. (1999). "Uniform Domain Name Dispute Resolution Policy." Available: http://www.icann.org
Kaplan, C. (2000). "Auction Dispute Centers on Question of Control over Data." *CyberLaw Journal*, April 14.
Lessig, L. (1999). *Code and Other Laws of Cyberspace*. New York: Basic Books.
Lessig, L. (2000). "The Limits of Copyright." *Industry Standard*, 26 June, 51–52.
Levy, S. (2000). "The Great Amazon Patent Debate." *Newsweek*, 13 March, 74.
Litman, J. (2000). "The DNS Wars: Trademarks and the Internet Domain Name System." *Journal of Small and Emerging Business* 4: L.149.
Locke, J. (1952). *The Second Treatise of Government*, edited by T. Peardon. Indianapolis, Ind.: Bobbs-Merrill.
McSwain, W. (1999). "The Law of Cyberspace." *Harvard Law Review* 112: 1574.
Nietzsche, F. (1962). *Also Sprach Zarathustra*. Stuttgart: Phillip Reclam.
Nimmer, M. (1970). "Does Copyright Abridge the First Amendment Guarantees of Free Speech and Press?" *UCLA Law Review* 17: 1180.
Nozick, R. (1974). *Anarchy, State and Utopia*. New York: Basic Books.
Reeve, A. (1986). *Property*. Atlantic Heights, N.J.: Humanities Press.
RIAA, Plaintiff's Brief. (2000). *A&M Records, Inc. et al. v. Napster*, 239 F 3d 1004 (9th Cir.).
Samuelson, P. (2000). "Towards More Sensible Anti-Circumvention Regulations." Working paper. Available: http://www.sims.berkeley.edu/~pam/papers/Samuelson
Schumann, Robert W. (2000). Supplemental Declaration in Support of Plaintiff's Motion to Modify the January 20, 2000 order of Preliminary Injunction and for Leave to Amend the Complaint, re *Universal City v. Reimerdes* 00 Civ. 0277.
Stefik, M. (1997). "Trusted Systems." *Scientific American*, March, 79.
Tedeschi, B. (1999). "Ticketmaster and Microsoft Settle Suit on Internet Linking." *New York Times*, 15 February.
Weintraub, A. (2000). "MP3.COM Faces the Music." *Business Week*, 9 April, 89–90.

8

Privacy Rights and the Internet

It did not take long for DoubleClick's executives to conclude that the shrill headline in the *Wall Street Journal*, "A Privacy Firestorm at DoubleClick," would thrust the company into an unwanted spotlight. DoubleClick was on the defensive for its data-collection and profiling practices. DoubleClick is an online ad agency founded in 1996 by Kevin O'Connor. It sells advertising space on over 1,500 Web sites; it also offers a service that will deliver targeted online ads to specific Web pages. In 1998 the company acquired a smaller firm called Abacus Direct, which owns a massive database containing information on consumers such as their names, addresses, and buying habits. DoubleClick saw a gold mine of rich consumer data in the linkage of the Abacus database with the information it had collected online through cookie technology. Its goal was to use offline data to target ads on Web sites and to recombine its once-anonymous online user profiles with offline data such as names, addresses, genders, and buying propensities.

In the face of negative publicity and a Federal Trade Commission investigation, DoubleClick ultimately backed down. It agreed not to link personally identifiable information with the anonymous Web behavior it had collected at the sites running its ads. The company, however, has not ruled out connecting such offline and online data in the future, once the government sets some better ground rules.

DoubleClick is not the only company to suddenly reverse course after a public outcry over aggressive information-management policies. Lotus, America Online, Microsoft, Lexis–Nexis, and many other companies can be added to this long list. They are all walking a slightly more cautious line on privacy issues these days. While companies like DoubleClick are more wary about the consumer's interest in online privacy, they also argue that privacy concerns cannot overwhelm economic concerns. According to DoubleClick's CEO, Kevin O'Connor (2000), "The future of the Internet must involve both the protection of individual online privacy and the ability of online advertisers to compete and deliver effective ads." O'Connor's point is that targeting is essential to making Internet ads uniquely valuable, and targeting can't happen unless Web sites "watch" users and record their activities.

The wave of dot-com liquidations during 2001 also put privacy issues and the ownership of consumer data under scrutiny. Internet companies have generally regarded consumer data as assets that can be sold off in order to help pay creditors. When ToySmart.com went bankrupt in the summer of 2000 it placed an ad in the *Wall Street Journal* looking for a buyer for its customer database. Privacy advocates quickly objected, observing that ToySmart had promised customers in its online privacy policy that it would never share that information with third parties. The FTC then stepped in and filed suit against ToySmart, accusing the company of deceptive trading practices. Fortunately, a settlement was reached: ToySmart agreed to sell the database, but only to a company in a related business that had to purchase the whole Web site and promise not to resell the data without the customer's permission. This settlement was still sharply criticized by some privacy advocates, and the whole affair raises questions about the ownership rights of those companies that have collected valuable consumer data. Privacy and property issues are deeply intertwined and the debate about privacy often focuses on the ownership status of information. It is not evident, however, that framing the debate about privacy in these terms is the most fruitful avenue for analysis.

As these cases illustrate, privacy is an enormous technical and public policy challenge, and it deserves considerable attention. This chapter will dwell on this topic and, more specifically, on the theme of information privacy, an individual's right to control his or her personal information collected by others. For the most part we will focus on some of the legal and technical privacy dilemmas posed by the Internet. As background, we will briefly review the moral and legal basis of the right to privacy, along with some of the more important pieces of legislation that attempt to translate this right into a regulatory framework.

We will also look at how different legal systems around the world address privacy, and we will attempt a comparison between the U.S. and European approaches. While the United States has sought to rely heavily on industry self-regulation, the European countries have adopted more stringent regulations that are consistent with the European Union Directive on Privacy. Other countries outside of Europe have also begun to embrace this directive. But is this "command and control" approach the most viable way to safeguard privacy? The loss of privacy is a market failure, but is government intervention the optimum method of dealing with this failure? Finally, we will consider privacy-enhancing technologies like P3P (Platform for Privacy Preferences). What role can this type of code play in protecting one's personal privacy, and can code mitigate the need for extensive regulation?

A related theme that will be discussed in this chapter is privacy at work and the widespread corporate surveillance of employees. Is such ubiquitous surveillance really necessary? How far can employers go without warning their employees? Should there be stronger privacy rights in the workplace, such as a limited right to e-mail privacy? The espousal of strong worker privacy rights is an unpopular position in this network society, but few corporations have calculated the human costs of transforming the workplace into a virtual panopticon.

Online Surveillance and the Threat to Privacy

The Internet's impact on privacy is certainly beyond dispute, but the loss of privacy at the hands of computer technology has happened in discrete stages. During the 1960s and 1970s personal and financial data were selectively collected and stored in massive mainframe systems. These data were fairly expensive to maintain, and were never easy to access except by the highly technical data managers and systems operators who controlled these "black box" systems. But the steady migration to personal computers, distributed technologies, and local area networks eventually made these data much more accessible. Most of the mainframe data could be reproduced on the desktop with relative ease and made readily available throughout the corporate hierarchy. Since expensive mainframes were no longer a requirement, smaller organizations could also get into the act. Thus, the power to gather and disseminate electronic data had now become decentralized. The Web, of course, makes it even easier to get at this information. The Web seamlessly links together organizational data from remote sources, making possible asynchronous access for users throughout the world, and the Web is only part of a pervasive and widening global network that seems almost omniscient in its knowledge and voracious in its appetite.

These advances in information technology, then, have made it easier to collect information that was at one time unrecorded. Think of supermarkets, which now record every item that is purchased by any customer using a discount card. Thanks to inexpensive memory and processing capabilities, it is also easier to store, analyze, recombine, and retrieve this information in ways that were virtually impossible until quite recently.

But what is behind this unprecedented drive to collect so much data? Why do companies strive to profile their customers so thoroughly? The presumption is that all these data will yield valuable knowledge about consumer buying habits and preferences. Data are valued primarily for their predictive power. Companies in this market-driven culture believe that the more information they gather about people, the more accurately they will be able to predict their preferences (Cohen 2000). Companies assume that the possession of copious consumer information reduces their uncertainty and helps them in product planning and marketing strategies. For example, if companies can figure out which ads work with different segments of the population, they can use these invaluable data to plan targeted advertising campaigns.

To some extent, this quest to rationalize and predict represents a broader social trend. According to Borgmann (1992), "The distinctive discourse of modernity is one of prediction and control." Whether corporate America's assumptions about the predictability of consumer preferences are justifiable is an open question. Can consumers be reduced to the sum of their transactions and online interactions and is that behavior a reliable indicator of their preferences and aspirations? While learning about one's customers is valuable, one suspects that the process of understanding consumer behavior is more complex than extrapolating from past purchases or clickstream data. We cannot enter into an in-depth discussion on this question, but it would seem that this liberal data collection philosophy is at best too simplistic. Nevertheless, that philosophy seems firmly entrenched in the corporate mentality and so the creative aggregation of rich amounts of consumer data is likely to remain a high priority in the new economy.

Our primary concern is with the privacy issues in cyberspace that involve not just data collection and dissemination, but the ubiquitous surveillance enabled by this watchful global network. Our focus is on how firms collect data in this new context. Cyberspace has generated a new species of privacy problems thanks to the surveillance possibilities created by shopping or even browsing in a network environment where one is constantly leaving behind traceable "digital footprints."

How is this covert surveillance of consumers possible? In large part it stems from technologies that companies use for Web personalization; that is, tailoring Web content and advertising directly to a specific user. This is often accomplished through the use of cookies and "Web bugs." Cookies are small data files automatically created by a Web server and stored on a user's computer for future access. The file is usually created the first time one visits a site; it contains a unique tracking number that can be read by the Web site on subsequent visits. Web sites rely on cookies to remember their users from one visit to the next. Cookies reveal what you purchased or looked at on your previous visits and tailor content and probably advertisements accordingly. Web sites can use cookie information to build profiles of online behavior that can be matched to an IP address or some other identifier.

Web bugs are another Internet monitoring technology used to collect information on visitors to a Web site. A Web bug, sometimes called a Web "beacon," is embedded as a miniscule and invisible picture on the screen and can track everything one does on a particular Web site. Some uses of these Web bugs are innocuous enough; they are often used to count visitors to sites or to gather other statistical data. They are also used by online advertising agencies to collect data about those who visit their clients' Web pages, such as which ads they click on. Web bugs are not as common or as versatile as cookies, but they might allow two different Web sites to work together as strategic partners in tracking the movement of consumers.

These covert technologies have been designed for a single purpose: to facilitate the search for richer and more precise consumer information. Among other things, this type of information makes possible tailored and more individualized advertisements, which are far more valuable and cost effective than nontargeted advertisements. The Net allows advertisers to reach targeted individuals who have demonstrated some interest in or buying propensity for the advertised product. This targeted approach differs from commercial advertising in traditional media, which is directed at an undifferentiated mass of people. Sometimes all of this happens without the user's knowledge or consent, and at other times users may cooperate in the process, voluntarily trading their information for certain rewards or even for monetary compensation.

Of course, these intrusive technologies are not the only reason behind the encroachment on personal privacy that has disturbed so many cyberspace users. Even information that we provide voluntarily in various ordinary transactions can be collected and sold or shared with third parties. Qwest Communications sent their customers a notice saying that they plan to share with their subsidiaries and marketing partners data such as "telephone services used, billing information, and places called" (Schwartz 2002). Customers will have a chance to opt out of this, but many will probably not take the time to make this effort.

Digital network technology seems to coexist uneasily with privacy values. According to Moor (2001), "When information is computerized, it is greased to slide easily and quickly to many ports of call." This "greasing of information" makes it accessible and easily reusable, and the network provides many paths for those data to take. Also, computers systems have elephantlike memories, and they can store data forever at a trivial cost. Data elements never seem to be forgotten. If one is a customer of Amazon.com, one must realize that this company has an indelible record of all the books, music, and videos that one has purchased over the years. This information, which can reside in a database forever, can be effortlessly transmitted to other organizations if Amazon.com ever decides to sell its customer profiles.

One might ask where the harm is in all of this. What's the big deal if a Web site knows my shopping habits or what music I listen to? But consider, for example, the social ramifications if books and other reading material were used as evidence against their reader. Should law-enforcement officials or others be allowed access to this information? Probably not, and yet the trend toward treating reading material as evidence is ominous. The Borders bookstore chain has been embroiled in several controversies over this issue. Borders bookstores in two states, Kansas and Massachusetts, have been served with subpoenas for book-buying records of suspected criminals (Barringer 2001). The company resisted, but in the end it had no choice but to comply. And Borders is not the only target. According to Barringer, on a more informal but periodic basis, "law enforcement officials have also sought information about books, music, and video purchases made by customers of Amazon.com."

While privacy advocates are appalled at this trend, many prosecutors believe that privacy rights are subordinate to the need for collecting evidence about criminal suspects. Obviously, computerized records of online bookstores like Amazon.com and Barnes & Noble, which have a quasi-permanent status, will make it much easier to track down this sort of information. However, the specter of building a case against someone based upon novels they enjoy or the ideas they have chosen to explore in their reading is chilling. Such investigations could easily lead to all sorts of presumptive conclusions about a suspect's culpability.

Herein lies the problem with such easy accessibility to personal information. There are potential dignitary injuries caused by the invasion of our privacy. According to Rosen (2000), when we lose our privacy we run the risk of being "judged out of context." Our spending or reading habits become subject to public scrutiny and suddenly people are making unwarranted assumptions about our behavior. Innocent lists of data begin to take on sinister overtones. Monitoring technologies and far-reaching searches threaten the presumption of innocence. According to Lessig (1999), in these situations "the burden is on you, the monitored[,] first to establish your innocence and second, to assure all who might see these ambiguous facts that you are innocent."

Although there are many problems with the erosion of boundaries between the public and private, this affront to human dignity is perhaps the most consequential. Thanks to computer technology, monitoring behavior or searches through our records need not be terribly intrusive. Unlike physical searches of one's property, they can usually be done clandestinely, without much disruption of our normal activities. But these activities can still offend our dignity, since they can put us in compromising positions where we must defend what books we like to read or what movies we like to watch.

Consider what often happens with the data collected at most Web sites. Many companies (like DoubleClick) construct profiles and pitch their products and advertisements accordingly. But this often leads to subtle manifestations of discrimination, as Oscar Gandy (1993) pointed out in his pioneering work, *The Panoptic Sort*. Profiling diminishes the level of equality in economic transactions as certain individuals get offered discounts, special products, and so forth based on demographic data and their purchasing habits. According to Gandy (1996), "The panoptic sort operates by transforming transaction information into intelligence that guides the presentation of inducements and offers to some, but not all, who might come to consume goods and services through the market."

If we assume privacy is under assault and needs better protection, how should that protection be established? Is comprehensive legislation necessary? Does self-regulation have any chance of success? Can users themselves exercise better discretion and be more conscientious in safeguarding their personal privacy? Or should we think about simple legislation that gives everyone a property right in his or her personal information? Is the privacy debate reducible to a deliberation about ownership rights? Finally, is there a corrective role technology can play in restoring this imbalance between the public and the private?

A THEORY OF PRIVACY

It is instructive to review at this point some background about the nature and importance of privacy. The public and the private have always been in tension, and culture, in its broadest sense, mediates that tension. Many novels, such as those of Thomas Hardy, deal with the conflicts that occur when questionable private behavior becomes revealed and reputations are irreparably damaged. Too much privacy can be a threat to public life, but our concern recently has been the encroachment of the public on the private as greater quantities of personal data become accessible to corporations and government authorities.

There are many definitions and concepts of privacy, and this can make the exploration of this topic complicated. Some theories, for example, see privacy in physical terms, as a repository of confidential information that can be emptied out or depleted. Others use spatial imagery, as they define privacy in terms of a "zone" that can be encroached upon or invaded in some fashion.

The Europeans have adopted a more simplified and direct approach to privacy. They look at privacy issues strictly in terms of data protection. The state has an interest in protecting personal data, and hence it must develop appropriate regulatory mechanisms. This premise is taken for granted and is not a matter of endless debate. Unlike Americans, they do not see privacy "in terms of a normative concept that needs philosophical analysis" (Spinello and Tavani 2001). The right to privacy is widely accepted in most of Europe, and it is not subjected to esoteric legal and philosophical discussion as it is in the United States.

Gavison (1984) is typical of those who see privacy as a normative concept. She defines privacy as the limitation of others' access to an individual with three key elements: secrecy, anonymity, and solitude. Anonymity refers to the protection from undesired attention, solitude is the lack of physical proximity to others, and secrecy (or confidentiality) involves limiting the dissemination of knowledge about oneself. We are less concerned these days with threats to solitude and physical invasions into where we live and more worried about confidentiality, limiting the dissemination of our personal information.

Most early legal cases about privacy involved the Fourth Amendment, which was written to protect against unwarranted searches and seizures. It protects the fundamental right to be left alone in the confines of physical spaces such as our homes and offices. But thanks to digital technology, our attention has shifted to information privacy, an individual's right to control personal information held by others.

There are two prominent theories of information privacy: the control theory and the restricted access theory. Gavison (1984) represents a prime example of the restricted access theory, which argues that privacy is equivalent to having information about oneself restricted or limited in certain ways. According to the control theory, advocated by Fried (1984) and Rachels (1975), "One has privacy if and only if one has control over information about oneself" (Spinello and Tavani 2001). But is it really possible to control our information in a society that records and collects data from almost all of our everyday transactions?

Moor (2001) has sought to integrate these two viewpoints into a more robust theory of privacy that he calls the control/restricted access theory. Moor distinguishes between natural privacy, the privacy one may enjoy by living a life of solitude, and normative privacy. A normatively private situation is one protected by ethical and/or legal standards. Discussions with one's lawyer or a psychiatrist represent such situations. Unless a person expresses an intention to commit a crime involving serious bodily harm, confidentiality cannot be breached in these professional contexts. We need "zones of privacy" or normatively "private situations" for our protection, so first we must be able to restrict access to our personal information by setting up these zones of privacy. According to Moor, "To protect ourselves we need to make sure that the right people and only the right people have *access* to relevant information at the right time" (emphasis in original). This basic objective should guide privacy policies. Notice that privacy or confidentiality according to this theory is situational; it is not a property of the information itself. The Internal Revenue Service is entitled to know how much money I made last year and how much taxes I paid, but my nosy neighbors have no right to this information.

This version of the restricted access theory has the advantages of the control theory as well, since one of the goals in establishing privacy policies is to give individuals "as much control over their personal data as realistically possible" (Moor 2001). The mechanism for exercising this control is usually "informed consent." Through informed consent we can establish the zone of privacy we prefer as we authorize information to be released only to the people or institutions we approve. Through the purchase of books at Amazon.com I allow this company to become privy to my reading habits. But if Amazon.com wants to sell my book purchases to a magazine vendor, it should inform me of its intention to dispose of my information in this manner. If I have no objection, I can give them my consent to consummate this transaction.

The reality, of course, is that most people do not feel they have any control over their personal information flows, and hence they are worried about the expansion of information-gathering practices. Qwest's customers, for example, might be justly agitated because data on their phone use are being shared so broadly. Policy makers have not been oblivious to general concerns about privacy, and they have passed laws to deal with selected areas of information.

PRIVACY, THE LAW, AND PUBLIC POLICY

In virtually every democratic society a right to privacy is recognized by the legal system. This reflects its great importance in providing us with security against the intrusive activities of others. In the United States privacy has deep common law roots that are well summarized in the 1890 law review article by Brandeis and Warren that was a response to new invasive technologies such as photography. According to these jurists, "Recent inventions and business methods call attention to the next step which must be taken for the protection of the person and for securing the individual . . . the right 'to be let alone.'" They argued further that the "invasion of privacy constitutes a *legal injuria*" (emphasis in original). This landmark article, then, created a new cause of action for privacy invasions where none had previously existed.

The common law doctrine of personal privacy implicit in the Brandeis and Warren article includes four grounds for tort liability:

- unreasonable intrusion upon the seclusion of another.
- unreasonable publicity "to a matter concerning the private life of another."
- "publicity to a matter concerning another that places the other before the public in a false light."
- the appropriation "to one's own use or benefit the name or likeness of another." (*Restatement of Torts*, §652B, C, D [1965])

It is unlikely that questionable online activities such as profiling or the use of surveillance technologies could be grounds for liability under this common law doctrine. Nonetheless, the common law of privacy does offer some protection, even in cyberspace. According to Gindin (1997), the second tort "may be a basis for suit in cases in which personal information (i.e., medical condition, tax return, or other confidential information) is disseminated electronically to a significant number of people, for instance, on a public bulletin board or newsgroup." And the third tort "may provide basis to sue for the online dissemination of erroneous information where the database provider has not taken proper steps to ensure its correctness."

In the 1960s the legal right to privacy, recognized by Warren and Brandeis, became less tenuous and achieved a more formal status thanks to several landmark Supreme Court cases, such as *Griswold v. Connecticut* (381 U.S.

479 [1965]). In this pivotal case the Supreme Court ruled that a Connecticut law that barred the dissemination of birth-control information violated the right to marital privacy. The majority opinion also stated that each individual was entitled to "zones" of privacy created by the First, Third, Fourth, Fifth, and Ninth Amendments to the Constitution. The Justices agreed that privacy was a right "so rooted in the traditions and conscience of our people as to be ranked as fundamental." The right to privacy was still an amorphous notion and its scope was still unclear, but thanks to this opinion it was now formally regarded as guaranteed by the Constitution.

Shortly after the Griswold decision, Congress began to enact legislation to protect privacy. These early laws were focused on the government's use of information, which was the more pressing concern at the time. In 1970 Congress passed the Fair Credit Reporting Act (FCRA), which regulated and restricted disclosures of credit and financial information by credit bureaus. The FCRA gave consumers certain rights: access to their credit files, the ability to demand an investigation of inaccurate information, and the right to include a statement disputing information. The FCRA was quickly followed up by the Federal Privacy Act of 1974, which put restrictions on government record keepers, and in 1978 Congress enacted the Right to Financial Privacy Act. The latter act required a search warrant before banks could divulge financial data of their customers to federal agencies. In these laws privacy claims were being translated into a statutory framework and the legal right to privacy was becoming more substantial and nuanced.

In the 1980s Congress continued to pass legislation that it hoped would formalize the privacy rights of U.S. citizens. In 1984 it passed the Cable Communications Policy Act, which prohibited cable TV companies from collecting or disseminating data about the viewing habits of their customers. A related piece of legislation was the Video Privacy Protection Act of 1988, which bars rental video stores from disclosing a list of videos watched by their customers. This act was passed in reaction to public outrage after journalists were able to retrieve Robert Bork's video rental records during his contentious (and unsuccessful) Supreme Court confirmation hearings.

Some have argued that the Video Privacy Act was an overreaction, but there are good reasons behind protecting this sort of information. We have alluded to the problems that can occur when one's viewing habits become public. Rosen (2000) makes a similar point in his book, *The Unwanted Gaze*: "People are reluctant to have their reading and viewing habits exposed because we correctly fear that when isolated bits of personal information are confused with genuine knowledge, they may create an inaccurate picture of the full range of our interests and complicated personalities."

In 1994 Congress moved to protect motor vehicle records, as it passed the Driver's Privacy Protection Act. This piece of legislation prohibits the release or sale of personal information that is part of the state's motor vehicle record (social security number, name, age, address, height, and so forth) unless drivers are provided an opportunity to opt out. Prior to the enactment of this legislation the sale of these data to third-party marketers, a lucrative business for many states, would usually occur without permission or notification. The catalyst for the passage of this act was the murder of actress Rebecca Schaeffer by a crazed fan who obtained her address from the California Department of Motor Vehicles.

More recently, in 1998, Congress passed the Children's Online Privacy Protection Act (COPPA), which forbids Web sites from collecting personal information from children under age thirteen without parental consent. Consent can be provided in several ways: a physically signed note, a credit card number, or an e-mail message with a password. Most privacy experts and ordinary citizens felt that this legislation was long overdue and that COPPA solved a serious problem. Enforcement of COPPA, however, has not been so easy. Many child-oriented Web sites just meet the letter of the law: They either post disclosures that the site is not for children (but go no farther) or they make it trivially easy for children to lie about their age. In the summer of 2000 the FTC conducted a "sweep" of these child-oriented sites and "found that only about half posted their privacy policies and obtained parental consent, as the law mandates" (Wasserman 2000).

In 1999 Congress passed the Financial Services Modernization Act. The main purpose of this legislation was to tear down barriers between banks, brokerage houses, and insurance companies, but the act also contained a provision requiring financial services companies to disclose their information privacy policies in writing to their clients once a year. They must also provide their customers with an opt-out form that enables consumers to forbid the selling or sharing of their financial information. The burden is on the customer to return the form and thereby protect his or her privacy. So far, the opt-out options are being returned at a surprisingly slow rate. According to Hall (2001), "Financial services companies have thus far received a piddling 0.5% to 0.75% response rate from customers demanding that all of their data be kept under wraps." Critics of the Modernization Act's implementation make two points: The privacy notices are confusing, several pages long, and enshrouded in legal terminology, and an opt-in system where privacy is the default would have been a better solution (to opt in is to accept some condition, such as the sale of one's personal data, ahead of time). The first criticism is particularly pertinent: The less expensive opt-out option has some chance of working, but only if consumers are clearly informed about threats to their privacy and given an opportunity to return a simple, postage-paid opt-out form (most companies now require customers to write a letter and pay for their own postage). It is hard to assess whether the low response rate is due to indifference or to the inconvenience of opting out.

A concise summary of U.S. privacy legislation is provided at the end of this section. What becomes evident as one examines this legislation is that the attempt to protect personal privacy is highly reactive and unsystematic.

Legislation has been triggered by various catalysts, such as the high-profile murder of an actress and the embarrassing revelations of a Supreme Court nominee's video viewing habits. As a result, what we have is an ad hoc, fragmented approach rather than a coherent and comprehensive body of privacy legislation. Also, as Smith (2000) observes, there is something disingenuous about many of these pieces of legislation: "In each instance when it enacted 'privacy-protection' legislation, Congress played tricks on the American people." For example, the video privacy law does allow video stores to release the names and addresses of their customers, along with the categories of movies they have rented. If someone makes a habit of renting "dirty adult movies," this disclosure could be embarrassing. Further, the Driver's Privacy Protection Act has sizable loopholes, since it allows the sale of social security numbers and photographs to private businesses. In 1999, Image Data, a small New Hampshire firm, started buying these photographs in order to construct a national database, but the company backed off after a spirited e-mail campaign.

Why isn't there more comprehensive and sweeping legislation that protects all types of information? Why isn't plain consumer data, information about one's Internet transactions, included in any of this protective legislation? There are a number of reasons for this. The Clinton administration, for example, embraced a philosophy of self-regulation for privacy matters. Recall that Clinton's guiding manifesto for the Information Age, "A Framework for Global Electronic Commerce" (see Chapter 3), argued for a minimalist approach to regulation. It also maintained that responsibility for privacy protection belonged primarily with the private sector and not with the government. There were some exceptions, such as children's privacy and medical privacy. Furthermore, there is no reason to believe that this minimalist approach to privacy regulations will change with the Bush administration. There are, however, some signs of public discontent and concern that may prompt a new wave of more stringent privacy regulations along with better defined standards.

The following is a summary of selected privacy policy initiatives:

- Fair Credit Reporting Act (1970): Approves only certain uses for credit reports, for credit transactions and for insurance underwriting; also for employment purposes, for a "legitimate business need [and] to determine the consumer's eligibility for a license or other benefits granted by the government."
- Family Educational Rights and Privacy Act (FERPA) (1974): Federally funded school systems and universities must protect student data and provide rights for access to and correction of those records.
- Federal Privacy Act (1974): Requires government record keepers to abide by the federal Code of Fair Information Practices, which stated that there could be no secret personal data record-keeping systems, that people must be provided with the opportunity to determine what kind of personal information is being kept about them, that this information in the record system not be used for other purposes without their consent, and that they be given the opportunity to correct or modify that information.

- Right to Financial Privacy Act (1978): Safeguards confidentiality of financial records, which can be provided to government authorities only under certain conditions, such as customer authorization or in response to an "administrative subpoena and summons."
- Cable Communications Policy Act (1984): Cable TV providers must notify subscribers regarding the information that is maintained about them.
- Video Privacy Protection Act (1988): Forbids video-rental companies from disclosing the names of videos rented by their patrons.
- Telemarketing Protection Act (1991): Limits use of autodialers and requires that telemarketers honor consumers' requests to be taken off their calling lists.
- Driver's Privacy Protection Act (1994): Requires the Department of Motor Vehicles to provide a means for drivers to opt out of the sale of their personal data to third parties.
- Children's Online Privacy Protection Act (1998): Requires parental consent before Web sites can collect data from children who are under the age of thirteen.

MEDICAL PRIVACY

Breaches of medical privacy are particularly disturbing because the information involved is so sensitive. Consider the case of an AIDS patient who sued Consumer Value Stores (CVS) Corporation over how it obtained his prescription records from a family-owned drugstore and incorporated those records into its massive database. CVS purchased this small midtown Manhattan pharmacy and, as is its policy, acquired the small pharmacy's customer prescription files as part of the transaction. CVS allegedly prevented this pharmacy from notifying its customers of this transfer of data. Such "file buying" is a common practice in this industry, so CVS was surprised by the judge's ruling in early 2001 that it could be sued for breaching this patient's confidentiality. The judge in this case appeared to sympathize with the plaintiff's concern that his sensitive data regarding his AIDS condition was transferred to a new context where the same safeguards might not be employed to protect his confidentiality.

Security lapses have also been responsible for compromising confidential medical data. In 2000 a Dutch computer hacker broke into one of the University of Washington Medical Center's computer systems and easily downloaded thousands of files of patient data. Most doctors do not keep their patient records in an online database and hence do not have to be concerned about this sort of problem, but hospitals, pharmacies, and insurance companies rely heavily on electronic databases. Data maintained here are more vulnerable, not just to security lapses but to illegitimate access.

Privacy experts, therefore, have long argued that the medical industry's vigilance and self-monitoring would be inadequate to ensure medical data protection. Specific and comprehensive regulations were essential. Policy makers in the Clinton administration had been edging toward this view and they finally developed new rules that took effect on April 14, 2001. These rules, mandated by the Health Insurance Portability and Accountability Act (HIPAA), prohibit health care providers from releasing patient information without the patient's consent. For example, hospitals can no longer sell the names of pregnant women to manufacturers of products such as baby formula. Patients also have the right to access, examine, and copy the information in their medical records. Finally, the restrictions limit the disclosure of health information to the "minimum necessary" for a specific purpose (such as paying bills). Some health care providers release a patient's whole record when only several specific pieces of information are needed. The Bush administration has indicated that this should not be interpreted as a strict standard that would prohibit doctors or nurses from sharing necessary information when treating a patient.

HIPAA also includes tight security provisions. According to Johnson (2001), "The law requires organizations to define clear procedures to protect patients privacy, designate certain individuals to monitor privacy practices, and hear patients' complaints."

President Bush originally indicated that his administration might oppose the enactment of these rules in response to heavy criticism from the health care industry. The rules were criticized for being so restrictive that they "could impede patient care and disrupt essential operations" (Pear 2001). Pharmacists, for example, claim that the broad consent requirement would mean that a patient would have to provide written consent before another family member or a neighbor picked up his or her prescription. Health and Human Services Secretary Tommy Thompson has indicated that some of the more problematic rules would be modified after a more extensive review. Patients will be allowed to have friends or relatives pick up their prescription drugs. Once they are put into effect in 2003, these privacy regulations are estimated to cost hospitals about $225 billion during the next five years (Dash 2001).

This experience with these HIPAA privacy rules points to the difficulty of formulating effective but flexible privacy regulations. The trick, of course, is to protect privacy without a negative impact on efficiency and productivity. Good legislation seeks to balance society's need for knowledge and information sharing with due respect for an individual's privacy rights. Some medical information must sometimes be released to protect the public from infections and epidemics, or to help apprehend a criminal, to conduct medical research, or even to help treat the patient. These rules appear to be a major step in the right direction, but more clarity and precision may help to achieve a better balance between privacy and productivity.

DATA PROTECTION IN EUROPE

We have seen in its essentials U.S. policy on privacy and we now wish to consider privacy protection in other countries and in other types of political systems. To some extent, Europe seems to be way ahead of the United States in its approach to respect for privacy rights and "data protection." While this term's meaning has changed over the years, it is still widely used to describe an individual's right to control his or her personal information. Most countries, such as Italy, Germany, and Sweden, have adopted a much more proactive approach than the United States.

Sweden, for example, passed its landmark Data Act in 1973. It was enacted to prevent "undue encroachment on personal privacy." The act established a Data Inspection Board (DIB), an independent agency responsible for monitoring and licensing those who maintained electronic data files. These files "could be kept only for specific purposes" and "data could not be disseminated or used for purposes other than specified without permission of the registered person or in accordance with the law" (Paine 1992). On-site inspections by DIB staff in order to ensure compliance were not uncommon.

The development of data-protection legislation in Europe closely mirrors the evolution of technology. Sweden's Data Act belonged to the first generation of data-protection laws, along with the Austrian Data Protection Act (1974) and the German Federal Data Protection Act (1977). This legislation was a response to the emergence of large government or corporate databanks. The government's centralized databases were used to manage their growing social welfare systems. Social planning is virtually impossible without sophisticated data-collection and processing mechanisms. Data protection was originally interpreted as a means of protecting citizens from the abuses or negative effects of the centralized databanks, where personal data were processed and frequently recombined. The legislation sought to license these huge databases and put some restrictions on how these data could be employed.

But as technology changed, so did the European understanding of data protection. During the late 1970s and the 1980s, data processing became decentralized; there were no longer just a few massive central databases, but a variety of databases on mainframe and minicomputer systems dispersed throughout Europe. According to Mayer-Schonberger (1997), this gave rise to a second generation of data-protection laws, where "existing individual rights were reinforced, linked to constitutional provisions, broadened, and extended." In this second-generation legislation the focus shifted to the individual, who was given a much stronger voice in the process of data collection and transfer. The Danish data-protection laws (1987), for example, gave individuals the right to control the transfer of personal data from public to private databases, along with control over the exchange of their data. Thus, as Mayer-Schonberger puts it, "Data protection as an attempt to regulate technology was transformed into an individual liberty of citizens."

Subsequent versions of data-protection laws in Europe have put more emphasis on "informational participation and self-determination" (Mayer-Schonberger 1997). In addition, general data-protection laws were supplemented with specific sectorial data-protection rules. For example, the

Norwegian Data Protection Act tightly regulates credit reporting. These sectorial enhancements are seen as essential to reinforce protection for data that are especially sensitive, such as financial or medical information.

Unlike the United States, there has been a long tradition of safeguarding privacy by translating protections into a statutory framework. It is no surprise, therefore, that the European Union would develop its own inclusive guidelines that have taken the form of a data directive (Directive 95/46/EC 1995) that sets forth the requirements of privacy policies and practices in its member countries. This directive was a culmination of earlier efforts to unite and harmonize European data-protection policies. The primary goal of this directive is to "ensure a high level of protection for the privacy of individuals in all member states" (Bennett 1997).

The directive is a profuse and intricate document, but several features stand out. According to Articles 6 and 7, every individual has the right to notice about the processing of his or her data, the right to access those data and correct mistakes, and the right to opt out of transfers to third parties for marketing purposes. Also, according to Article 6, personal data must be accurate and, where necessary, kept up to date. Under this directive, European companies must notify individuals of the intended uses for personal data and may not use or release those data for other purposes without the individual's consent. The basic principle is that personal data may not be processed without the user's consent unless "processing is necessary for the performance of a contract to which the data subject is party" (Directive 1995.) In addition, the directive mandates the establishment of a national privacy agency to enforce all this. This is not a big problem for most European countries, since most of them already have privacy bureaucracies. The Italian Data Protection Commission, for example, has the responsibility to ensure Italy's strict privacy laws. Finally, Article 25 forbids the transfer of personal data pertaining to EU citizens to countries that do not have in place "adequate" privacy laws. In January 1999 the European Union, as expected, concluded that U.S. privacy laws were inadequate under the terms of the directive. As a consequence, it prohibited all data transfer from the United States after June 2001.

The United States and the European Union have, however, reached agreement on a "safe harbor" provision that would exempt U.S. companies from Europe's privacy rules provided they follow rules that revolve around the privacy principles, such as notice, choice, security, data integrity, and access to correct one's information. Most U.S. companies do not yet comply with these principles and have not taken advantage of this safe harbor arrangement. The cost of such compliance would be significant: Some businesses estimate that it would cost hundreds of thousands of dollars to develop a process that allows people to access their data, which is a directive requirement.

The disruption in data flows that may come about because of the asymmetries between European and American privacy laws underscores the need for an international set of norms. There is some chance that the E.U. Directive will become the basis for an international standard. Argentina, Australia,

Canada, Switzerland, and New Zealand have either adopted the E.U. Directive or are working on a set of rules that are heavily influenced by that directive (Thibodeau 2001). While some in the United States may see this trend toward convergence as a threat to national sovereignty, others believe that a simple global standard is the only way to ensure that privacy rights are recognized and enforced throughout the world.

THE ARCHITECTURES OF PRIVACY

Privacy or data protection, especially the European version, comes with a price. Not only does it require an overarching system of regulations, it also requires a bureaucracy, a federal privacy agency to enforce those regulations. We should recall Coase's admonition about the need to weigh carefully the benefits and costs of regulation. Government intervention is not necessarily the most appropriate solution to the externality problem of privacy erosion.

There are, however, some alternatives to the top-down regulatory approach that has been so unequivocally embraced by the European Union. Perhaps technology can help to solve the very problem it has created. There are certain architectures that have been designed to protect privacy, and they are sometimes referred to as privacy enhancing technologies (PET). Obviously these architectures cannot fully resolve the privacy conundrum, but is it possible to architect systems that give users reasonable control over their privacy? To what extent should individuals take the initiative to protect their own privacy with these tools? Is this sort of individualistic and decentralized approach preferable to the more paternalistic philosophy that is typical of Europe? If these architectures work, it might be possible to preserve end user autonomy while safeguarding personal privacy.

The most common architectural platform is still Platform for Privacy Preferences. P3P is a protocol designed by the World Wide Web Consortium that standardizes the comparison between Web site privacy polices and users' privacy preferences. The P3P protocol includes rules that allow Web sites to translate their privacy policies into P3P's machine-readable language. These policies will specify whether the site uses cookies or shares data with third parties. The users' privacy profile will be embedded into his or her browser software and it will specify allowable and nonallowable uses of personal data. P3P will only permit users to provide their personal data at sites that are consistent with those preferences. If a Web site offers less privacy protection than a user desires, P3P will warn the user and block the transfer of personal information, but it will provide the option of overriding the users' privacy preferences and conducting business on the vendor's terms. The goal of P3P is to empower users to make informed choices about whether to transact business at a given Web site based on that site's privacy policies.

Obviously, P3P will work only if commercial Web sites adopt this standard and express their privacy policies in P3P's special machine-readable language. Only then can the browser software compare that policy with the user's profile. Major software vendors such as Microsoft have thrown their weight behind this standard. Microsoft is incorporating this protocol into version 6 of its Internet Explore browser. In addition, some of the Internet's biggest companies, such as AOL–Time Warner, IBM, and AT&T, have made a firm commitment to P3P, and they have vowed to make their Web sites P3P compliant. But others, including Amazon.com and Disney, have adopted a wait-and-see attitude for the present time.

There are other privacy-enhancing technologies, of course, besides P3P. A New York software company called Ponoi has developed software that will allow Web sites to offer consumers anonymous access; that is, without the need to disclose their identities or IP address. According to Ricardo (2001), "Ponoi's software will allow companies to place a feature on their Web sites that lets users browse and gather information in a private space—that is, without having information stored on any outside computer." Ponoi is not alone in developing such protective software. We will most likely see similar privacy technologies embedded into browsers and other systems in the near future.

P3P and other privacy tools are surely not a panacea for privacy protection. Even if this architecture is widely embraced by commercial Web sites and all of its bugs are worked out, it has limitations. In its current form P3P only screens a user's broad privacy preferences and there is some question about this protocol's ability to "understand" in-depth privacy policies. There is also an ongoing debate over P3P's default settings, which guarantee a minimal level of privacy, especially for more unsophisticated users. In the case of the Internet Explore browser, Microsoft will determine that default setting, and some privacy advocates find fault with this. According to Simpson (2001), "Microsoft's default P3P setting will reject cookies from any third-party company working with the host site unless that company also complies with P3P and has an 'opt-out' mechanism on its own site allowing users to stop placement of cookies. This will have the effect of forcing all Internet advertisers and data-collection companies to adopt opt-out policies." The problem with this default setting is that consumers will need to visit these sites and opt out of cookie placements, and some may not take that initiative.

These deficiencies in P3P have engendered skepticism about its efficacy as a reasonable, albeit partial, solution to protecting consumer privacy. P3P has been characterized as "too little, too late" and as "a complex and confusing protocol" (Clausing 2000). But why not give this young and admittedly imperfect technology a chance to mature? Why not give vendors like Microsoft the opportunity to work out the kinks that have surfaced through public feedback and criticism and to make refinements. If implemented properly and responsibly, P3P can surely play at least a moderate role in achieving the goal of data protection.

The ethically responsible implementation of P3P implies that consumers will be given specific and clear information about the sharing of their personally identifiable information, including its secondary and tertiary uses. According to Cohen (2000), "To assess the benefits and costs of a trade accurately, individuals must understand the uses contemplated for the information they are asked to disclose." This means that recipients of a user's data must be identified in more than general terms and the secondary or tertiary uses of that data are also spelled out in specific terms. Otherwise users will not be able to make an adequately informed decision. It will be vitally important then that vendors develop well-articulated privacy policies that prevent information asymmetry. Lack of transparency will mean that the user's apparent empowerment is a mere illusion. Incorporating such fine-grained privacy policies into architectures such as the P3P will be a technical challenge; if successful, however, P3P may offer individuals the opportunity to restrict access and control the flow of their information without excessive risks.

Some have also questioned the most significant premise behind P3P, which is implied by its name. Is privacy really a preference, something that is within the ambit of the consumer's discretion, or is it a fundamental right that deserves a certain level of protection no matter what one "prefers"? Should all personal information be treated with the same level of protection and confidentiality? We argue that everyone deserves a baseline level of privacy; that is, unambiguous legal protection for very sensitive personal data, such as one's medical and financial background. But consumer data, which are mostly at issue here, are another matter. We tend to find a spectrum of privacy preferences when it comes to this sort of information: Some people couldn't care less that Amazon.com knows what books they read and might sell that information to a third party; others prefer that Amazon not include their data in any such sale for the reasons enumerated earlier. It is far from evident that there is a consensus on what types of consumer data should or should not be protected. P3P therefore has potential to become a tenable code-based solution, since it empowers users to express their preferences as rules and to restrict access if they so prefer.

Finally Cohen (2000) worries about P3P and the "privacy-as-choice" model because the vendor is still free "to decide what terms to offer in the first place." If all vendors in a given market insist that "the surrender of personal information is non-negotiable," users will be foreclosed from making a purchase unless they comply. This scenario seems unlikely, however, in an efficient marketplace where demand for privacy would ultimately be satisfied by opportunistic vendors.

SELF-REGULATION OR FEDERAL STANDARDS?

The loss of privacy is a market failure. More precisely, it is a negative externality analogous to various forms of environmental degradation. The sale or exchange of data between two parties imposes a cost on the data subject: His or her information is being sold, and this results in a loss of privacy. The cost is not borne by the two parties who engage in the transaction, but instead it is borne involuntarily by the data subject. It is important to realize that this transaction has certain benefits: The exchange of information, the primary input in an information economy, serves important social and economic value. The challenge is to weigh those benefits against the cost, an encroachment on one's privacy, which is more difficult to quantify.

What is to be done about this market failure? Do we need a forceful policy response similar to the one that gave us strict environmental regulations and the EPA? Is it time for the United States to adopt stricter, across-the-board privacy laws such as those we find in European countries? Is such government intervention welfare enhancing?

The past two presidential administrations have relied on a philosophy of self-regulation. However, we must admit that many commercial Web sites have not been conscientious about formulating and abiding by fair privacy policies. The policy vacuum and the disingenuousness of some corporations has led to calls for federal legislation, an American equivalent of the E.U. Directive, that will better protect the consumer.

We cannot assume that full-scale government intervention will increase aggregate welfare in this case. I would argue instead for the continuation of a more focused and sectoral approach to privacy protection. For medical and financial privacy a more paternalistic philosophy does seem called for, given the stakes of disclosure of such sensitive data and the potential for significant dignitary harm. Government regulations or rules (such as HIPAA) are essential to protect such sensitive medical and financial data. There is a need for uniformity in the way computer medical records are managed. But for more generic information, such as consumer data (including information about shopping habits, clickstream data, ads we look at, etc.) collected by cookies or through other means, we can afford to try a different approach. We may not need command and control regulations, since these data are not nearly as sensitive, and the user can probably rely on code-based solutions for protection. Thus, once we have worked out a baseline level of absolutely essential privacy protection (e.g., medical privacy), why not rely on a scheme of ethical self-regulation for other types of information?

As argued in Chapter 3, government regulations should only be adopted when the transaction costs of settling the problem without government intervention are prohibitively high. Privatized solutions are generally preferable to ones imposed by the government. It might be possible to resolve consumer privacy without elaborate legislation and the accompanying bureaucracy. The efficacy of a privatized solution is enhanced by the availability of technologies such as P3P, which can help users achieve the control over personal information by restricting access. Corporate self-regulation supplemented by responsibly implemented technology can go far to protect privacy without the excessive costs and negative effects of a more elaborate regulatory infrastructure. If we assume that vendors like Microsoft are sensitive to consumer demands and to criticisms of P3P, products like P3P will continue to evolve and become more efficacious protectors of privacy. Consumers will have the tools to control their environment, and this will enable them to make the tradeoffs they prefer when they engage in Web site transactions. No one disputes that consumer data need some protection, but let's find the simplest and most cost-effective approach that empowers consumers and optimizes the social good.

The problem with European-style regulations of consumer data is the high transaction costs of the regulatory infrastructure, which can yield a suboptimal result. As in Europe, so in America; if we regulate privacy heavily and adopt the equivalent of the European Directive, the government will be forced to set up a privacy bureaucracy (an EPA for privacy) and perhaps appoint a privacy czar who will enforce the government's regime of extensive privacy laws. As a result of the massive exchanges of information that lubricate our economic system, those enforcement costs will be quite expensive and impose huge burdens on the economy. Given the magnitude of these costs, the potential for allocative inefficiencies that often accompany government regulations, and the availability of viable alternatives of code and user empowerment, it is by no means self-evident that comprehensive data-protection laws will create the most value. At the very least, before we emulate the European approach there should be a careful reckoning of the estimated costs of government polices along with their potentially harmful effects on electronic commerce. Privacy-policy analysis that fails to study these effects of government regulation is impractical and incomplete.

One last word about self-regulation. It will not work without the cooperation of commercial Web sites, and if those companies are serious about self-regulation they must begin by developing a careful and nuanced privacy policy that should ultimately be expressed in machine-readable format for the sake of P3P and other technologies. Companies are not legally obligated to develop such policies, but there are compelling moral and economic reasons for doing so. Nuanced privacy policies increase consumers' confidence and trust in a particular site. They also manifest respect for the user's autonomy. There is something morally reprehensible about the clandestine collection of data under ordinary circumstances. It is far more responsible to be up front with customers about the data being collected and to abide by the key moral principle of informed consent. Consumers will reward that site's candor and integrity in the long run. Once a company decides on a set of policies, it must ensure that those policies are enforced throughout the organization and closely followed by their employees. At the end of this section is an example of a generic privacy policy for a typical Web site; it is not necessarily a complete list of what such a policy should include, but it does provide some general sense of direction. In addition, the policy should be prominently displayed so that consumers who visit the site will not miss seeing it.

Finally, the scheme of self-regulation depends on consumer cooperation as well. Some consumers may feel that the maintenance of their privacy is not worth the trouble, and it is surely their prerogative to discount privacy concerns. But those consumers who think it is worth the trouble must begin to take some responsibility for the protection of their personal information if they want commercial Web sites to respect their privacy rights and to abide by their preferences. Instead of relying on the government to be a paternalistic intermediary between commercial Web sites and the consumer, why not let individuals take some responsibility for safeguarding their own data with the assistance of technologies like P3P?

The following is a privacy policy outline:

Section A: Notice of Data Collection and Usage

- The policy should inform users about what data are being collected and how those data are collected. Does the site use cookies or Web bugs?
- What is the primary use of the data being collected? What about secondary and tertiary uses?
- Which third parties (if any) will have access to the data?
- Explanation of security mechanisms that are in place to protect confidentiality and integrity of the data.

Section B: Giving the Consumer a Choice

- Companies should explain whether they will allow the consumer to opt out or to opt in. Under the opt-out approach, the default choice is to allow use of one's personal data, but under opt in the default choice is to prohibit any such use of those data for secondary purposes unless the user explicitly provides his or her permission. The consumer should also be provided with a convenient mechanism to exercise this choice.

Section C: Access and Correction Process

- Companies must make a choice about access by the data subjects: Will they have the right to access their data and to make necessary corrections? If they intend to allow this, the process for making corrections must be spelled out.

Section D: Due Process and Enforcement Issues

- An explanation of how the policy is to be enforced along with the procedure that the consumer can use for informing the company that their privacy rights have been violated. (Michigan Attorney General's Office 2000)

PRIVACY IN THE WORKPLACE

"Big Brother" has always been a presence in the workplace, but thanks to new networking "technologies of control," electronic-eavesdropping capabilities are being extended into every office that uses the Internet. These technologies are also changing the nature of work beyond the office. The U.S. Department of Transportation recently proposed a requirement that long-haul truck drivers use electronic recorders, ostensibly to make sure that they were taking time off to rest in accordance with federal safety rules. These onboard recorders can track every move the truck makes, when it is out of commission, and when a driver uses windshield wipers or puts on the headlights. In the future trucks could be equipped with a global positioning system chip that will also keep track of their precise whereabouts.

With these new surveillance techniques come great anxieties for many workers. Indeed, the level of surveillance and monitoring in the workplace is unprecedented. Employers track employee e-mail along with every Web page that an employee visits. For example, some companies use a software product called Telemate.Net, which reports Web site visits by employees and categorizes them into groups such as pornography, job hunting, or shopping. Few employers appear to give much consideration to the privacy implications of this incessant monitoring or its effect on morale.

There is even surveillance software called Investigation that secretly monitors each keystroke an employee makes, even if that keystroke is immediately deleted. If an employee in a fit of rage begins to write the first few sentences of an inflammatory letter critical of his employer, changes his mind, and then erases his vitriolic prose, he has still left an indelible trace of anger that will be recorded by this software system. Even among the welter of prying monitoring systems that one finds in the workplace, this one seems particularly invasive, a potent threat to personal autonomy that gives the employer a window into the thought processes of its workers.

The rationale behind this keystroke software and other systems is the need for better offline surveillance as well as online surveillance. According to McCarthy (2000),

> Many companies are concluding that they may be missing computer mischief that doesn't involve the Internet or the corporate network, both of which they can monitor; right at their own desktops employees could be copying sales leads or pornography to or from disks or CD-ROMS or downloading bookkeeping software to run their own business—all of which could elude conventional surveillance methods.

Since communications within a company-owned computer system are not considered private in the eyes of the law, there is nothing legally questionable about using software like Investigation. Whether its utilization is within the bounds of ethical probity, however, is quite another matter.

While the use of such keystroke software may not yet be widespread, nearly every organization monitors employee e-mail. At most companies it is common to find systems that monitor both incoming and outgoing electronic mail. Companies claim that such monitoring is essential to protect their systems from misuse and to protect their intellectual property. But companies seem especially worried about liability for their employee e-mail. According to a *Computerworld* poll, 57 percent of corporations that monitor e-mail say that one of the top two reasons is "potential legal liability from information contained in e-mail." Also, 47 percent cite "uses of e-mail for racial and sexual harassment" (Deckmyn 1999).

When companies find e-mail abuse they often take aggressive action. In November 1999 the *New York Times* fired twenty-three support workers because they allegedly distributed offensive jokes on the company's e-mail system. Predictably, there was a backlash when this incident became public, but the *Times* did not reverse the termination. Corporations like Nissan, Edward Jones & Co., and Pillsbury have also fired employees for improper use of the corporate e-mail systems.

Most companies that do rely on systematic monitoring of e-mail traffic have articulated an e-mail policy so that their workers will not be taken completely by surprise. That policy usually delineates (1) whether the corporation's computer can be used for limited personal purposes (or is it for business use only), (2) the proper uses of the e-mail system, (3) to what extent e-mail content will be monitored, and (4) sanctions that will be imposed for violating policy.

Simply having a policy, of course, does not imply that monitoring is legally acceptable or that it doesn't infringe workers' privacy rights in some way. Where have the courts sided on this issue? It is important to note that there are no federal laws that could be invoked to protect e-mail privacy. The Electronic Communications Privacy Act of 1986 (discussed in the next chapter) does extend to "electronic" communications, but it exempts the providers of the communication medium (in this case the corporation providing the e-mail system) from liability. Most states recognize a common law right of privacy; to prove an infringement of this right the plaintiff would be required to demonstrate "an intentional intrusion into his or her private affairs or concerns which would be highly offensive to a reasonable person" (*Restatement of Torts*, §652B [1977]). An employee would have to establish a "reasonable expectation of privacy" in the content of his or her e-mail messages; if so, the messages could be considered private and off limits to the company. The plaintiff would also have to demonstrate that the employee's monitoring of e-mail communications was unreasonable under the circumstances. Most legal experts, however, believe the common law approach will be a difficult way of establishing the propriety of e-mail privacy.

Some employees who have been terminated for alleged e-mail abuse have fought back with lawsuits. But in cases such as *Shoars v. Epson America* (BC007036 Cal. Sup. Ct. [1991]) and *Bourke v. Nissan Motor Corp* (B068705 Cal. Ct. Appeals [1993]), the employers have easily prevailed. Both of these cases have minimal value as precedents, but that isn't true of *Smyth v. Pillsbury Co.* (914 F. Supp. E.D. PA [1996]), which was decided by a federal court. Michael Smyth claimed that he was wrongfully discharged from his position at Pillsbury as regional operations manager. The reason was an inappropriate use of the company's e-mail facility that took place in October 1994. In an e-mail exchange with another employee concerning recent developments pertaining to Pillsbury's sales-management staff, one of Smyth's messages said that he would "kill the backstabbing bastards." In another message he likened an upcoming company party to the "Jim Jones Koolaid affair." Unbeknownst to Mr. Smyth, his e-mail messages were intercepted by one of his mangers. In January 1995 Smyth was terminated for transmitting "inappropriate and unprofessional comments" over the Pillsbury e-mail facility. Smyth argued for wrongful discharge, claiming that Pillsbury had informed employees that e-mail communications were confidential and would not be used as a basis for reprimand or discharge. Pillsbury contested this claim by reference to an automated message that employees received when they invoked the e-mail system. That message indicated that electronic mail should not be considered "secure" and could be inspected by the company at any time.

The U.S. District Court for the Eastern District of Pennsylvania ruled in Pillsbury's favor. The court stated that company e-mail does not warrant privacy protection because e-mail by its very nature is a public form of communication (i.e., messages are transmitted over the network in an open, insecure fashion). Thus, employees should have no expectation of privacy in their e-mail messages. Also, according to the court, Pillsbury had a legitimate need to monitor its e-mail communications in order to protect its assets and to ensure worker productivity. This interest overrides any privacy rights, even if the employer did characterize its e-mail messages as confidential.

The *Smyth* case is significant because it is the first legal decision at the federal level that repudiates any employee right to privacy in the content of his or her e-mail transmitted over an employer's e-mail system. One could argue, however, that the court's reasoning in this case is flawed. For example, the court's claim that the e-mail system was "utilized by the entire Company" and therefore assumed a "public status " is questionable. Yet the court seems to rely on this assumption to conclude that Smyth should not have an expectation of privacy. According to Dixon (1997), "The fact that a company's communication system is used widely by multiple users should not thereby transform the contents of any message sent through that system as statements devoid of any expectation of privacy." Does Smyth's use of Pillsbury's e-mail system mean that he has no privacy expectations merely because his fellow employees use that same system? It would seem that a rational expectation of privacy depends more on Smyth's beliefs about whether his employer would intercept and scrutinize his messages and less on how pervasive e-mail had become within the organization. Also, the use of encryption technology would heighten an expectation of privacy, even though the Internet is an open and unsecure system. In other words, there are factors that could certainly elevate one's privacy expectations in e-mail communications. The court's argument, therefore, appears to be tautological: Since the employer has the ability to read the e-mail, there should be no privacy expectations. For these and other reasons the conclusions reached by the court in this case need to be reassessed.

It is also highly debatable whether the conservation of privacy rights should be so dependent on the subjective expectations of employees. As the information network becomes more ubiquitous we may expect less and less privacy, but does that mean we deserve less privacy? In his dissent on *Smith v.*

Maryland (442 U.S. 750 [1979]) Justice Thurgood Marshal wrote, "Whether privacy expectations are legitimate depends not on the risks an individual can be prepared to accept when imparting information to third parties, but on the risks he should be forced to assume in a free and open society." The question here is whether employees should be forced to assume some "risk" when they receive or send e-mail at work.

In addition, most of the arguments advanced by corporations on behalf of e-mail monitoring are not persuasive. Corporations contend that e-mail surveillance is necessary not so much to acquire relevant information but to protect their assets; that is, in order to ensure that their computer resources, including electronic mail software, are being used exclusively for work-related matters. They contend that the property owner should have prerogative to monitor how his or her property is being utilized in order to prevent the threat of abuse. To some extent, then, this disagreement over the propriety of e-mail monitoring can be reduced to a conflict between property rights and privacy rights. A corporation asserts that its property rights must take priority, while workers contend that their privacy rights ought to come first.

To be sure, property rights cannot be casually dismissed or ignored in the debate about e-mail privacy. Corporations must have the capacity to use reasonable means to protect their valuable resources from waste and misuse. I would submit, however, that at least when it comes to e-mail this can normally be accomplished with less intrusive methods than e-mail surveillance. When most organizations want to make sure that telephone communications are not being misused for expensive personal long-distance calls, they might compile and check selective phone numbers called by their employees looking for patterns of abuse, but they do not routinely listen in on the content of those communications.

There is something to be said, however, on behalf of e-mail monitoring for the sake of avoiding or limiting liability claims. Federal and state regulatory agencies responsible for enforcing racial and gender equality statutes put pressure on companies to have systems in place that can swiftly identify expressions of bias and effect necessary remedies. If harassment is taking place through the electronic mail system, monitoring might allow a company to ferret it out before it escalates. The problem is that sexual harassment law imposes more liability on the employer than on the harasser. Harassment law therefore perversely encourages e-mail and Web surfing monitoring, and employees must often pay the price when their presumably private comments are exposed within the corporate hierarchy.

According to legal scholars, the problem with harassment law based on interpretations of Title VII of the Civil Rights Act is the "hostile environment test." According to Rosen (2000),

> By allowing women (or men) to complain about any sexually oriented speech or conduct that they found hostile or abusive, the new test allowed aggrieved coworkers to object to overheard jokes and to e-mail, suggestive pictures or even their colleagues

consensual flirtation, even if the men in question never intended their conduct to be offensive, and the women to whom the conducted was directed didn't perceive it to be offensive.

Many have been quick to point out the threat this law poses to privacy and to speech. It's certainly possible that sexual harassment law can be refined so that it does not pose such a great threat to privacy and speech. As Rosen observes, it can focus on the question of whether the disputed conduct (or speech) really constitutes a form of discrimination because of sex. He also argues that hostile environment (when there is no employment issues) sexual harassment can be reinterpreted as an invasion of privacy. This would reduce the employer's incentive to punish trivial offenses, since the costs of regulation might exceed the harm that the regulations are seeking to prevent.

If the regulatory burden is eased by these changes or other legal refinements, corporations may not feel the same pressure to monitor every move their employees make. The goal of the legal system should be a balance between corporate liability for harassment and other rights violations and preservation of the employee's privacy rights. Right now, there is a gross imbalance, with privacy rights being sacrificed for the sake of avoiding expensive liability litigation.

The preservation of some type of private space or "zone" in the workplace is not a trivial concern. Blanket workplace monitoring that turns the work environment into a virtual panopticon is an affront to a worker's dignity, since it deeply affects his or her personal autonomy. When we are watched we are inhibited, stripped of our freedom to behave spontaneously. This panopticon effect has been described by Foucault (1979) and also by Goffman (1961), who used the term "total institution" to describe a place where one's behavior and actions are almost completely transparent. According to Goffman, "On the outside, the individual can hold objects of self-feeling—such as his body, his immediate actions, his thoughts and some of his possessions—clear of contact with alienating and contaminating things. But in total institutions these territories of the self are violated; the boundary that the individual places between his being and the environment is invaded and the embodiment of self profaned." In order to prevent the devolution of the corporation into a "total institution," companies must begin to take the privacy rights of their workers more seriously. Despite the risks of liability, which should be corrected, we maintain that the corporation should recognize at least a conditional or prima facie right to e-mail privacy. There are as yet no legal precedents that insist upon e-mail monitoring as a way to deter future workplace harassment; if companies take swift action as soon as they are put on notice that there is e-mail abuse, courts will be more lenient in the allocation of liability. Many of the same issues could apply to telephone communication systems, including voicemail, which most firms have chosen not to monitor because it is too expensive. To prevent harassment, companies must strive for vigilance without intrusiveness.

As we have argued elsewhere (Spinello 2002), workers should not be forced to surrender their privacy rights when they walk into the workplace, although those rights must be balanced against the company's "need to know." We claim that there must be a strong presumption in favor of privacy rights in the workplace. Corporations can maintain the right equilibrium if they seek only relevant knowledge about their workers, using ordinary means of inquiry. DesJardins (1985) is one of many business ethicists who have argued that extraordinary means of data collection such as "blanket surveillance of all employees" are illegitimate because they are so intrusive and potentially harmful. Hence, they should not be adopted unless there are extraordinary circumstances. This stipulation that the means of gathering information about employees will be confined to ordinary methods precludes routine electronic surveillance (such as monitoring and intercepting e-mail), and it reinforces the notion that workers should have at least a prima facie or conditional right to the confidentiality of their e-mail communications. The burden of proof is on the organization to make the case that a particular situation warrants the use of extraordinary methods of inquiry such as e-mail surveillance. If there is no just cause, if a case cannot be made that would satisfy a reasonable, objective person, then there is no justification for using these extreme methods, and the employee's prima facie right to e-mail privacy must be safeguarded.

CONCLUSIONS

Few of us are really seers of the future, but it does not take much foresight to recognize that the slow evanescence of personal privacy is not likely to abate anytime soon. In ten or fifteen years we may wistfully look back to the abundant privacy we enjoyed at the inception of this new millennium. The reasons for privacy's gradual demise are complex and varied, ranging from sheer indolence and indifference to our enthusiasm for embracing the huge benefits that the new economy promises without reckoning the costs. The surrender of privacy may seem like a small price to pay for more convenient and secure shopping, but many of us may come to regret these tradeoffs when there is little privacy left. Privacy has always been an abstract and almost ineffable value, and this makes it easier to sacrifice for tangible and more immediate benefits.

Thus, although the dissipation of privacy is a market failure, it is also a personal failure. There are tools and capabilities that can help users protect privacy. Some of these are simple, such as the capability to disable the cookie functionality of a browser. But for most users taking these precautionary steps doesn't seem to be worth the trouble. It is hard to explain this inertia: Perhaps consumers really do not care so much about privacy, and if that is so, why should we enact costly laws that fill a policy vacuum about which consumers are indifferent?

I have expressed some optimism here that the same technology that destroys privacy may also protect it and that self-regulation for generic consumer data should be given a chance to work. The scheme of self-regulation requires that users take some responsibility for their own privacy protection by adopting technologies with embedded safeguards. It also depends on corporations to recognize their moral duty to respect privacy rights and to adopt policies that will allow for informed consent facilitated by privacy enhancing architectures. The alternative is to rely on the state as a paternalistic intermediary between companies like DoubleClick or Amazon.com and the consumer. While elaborate legal solutions and remedies such as the E.U. Directive may help forestall the further encroachment on one's privacy, they may do so at too high a cost. I am still inclined to put some faith in the conscientious utilization of privacy-enhancing technologies, including protocols such as P3P.

I concede that the Europeans *may* be right about all this and that in the end the only viable modality of regulation will be the law. But let's give companies and consumers a little more time to adjust to the remarkable transformative effects of electronic commerce, and let's give protocols like P3P a chance to mature. We might find a solution that creates value other than government intervention. Such a solution is likely to depend upon the proficient use of code, the user's willingness to assume some responsibility for demarcating a desired privacy zone, and the development of responsible corporate privacy policies.

REFERENCES

Barringer, F. (2001). "Using Books as Evidence Against Their Readers." *New York Times*, 8 April, sec. 4, p. 3.

Bennett, C. (1997). "Convergence Revisited: Toward a Global Policy for the Protection of Personal Data." In *Technology and Privacy: The New Landscape*, edited by P. Agre and M. Rotenberg. Cambridge: MIT Press.

Borgmann, A. (1992). *Crossing the Postmodern Divide*. Chicago: University of Chicago Press.

Brandeis, L., and Warren, S. (1890). "The Right to Privacy." *Harvard Law Review* 4: 193.

Clausing, J. (2000). "New Technology Is Aimed at Increasing Web Privacy." *New York Times*, 22 June, C6.

Cohen, J. (2000). "Examined Lives: Informational Privacy and the Subject as Object." *Stanford Law Review* 52: 1373.

Dash, J. (2001). "HIPAA Rules Go into Effect." *Computerworld*, 16 April, 77.

Deckmyn, D. (1999). "More Managers Monitor E-Mail." *Computerworld*, 18 October, 97.

DesJardins, J. (1985). *Contemporary Issues in Business Ethics*. Belmont, Calif.: Wadsworth.

Directive 95/46/EC of the European Parliament on the Protection of Individuals with regard to Processing of Personal Data. (1995). Available: http://europa.eu.int/eur-lex/en/lif/dat/1995

Dixon, R. (1997). "Windows Nine-to-Five: *Smyth v. Pillsbury* and the Scope of an Employee's Right of Privacy in Employer Communications." *Virginia Journal of Law and Technology* 2: 4.

Foucault, M. (1979). *Discipline and Punish: The Birth of the Prison*. New York: Vintage Books.

Fried, C. (1984). "Privacy." In *Philosophical Dimensions of Privacy*, edited by F. Schoeman. New York: Cambridge University Press.

Gandy, O. (1993). *The Panoptic Sort*. Boulder, Colo.: Westview Press.

Gandy, O. (1996). "Coming to Terms with the Panoptic Sort." In *Computers, Surveillance & Privacy*, edited by D. Lyon. Minneapolis: University of Minnesota Press.

Gavison, R. (1984). "Privacy and the Limits of the Law." *Yale Law Journal* 89: 421.

Gindin, S. (1997). "Lost and Found in Cyberspace." *San Diego Law Review* 34: 1153.

Goffman, E. (1961). *Asylums: Essays on the Social Situation of Mental Patients and Other Inmates*. Chicago: Aldine.

Hall, M. (2001). "The Politics of Privacy." *Computerworld*, 13 August, 32–33.

Johnson, A. (2001). "Getting a Grip on HIPAA." *Computerworld*, 7 May, 45.

Lessig, L. (1999). *Code and Other Laws of Cyberspace.* New York: Basic Books.

Mayer-Schonberger, V. (1997). "Generational Development of Data Protection in Europe." In *Technology and Privacy: The New Landscape*, edited by P. Agre and M. Rotenberg. Cambridge: MIT Press.

McCarthy, M. (2000). "You Assumed 'Erase' Wiped Out That Rant against the Bosses? Nope." *Wall Street Journal*, 7 March, A1, A16.

Michigan Attorney General's Office. (2000). "Guide to Privacy Policies." Available: http://www.ag.state.mi.US/inet_info/priv_guide.htm

Moor, J. (2001). "Towards a Theory of Privacy for the Information Age." In *Readings in CyberEthics*, edited by R. Spinello and H. Tavani. Sudbury, Mass.: Jones and Bartlett.

O'Connor, K. (2000). "The High Cost of Net Privacy." *Wall Street Journal*, 7 March, A27.

Paine, L. (1992). *Note on Data Protection in Sweden*. Boston: Harvard Business School Publications.

Pear, R. (2001). "Medical Industry Lobbies to Rein in New Privacy Rules." *New York Times*, 12 February, A1.

Rachels, J. (1975). "Why Is Privacy Important?" *Philosophy and Public Affairs* 4, no. 4.

Ricardo, C. (2001). "Privacy: Technology Has Taken Away Privacy, Now Promises to Give It Back." *Wall Street Journal*, 25 June, R17.

Rosen, J. (2000). *The Unwanted Gaze: The Destruction of Privacy in America*. New York: Random House.

Schwartz, J. (2002). "Qwest Plan Stirs Protest over Privacy." *New York Times*, 1 January, C2.

Simpson, G. (2001). "The Battle over Web Privacy." *Wall Street Journal,* 21 March, B1, B4.

Smith, R. (2000). *Ben Franklin's Web Site*. Providence: Sheridan Books.

Spinello, R. (2002). "Electronic Mail and Panoptic Power in the Workplace." In *Perspectives in Business Ethics*. 2d ed., edited by L. Hartman. New York: McGraw-Hill.

Spinello, R., and Tavani, H. (2001). "Introduction to Chapter Four: Privacy in Cyberspace." In *Readings in CyberEthics*, edited by R. Spinello and H. Tavani. Sudbury, Mass.: Jones and Bartlett.

Thibodeau, P. (2001). "Europe's Privacy Laws May become Global Standard." *Computerworld*, 12 March, 77.

Wasserman, E. (2000). "Save the Children." *Industry Standard*, 28 August, 110–111.

9

Cybercrime, Encryption, and Government Surveillance

The crime sounded alarming: an audacious theft of 1 million credit card numbers from numerous e-commerce sites stretched across twenty states. This disturbing incident, announced by law-enforcement authorities in March 2001, was described by the FBI as the largest organized criminal attack on the Internet to date. The FBI devoted considerable resources to this case, but so far its quarry proved to be too erratic. At first, some thought this had to be the work of ingenious hackers, but as the FBI untangled the details of this crime it discovered that these hackers were not so ingenious after all. They merely exploited security flaws, unpatched vulnerabilities in the Windows NT operating system. Microsoft had provided patches (or fixes) for these problems in 1998, but the victims carelessly failed to install them. Had these e-businesses been more assiduous about security it is quite likely that this costly theft could have been prevented (Levitt 2001).

High-profile cybercrimes that underscore the Net's vulnerability are frequently the subject of headlines in major publications. The *Wall Street Journal* proclaimed the Internet "Under Siege" (Hamilton and Cloud 2000) as it described how cyberterrorists had temporarily paralyzed some of the country's biggest Web sites through a denial-of-service attack. The technique is relatively simple, but the results can be catastrophic. Denial of service now joins a long list of other weapons that "black hat" hackers or crackers use to disrupt

Web sites. These include packet sniffers, trojan horses, and malicious applets. Many companies fall prey to these damaging technologies despite their renewed vigilance and their heavy investment in security systems.

Privacy and intellectual property rights will be meaningless unless we can adequately secure the Net and thwart the efforts of those who engage in criminal activity. Also, as observed in Chapter 4, Internet commerce is unlikely to flourish in an environment rife with crime and theft. There must be a level of trust, but how can we achieve this trust with the opaqueness of so many Internet relationships and transactions?

In this final chapter we will cover some of the legal and technical background central to developing a lucid analysis of security and related policy issues. After a cursory overview of the Net's vulnerabilities and cybercrime, we turn to the new frontiers for law enforcement in cyberspace. Special focus will be on the encryption controversy in the United States, the uneasy issues raised by government surveillance, and the use of technologies such as the FBI's Carnivore. These issues have obviously assumed greater import thanks to the events of September 11. The problem is that some of the architectures used to secure the Net and protect privacy give succor to criminals and terrorists. Society must make difficult trade-offs between privacy and anonymity and the need for an Internet infrastructure that permits electronic surveillance by law-enforcement authorities. We will carefully look at how these trade-offs have been managed so far and how the balance between security and liberty may need to be recalibrated to help in the struggle against terrorism.

We then shift focus to the topic of digital identity as a way to promote trust and security. Mandating digital identity as a means of assuring authentication appears to have the force of inevitability, but is it a sound and responsible idea? We will argue that code has a role to play in resolving this problem, since there are architectures that can authenticate without creating a privacy hazard. Finally, we conclude with a laconic discussion on whether security achieved through architectures is the best path to a more trustworthy Internet.

THE NET'S VULNERABILITIES

Any discussion of Internet security must begin with a realization of the paradoxical nature of network security. As we have discovered, the Net's decentralized and distributed nature imply many positive security features. For example, it is virtually impossible for some organization or rogue government to seize total control of this information infrastructure. Networks are more resilient because they are not organized around a dominant power center. Thus, the Internet avoids the vulnerabilities intrinsic to a more centralized operation. On the other hand, the Internet's broad accessibility makes it a visible and inviting target, and the openness of Internet protocols makes it easier to launch attacks on the system. Also, it can be difficult to contain damage on a network that is susceptible to disruptive viruses that sometimes circulate with great virulence. Security in any network is only as strong as its weakest link.

The main goal of Internet security is to keep proprietary information confidential, to preserve its integrity, and to maintain its availability for those authorized to view that information. When information is accessed and examined by unauthorized individuals, it is no longer confidential. By connecting to the Internet organizations have made their information assets far more vulnerable to unauthorized access and breaches of confidentiality. If data are tampered with, modified, or corrupted by intruders there is a loss of information integrity. Sometimes this can happen inadvertently, but most often it is the intentional act of a hacker or a disgruntled employee seeking revenge. Finally, if information is deleted or becomes inaccessible to authorized users, there is a loss of availability. The denial-of-service attacks described earlier meant that information was unavailable to Web site customers for a long period of time.

Would-be intruders are well equipped to gain unauthorized access and compromise confidential information. In order to gain access to a computer system or a protected Web site, a username and password are usually required. Hackers probe systems seeking access, often trying to crack passwords by brute force or with the help of software programs written for this purpose. If they succeed, the Web site or account is compromised and the confidentiality and integrity of its information is in jeopardy. Sensitive data are in even greater peril when on the move (i.e., as the data are being transmitted over the network). Hackers might use packet sniffers, for example, which are programs that capture data from information packets as they move from one node on the network to another. The captured data could be a username and password or other proprietary information.

In addition, denial-of-service (DoS) attacks are becoming more common. Hackers are able to download software from underground Web sites that enable them to hijack scores of computers in which they implant the downloaded program. They then instruct these machines to send requests for information to some prominent target site such as Yahoo or Disney.com. These constant messages clog the system, and the whole process eventually brings the Web server of the target site to its knees. These attacks may also involve the disruption of the network's physical components or the manipulation of data in transit.

In February 2000, Yahoo, Amazon.com, eBay, and several other major sites were crippled by well-coordinated DoS attacks. The hackers bombarded these Web sites with phony requests from computers distributed around the world. According to one IT manager, "Our systems are designed to handle the normal wave action of Internet activity, and then a tidal wave comes in [and] we weren't prepared for that" (Yasin 2000).

One of the more ubiquitous and damaging security problems has been the use of malicious code, such as viruses and worms. The ILoveYou virus, for example, which infected numerous computers in the United States, Europe, and Asia in May 2000, caused $11 billion in total damage. Viruses are self-replicating programs, usually attached to documents, programs, or files and activated when a particular application is initiated. A virus is spread when someone passes along the infected code. Worms are similar to viruses, but unlike a virus, a worm can run independently and travel from one system to another without attaching itself to another entity. The Melissa virus, unleashed on the world in the late spring of 1999, was particularly promiscuous, infecting tens of thousands of computers around the globe. It was a hybrid creature, combining elements of both a virus and a worm, that exploited the macro program features of Microsoft Word. Melissa entered a computer concealed in a Word file attached to an electronic mail message. Once in the computer it would infect Word files opened by the owner. The virus searched for the Outlook address book and then sent a copy of itself, embedded in the Word file, to the first address on the list. Melissa is only one of the several insidious viruses and worms that have gained notoriety in the last few years. Our computers were once isolated systems and thus less susceptible to destructive infectious "diseases" from external forces. But this has all changed. As Markoff (1999b) observes, with the ascendance of the network we have struck a Faustian bargain, "gaining the potential of robotic software agents, which can flit from computer to computer to do their master's bidding almost intelligently, but accepting as well the darker prospect of software infections that can sow the destruction of cybernetic plagues."

CYBERCRIME AND CYBERTERROR

Thanks in part to the Net's visibility and vulnerability, it has become a breeding ground for certain forms of cybercrime. This term is rather nebulous and has multiple meanings, so some clarification of its use in this context is necessary. We will define "cybercrime" as a special category of criminal acts that can only be executed through the utilization of computer and network technologies. Cybercrime includes three basic categories: (1) software piracy, (2) electronic break-ins, and (3) computer sabotage (Tavani 2001).

Software piracy involves the unauthorized duplication of proprietary software and the distribution or making available of those copies over the network. The unauthorized copying and distribution of proprietary operating system software or MP3 files would fall under this category. Electronic break-ins, discussed in the previous section, include gaining unauthorized access to a computer system or to a private, password-protected Web site. And computer sabotage involves the use of viruses, worms, and DoS attacks to interfere with computers and disrupt information flows. According to Tavani (2001), computer sabotage also involves using computer technology to "destroy data resident in a computer or damage a computer system's resources."

Not included in this narrow category of cybercrime are crimes that are facilitated thanks to the use of computer and network technologies. These crimes do not require computer technology and in most cases they have been going on long before the arrival of the Internet. One might include in this category stalking, theft (including fraud, swindling, and embezzlement), and the distribution of illegal material such as child pornography. Some argue, for example, that while stalking is not a new crime, the electronic version of stalking is on the rise because stalking is easier to do over the Internet. The stalker can use the Net to learn about his or her target; the stalker also has a better chance of remaining anonymous in cyberspace.

Finally, in addition to cybercrime and crime facilitated by computer technology, law-enforcement officials must deal with the use of the Internet as a communications medium to plan crimes in the physical world. For example, some traditional crimes like bank robbery might be coordinated by e-mail instead of the telephone. We might refer to these last two categories, crimes facilitated by the Internet or crimes planned and carried out with the help of the Internet and related technologies, as "computer-related crimes."

When certain forms of cybercrime such as computer sabotage is perpetrated on a massive scale it becomes "cyberterror." Since the tragic events of September 11, 2001, the threat of cyberterror is no longer an abstraction. Networks provide crucial linkages for the world's economy and their disruption could have a devastating impact. While some worry that an "electronic Pearl Harbor" is imminent, others believe that cyberterrorism will not occur apart from a substantial terrorist attack: Hacking might be used "to further complicate matters, perhaps by taking down key computers in financial or communications industries, after a bombing" (Schwartz 2001a). But adept hackers could all too easily disrupt critical facilities in the real world such as air traffic control, power-switching capabilities at electrical power plants, or even 911 services.

There are no easy remedies for these threats, but computer users and Web site operators are not defenseless. What can be done to provide a more unified defense against cybercrime, computer-related crimes, and even cyberterror?

DEFENDING THE NET

While it may not be possible to build systems that are immune from the threat of cybercrime and other disruptions, organizations and individuals are far from powerless, and their involvement is consistent with the model of self-regulation we have been advocating. The firewall is the first line of defense, since it should prevent intruders from gaining access into the internal network. A firewall consists of hardware and/or software that is positioned between an organization's internal network and the Internet. Its goal is to insulate an organization's private network from intrusions by trapping any external threat such as a virus before it can penetrate and damage an information system. The simplest form of firewall is the packet filter, which relies on a piece of hardware known as a router to filter packets between the internal network and an outside connection such as the Internet. It operates by examining the source address of each individual packet along with its destination address within the firewall. If something is suspicious or the source address is considered to be an "untrusted" or suspect site, it can refuse the packet's entry. Every computer connected to the Internet should be protected by a decent firewall program.

Antivirus software is also an essential component of any sound security architecture. This software scans a computer system for malicious code and notifies the user once it has been located. Some of the better programs delete that code and fix the infected file. This software works pretty well against known viruses, but new viruses evolve all the time and this requires the constant updating of antivirus programs.

Filtering systems can also be a helpful security mechanism. Software such as MIMESweeper can scan incoming mail for spam or for viruses while searching outgoing mail for sensitive corporate data that should not leave the confines of the organization. This software may increase security, but it also diminishes employee privacy, and the trade-off needs to be carefully weighed.

One way of ensuring the integrity of information transmitted over an open network is to encrypt that information. Through the use of encryption this information can be protected against interception and tampering. Data encryption has its roots in cryptography; that is, the use of ciphers or algorithms that allow someone to speak and be understood through secret code. When a message is encrypted, it is translated from its original form or plain text into an encoded, unintelligible form called ciphertext. Decryption, which is usually accomplished with a key, is the process of translating cipher text back into plain text.

The first encryption systems were symmetric; that is, the same key is used to encrypt and decrypt the data. In a simple encoding pattern the numbers 1 to 26 might represent the letters of the alphabet (1 = A, 2 = B, 3 = C, and so forth) so that the message 8-5-12-12-15 means "Hello." The "key" simply refers to the decoding pattern. In order for this method of encryption to work properly, both parties, the sender and the receiver of the data, must have access to this key. The key itself must then be communicated and maintained in a secure fashion or it could be intercepted by a third party and fall into the wrong hands. Another disadvantage of private-key cryptography is that even highly sophisticated codes, generated by algorithms, can be deciphered by computer systems when only one key is involved.

This problem was solved by cryptographers like Whitfield Diffie, who developed public-key cryptography, which divides the key into public and private parts. Each party gets a pair of keys, one public and one private; the public key is usually kept in a directory and is used to encrypt a message, while a secretive private key is available only to the recipient who uses it to decrypt the message. Public-key cryptography also provided a secure means of authenticating the sender of an electronic communication. The sender signs the message with his private key and the recipient uses the sender's public key to unlock that signature. The private key is used to decrypt and to sign messages, but it is never circulated.

In practice, the Secure Socket Layer (SSL) protocol is most often used in e-commerce transactions. SSL is used to encrypt data sent between Web browsers and Web servers. Thanks to SSL, data such as a credit card number can be exchanged through a secure conduit that will prevent would-be intruders from seeing or tampering with those data. SSL also authenticates the server so that users know that they are at the Web site they intended to visit.

In addition to encryption, online transactions can be more secure if identification of both parties is authenticated. Authentication refers to the process whereby a security system establishes the validity of an identification. This is normally accomplished through digital signatures, which have become vital for the integrity of electronic contracts. These signatures had an equivocal status until the passage of the Electronic Signatures in Global and National Commerce Act in June 2000. This law gives uniform national legal recognition to a digital signature, which now has the same force of law as its handwritten counterpart. The law also paves the way for records of transaction and contracts to be stored electronically.

According to the Electronic Signatures Act an electronic signature is defined as "an electronic sound, symbol, or process, attached to or logically associated with contract or record and executed or adopted by a person with the intent to sign the record." The law makes a distinction between *electronic* signatures, such as those included on a smart card or on a digital pad using biometric technology, and *digital* signatures. Electronic signatures do not involve the use of encryption. Digital signatures, on the other hand, include only those signatures that rely on encryption. Digital signatures are usually implemented by means of public-key cryptography. The sender who wants to enter an agreement with an online business uses a private key. The sender affixes his or her private key to a particular contract or document. The sender's public key, which is accessible to all, is then used by the enterprise to verify the signature. A certification authority (CA) is often used to authenticate the keys. The CA issues a certificate guaranteeing that the owner of the public and private keys is the same person.

While digital signatures are not foolproof, they can help to reduce fraud, since e-commerce firms will have verifiable information regarding the identity of those using their services. According to Fitzgerald (2000), "The use of digital signature technology clearly establishes the necessary evidence for the integrity of the electronic contract." There are questions about the timely adoption of this technology, however. Will consumers be motivated to begin taking advantage of encryption software? Will they take the time to register with a CA? One can also debate the merits of using asymmetric cryptography. But the Electronic Signatures Act goes a long way to heighten awareness of this technology and to provide a uniform standard that had been lacking.

Some of the architectures (such as encryption code) used to enhance security on the Internet can interfere with law-enforcement's efforts to deal with cybercrime and computer-related crime. Should laws trump code in this case so that government surveillance of communications is not impeded? The U.S. government's encryption controversy, chronicled in the next section, underscores the drawbacks of such a strategy.

EXPORT CONTROLS ON ENCRYPTION PRODUCTS

Although numerous encryption algorithms have been developed, one of the most popular commercial versions is the Data Encryption Standard (DES), which the government has utilized as its standard since 1977. The DES was originally created in the 1960s by IBM researchers, but it was modified by the National Security Agency (NSA) before being adopted as a standard. The DES is currently used in many electronic mail and networking packages and was recently recertified by the government in 1993.

The DES is a symmetric private-key cryptography system. As noted, this simply means that the same secret binary key is utilized for both encryption and decryption. Usually a different session key is used for each piece of communication, and each party must know the secret key. Keys are 56 bits long, so there are 2^{56} keys. The Electronic Frontier Foundation (EFF) estimates that a special-purpose computer costing about $200,000 could crack DES in fifty-six hours.

In addition, there is the Rivest–Shamir–Adelman (RSA) algorithm, created by the three individuals at MIT with these surnames. This public-key system was developed into a commercial product sold by RSA Data Security, Inc. With this system the public key is distributed to other parties, usually by posting it on a Web site. Messages encrypted with this public key can only be decrypted with a private key available only to the recipient. Other vendors besides RSA include a company called Network Associates (NAI), which bought the Pretty Good Privacy (PGP) public-key encryption program from its creator, Phil Zimmerman. PGP was considered to be a well-designed program offering virtually unbreakable 128-bit encryption, and NAI was convinced of the product's commercial viability.

The commercialization of cryptography, however, quickly caught the attention of the National Security Administration. In the late 1980s the NSA adamantly opposed the shipment of Lotus Notes abroad because it included a hybrid encryption scheme (RSA for the key exchange and DES for the encryption code). The NSA and other government agencies developed strict rules that forbade the export of strong encryption products like NAI's PGP. What was the government's concern?

While few governments aside from China and Russia restrict the domestic use of encryption by their citizens, many have sought to establish export controls. The U.S. government was apprehensive about the export of sophisticated encryption systems beyond a certain strength (as measured in keys). As a result, it either prohibited the export of certain products or asked for "back-door access"; that is, some form of control over exported public and private keys. The United States worried that international terrorists or bands of criminals would get their hands on an encryption system to which law-enforcement authorities did not have the key, and which therefore could not be decoded. It was concerned, therefore, that the proliferation of these systems would diminish its capacity for wire taps and surveillance, activities important for intelligence gathering and tracking the movements of terrorists. The NSA argued that in the long run an inability to decipher encrypted communications could imperil national security.

U.S. firms lobbied intensely for relaxation of these controls. They argued that this ban on exports could constrain the Internet economy and threaten America's world leadership in information technology. In their view, encryption export regulation was only hurting America's competitiveness abroad, while it did little to deter the dissemination of encryption products. American software companies either had to produce two products, one with strong encryption for the United States and weak encryption for international markets, or sell all of their products with weak encryption.

In a first concession to the inevitable diffusion of this technology, the NSA relented and the government began to allow the exporting of cryptographic software with 40-bit keys. However, while a key of this length will protect a user against the casual cybersnooper, professionals could easily crack it. Until recently, government agencies have continued to steadfastly resist the export of high-end encryption systems unless a back-door entry is provided. This might take the form of key escrow or some other methodology. Most of these methods, however, collided with privacy rights, and this has sparked numerous controversies. It is enlightening to review these proposals for back-door entry along with some of the criticisms that they have provoked, since the basic premise of this approach is still embraced by some law-enforcement authorities.

The Clipper Chip

The government's attempt to get control over encryption technology has its roots in its Clipper system, which was first proposed by the Clinton administration in 1993. The Clipper system, which was developed by the National Security Agency, was designed for the encryption of telephone or computer communications. The Clipper chip itself is a microprocessor with an encoded algorithm known as Skipjack. When two individuals using computer communications equipped with these Clipper-chip devices decide that they want to secure their communications, they activate those devices to exchange a packet of information called a LEAF (Law Enforcement Access Field). The LEAF includes a special session key that allows the callers to encode and decode the contents of the phone call. The LEAF also includes the chip's serial numbers. The FBI would have a universal family key that would decode the serial number but not the session key. Whenever the FBI was granted a legal warrant to wiretap, it could then extract from the LEAF the serial numbers of the clipper chips in usage.

As part of this plan the government would maintain in escrow the master key to each Clipper chip. The proposal was to have these unique numeric keys divided between two government agencies, which would effectively act as custodial agents. One agency would hold one half of a key and the other agency would hold the other half. Once the FBI has the proper serial number, they can request the two portions of the unique key from the respective government agencies holding them in escrow; each agency looks up the serial number provided by the FBI and provides its portion of the key corresponding to that number. The FBI combines the two halves of the key and this enables it to decode the session key in the LEAF along with the contents of the encrypted call.

The Clipper-chip proposal provoked enormous criticism and touched off a divisive debate. Security experts were quick to point out its many technical flaws, but for many civil libertarians this technology would come to symbolize the government's overzealousness and its lack of sensitivity to privacy rights. Barlow (1994) described Clipper as "a last ditch attempt . . . to establish imperial control over cyberspace."

But export controls and even Clipper did have some supporters, who feared what might happen if wiretapping became impossible thanks to hard-to-crack encryption technologies without any back doors. They appreciated the government's well-intentioned goal to prevent the spread of uncrackable encryption code. According to Levy (2001), "The ability to listen in on the world—with a vast multibillion-dollar network of secret satellites, radar installations, and ground sensors—was a pillar of U.S. defense policy." But from the government's perspective the free trade in encryption technology would put that policy in jeopardy.

Key Escrow and Key Recovery

After the demise of the Clipper chip proposal the U.S. government promptly issued a new encryption plan. It was called Key Management Infrastructure (KMI) and was launched in 1996. As part of the KMI plan the regulatory oversight of encryption products was transferred from the State Department to the Department of Commerce. This effectively put an end to the NSA's involvement in the process of crypto exports. Encryption technology was no longer regarded as a weapon, but as a tool of commerce.

KMI authorized a government infrastructure with key-recovery services. Encryption products of any strength could be exported as long as they had key-escrow accounts that were accessible by law-enforcement authorities. The government or a specially authorized private organization would hold the keys and provide them to those authorities on demand. KMI would be implemented by registering the keys with a key-escrow agent and having them digitally signed by certification authorities. Companies could now export 56-bit keys, provided that they complied with this plan for handling keys that exceeded 56 bits.

This key-escrow plan met with the same recalcitrant opposition from privacy advocates, Internet activists, and commercial interests. They remained troubled because the U.S. government would not abandon the requirement of key recovery. Privacy experts warned that the involvement of a neutral third party, the central administrator holding the escrowed keys, had the potential to make sensitive communications more vulnerable. The government's plan left many unanswered questions: How costly would it be to have this massive key-escrow system? Would such a system be scalable? How could circumvention of the key-escrow system be prevented? In general, there was consensus that key-access schemes were a bad idea.

Revised Encryption Regulations

In January 2000 the Clinton administration finally reversed its stand on tight export controls. It issued a set of new encryption regulations that represented a fundamental change in U.S. policy. This new approach to encryption control was based on three key principles:

1. technical review of encryption products prior to their sale abroad.
2. an expedited postexport reporting system.
3. review process for approving exports of strong encryption to foreign governments.

In the U.S. government's view these revised principles would help achieve balance between the competing interests of e-commerce and national security. The specific policy changes included the following:

- Any encryption commodity or software of any key length can now be exported to any nongovernment end user in any country (except the seven countries that support terrorism); it must first undergo an initial technical review.
- A new product category was established called "retail encryption commodities and software"; these retail encryption products of any key length can be exported to any end user (except in the seven state supporters of terrorism).
- "Encryption source code which is available to the public and which is not subject to an express agreement for the payment of a licensing fee or royalty for commercial production or sale of any product developed with the source code may be exported under a license exception without a technical review."

- Postexport reporting is required for exports of products with keys above 64 bits (unless they are finance specific). (Center for Democracy and Technology 2000)

Some civil liberties groups such as the ACLU voiced their discontent with the government's change of heart, claiming that it did not go far enough. There was concern that "while the new regulations appear to permit free postings of encryption source code to Internet discussion lists, these postings may be illegal if the author has 'reason to know' that they will be read by a person in one of the countries that are banned from receiving such material" (Harrison 2000).

Nonetheless, the U.S. policy reversal has been applauded by many countries throughout the world. Those countries have followed suit by relaxing their own export controls. For example, in April 2000 the European Union liberalized regulations for exporting data-encryption software in the fifteen European Union countries and in the United States. E.U. countries will no longer need to get approval from national licensing boards or a national security agency before exporting their products.

The new export policy appears to have resolved the encryption dilemma that dogged the Clinton administration throughout the 1990s. Worldwide use of encryption is the best method for safeguarding the security of individuals, corporations, and the information infrastructure itself. Complete decontrol of encryption exports, however, is inadvisable and the revised policy correctly forbids exporting encryption products to terrorist nations like Iraq. Also, we cannot neglect the security side of the equation and the abuse of this technology. Hence, it may be advisable to pass legislation that stiffens penalties for those who use encryption in the commission of a federal crime. Because of security implications the United States must stay in the forefront of encryption research; consequently, it would be beneficial to provide government funding to both the public and private sectors for further research. It is possible that in the post–September 11 era, export controls will be reconsidered, but the government should avoid the temptation to reverse this policy change.

INTERNET WIRETAPPING AND CARNIVORE

In the absence of encryption export controls and key-escrow systems, there are widespread fears that the U.S. government will turn to extraordinary surveillance measures in order to obtain information about criminal suspects. This brings us to the issue of Internet wiretaps and the deployment of other surveillance techniques by law-enforcement officials. To what extent should the Internet infrastructure allow or support these electronic surveillance architectures? Are these architectures susceptible to any unacceptable risks? How can we balance privacy rights with the need to monitor some digital communications in order to combat cybercrime, computer-related crime, and cyberterrorism? In order to answer these questions some historical perspective is essential.

The legality of wiretaps has a long and convoluted history in the United States. The first-known telephone wiretaps can be traced back to 1890. Since that time, telephone wiretapping has become a favorite tool of law-enforcement authorities. The Internet creates new threats and problems for law-enforcement officials. In a world where crime, like all other activities, is facilitated by digital technology, the ability to tap Internet communications seems indispensable.

Telephone or Internet wiretapping cannot be indiscriminate or undertaken on a whim by local police or federal authorities. The relevant legal principle is embodied in the Fourth Amendment, which protects citizens against unwarranted searches and seizure. This Amendment stipulates, "The right of the people to be secure in their persons, houses, papers, and effects, against unreasonable searches and seizures, shall not be violated." While the Fourth Amendment is a simple and hallowed right, its application to wiretapping is quite complex. In *Olmstead v. the United States* (277 U.S. 438 [1928]) the U.S. Supreme Court held that wiretaps did not violate the Fourth Amendment, since they did not amount to a physical search or a seizure of any property. But in *Katz v. the United States* (389 U.S. 347 [1967]) and *Berger v. New York* (388 U.S. 57 [1967]), this controversial decision was overturned. In the former case, Charles Katz was convicted of illegal gambling in a federal court based on evidence collected through a tap on his phone. He appealed, and ultimately the Supreme Court ruled that the evidence based on the wiretapped conversations was inadmissible; on that basis they threw out the conviction. This Supreme Court, unlike the Court that decided the *Olmstead* case, regarded electronic surveillance as the equivalent of search and seizure, so it was covered by the Fourth Amendment. According to the majority opinion in the *Katz* ruling, "The Fourth Amendment protects people, not places. What a person knowingly exposes to the public, even in his own home or office, is not a subject of Fourth Amendment protection. But what he seeks to preserve as private, even in an area accessible to the public, may be constitutionally protected."

Since the *Katz* decision it has been necessary to get a court-issued warrant in order to conduct a wiretap, and that wiretap must generally be of short duration and must be narrowly focused. Congress affirmed these rulings by adopting Title III of the Omnibus Crime Control and Safe Streets Act of 1968. This legislation requires a court order based on probable cause in order to engage in wiretapping.

While the *Katz* and *Berger* decisions are regarded as a great advancement for privacy rights, civil libertarians believe that the Supreme Court moved in the reverse direction in the case of *United States v. Miller* (425 U.S. 435 [1976]). In *Miller* the Court held that personal information provided to a third party loses its Fourth Amendment protection. As a result, if one's credit records are made available to law-enforcement authorities in the course of an investigation, they are no longer entitled to Fourth Amendment protection. Finally, in what some consider as another blow to privacy, in *Smith v. Maryland* (442 U.S. 750 [1979]) the Supreme Court held that the numbers one dials to make a phone call, data collected with a "pen register" device, are not protected under the auspices of the Constitution. According to Dempsey (2000), "While the Court was careful to limit the scope of its decision, and emphasized subsequently that pen registers collect only a very narrow range of information, the view has grown up that transactional data concerning communications is not constitutionally protected."

In the mid-1980s, as the computer revolution accelerated, Congress attempted to anticipate privacy problems that would surface due to new electronic technologies. In 1986 it passed the Electronic Communications Privacy Act (ECPA). The ECPA clarified that wireless communications were to be given the same protection as wireline telephone communications. It amended the federal wiretap law so that it would now apply to cellular telephones, electronic mail, and pagers. According to Dempsey (1997), "The ECPA made it a crime to knowingly intercept wireless communications and e-mail, but authorized law enforcement to do so with a warrant issued on probable cause." The ECPA also established more precise rules for the deployment of pen registers, which identify the numbers dialed in an outgoing call.

Under this statutory framework, law-enforcement officials have enough latitude to engage in electronic surveillance whenever they deem it necessary. Empirical evidence also supports this supposition: The number of wiretaps has increased steadily from 564 in 1980 to 1,350 in 1999 (Schwartz 2001b). According to Steinhardt (2000), "In the last reporting period, the Clinton Administration conducted more wiretaps in one year than ever in history, and the number of 'roving wiretaps' (wiretaps of any phone a target might use, without specifying a particular phone) nearly doubled."

Civil liberties groups believe that this trend of more wiretaps and increasing numbers of intercepted communications will intensify thanks to the advent of digital communications along with growing concerns about terrorism. There are particular worries about the FBI's new system, called Carnivore, an Internet wiretapping system. Carnivore is a packet sniffer that enables FBI agents working in conjunction with an ISP to intercept data passing to and from a criminal suspect. This monitoring close to the source of data transfers makes it easier to trace messages. The data are copied and then filtered to eliminate whatever information federal investigators are not entitled to examine. For the most part, Carnivore is used to track and log the senders and recipients of e-mail, so it functions primarily as a pen register or a "trap and trace" device (A pen register collects electronic impulses that identify the numbers dialed for outgoing calls and a trap and trace device collects the originating number for incoming calls). The threshold for court approval for such wiretaps is low, since investigators need only demonstrate that the information has relevance for their investigation. According to Schwartz (2001), the FBI believes that Carnivore's value lies in its ability to be less inclusive than predecessor wiretapping technologies: "Agents can fine-tune the system to yield only the sources and recipients of the suspect's e-mail traffic, providing Internet versions of the phone-tapping tools that record the numbers dialed by a suspect and the numbers of those calling in."

Nonetheless, this sort of surreptitious surveillance exemplified by the FBI's Carnivore technology has provoked the ire of civil libertarians. For example, the Electronic Frontier Foundation objects to Carnivore because the use of packet sniffers on the Internet captures more information than the use of pen registers and trap and trace devices used for traditional telephone wiretapping. In Internet communications the contents of messages and sender–recipient header data are not separate. According to the EFF (2000), even though Carnivore will be filtering out unwanted e-mail and other communications information, "The Carnivore system appears to exacerbate the over collection of personal information by collecting more information than it is legally entitled to collect under traditional pen register and trap and trace laws."

In response to these criticisms, the FBI explains that it relies on a complex and finely tuned filtering system that selects messages based on criteria expressly set out in the court order. Thus, it will not intercept all e-mail messages, but only those transmitted to and from a particular account. If, for example, Joe is a Carnivore target who e-mails three companions, Mike, Nancy, and George, and the FBI is interested only in his communications with George, the communication with Mike and Nancy will be filtered out. It appears, however, that those messages that are intercepted do include content as well as the sender and recipient addresses.

Another problem for civil libertarians is the trustworthiness of the FBI. The FBI claims that it will only record e-mail communications to which it is entitled by the court order. But there is no way to ensure their compliance. It has access to a massive stream of communications over an ISP's network, and no one, including the ISP, will be able to verify which information is intercepted. According to the ACLU, this type of surveillance constitutes a repudiation of the Fourth Amendment, which has been based on the premise "that the Executive cannot be trusted with carte blanche authority when it conducts a search" (Steinhardt 2000).

There are indeed good reasons to be unnerved by Carnivore. The initial scope of surveillance—the entire stream of communications of an ISP's clients—is truly unprecedented. The proximity to all of these data near their source (the ISP) and lack of oversight clearly creates the potential for abuse. Moreover, the FBI's poor track record in recent years, such as its inability to detect spying within its own ranks and its failure to hand over all of the evidence in the trial of the Oklahoma City bomber, Timothy McVeigh, have not inspired the public's confidence in its discretion and ability.

Civil liberties groups have also expressed dismay regarding the FBI's heavy-handed approach to the implementation of a law passed in 1994 known as the Communications Assistance for Law Enforcement Act (CALEA). According to this law,

> A telecommunications carrier shall ensure that its equipment, facilities, or services . . . are capable of expeditiously isolating and enabling the government, pursuant to a court order or other lawful authorization, to intercept, to the exclusion of other communications, all wire and electronic communications carried by the carrier within [its] service area.

The thrust of this regulation is that telephone companies must redesign their telecommunications infrastructure so that law-enforcement officials will continue to have the capability to engage in surveillance and wiretaps. Such redesign might be necessitated by new technologies that could impede interception of communications. One problem with CALEA has been the FBI's peremptory insistence that this legislation mandates that phone companies build in capabilities that exceed traditional interception procedures. For example, they insist that wireless service providers have location tracking capability built into their systems. Clearly, this poses another new threat to privacy. As Dempsey (1997) points out, the FBI will continue to dominate the implementation process and ignore privacy concerns "unless the other government institutions exercise the authority granted them under the statute to promote the counterbalancing values of privacy and innovation."

Nonetheless, the FBI and other federal law-enforcement officials are entrusted with safeguarding national security and public safety and September 11 reminds us of the need for a heightened security consciousness. Hence, there is a need for responsible surveillance and wiretapping on the Internet that respects the delicate balance between order and liberty. If Carnivore is to be retained by the FBI, there must be more public oversight of its various uses. It may be necessary for Congress to raise the standard for the use of pen registers on the Internet, given the difficulty of separating origin and destination addresses from the content of e-mail communications. Also, there is no national reporting requirement for pen register court orders (as there is for wiretaps), and this too must be changed. There needs to be more publicity and accountability about the collection of these data. These and other measures will be essential if the integrity of the Fourth Amendment is to be preserved in the face of technologies like Carnivore.

Finally, the need for convergence is acute. We now have a patchwork approach to surveillance rules, with different standards for telephone, cable, and other communication systems. For example, according to the Cable Act of 1984 there is a high burden for government agencies to meet when requesting permission to monitor computers that use cable modems. The act also requires that the target of the surveillance be provided an opportunity to challenge the request. It would clearly be preferable to have one standard for all of these technologies, and that standard should give judges greater discretion over the process of granting requests for surveillance and wiretaps.

ANONYMITY AND DIGITAL IDENTITY

One of the biggest security problems for the Net is the fact that individuals and organizations can still misrepresent themselves with impunity. At present, there is no uniform system or mechanism for identifying users who frequent cyberspace. The Internet does support architectures that facilitate identification, such as password protections, biometric systems, and digital certificates. It is still quite possible for users to interact in cyberspace anonymously, and it can be difficult to trace the real identity of users who are deliberately trying to conceal their identity. While anonymity supports privacy and free-speech rights, it also interferes with security and the curtailment of cybercrime. Hence, the lack of an identifying infrastructure has sometimes been detrimental for electronic commerce and for effective law enforcement in the realm of cyberspace.

The interconnected issues of digital identity and anonymity are highly charged ones that stir deep emotions. This was evidenced by the heated response to Intel Corporation's announcement in February 1999 about its plan to embed identification numbers in its next generation of computer chips, the Pentium IIIs. The primary purpose of the embedded serial numbers was to authenticate a user's identity in e-mail communications, enhance security for electronic commerce by reducing the risk of fraud, and allow organizations to better track their computer equipment. Privacy advocates, on the other hand, argued that this unique identifier would enable direct marketers and others to surreptitiously track a user's meandering through various Web sites. While Intel capitulated to this intense pressure and agreed to ship its products with the serial numbers turned off, the incident seemed to elevate awareness about the tenuous future of electronic anonymity. Also, the incorporation of identity features into chip technology has not been abandoned by Intel.

Despite Intel's quick response, there is growing anxiety that these serial numbers are "harbingers of a trend toward ever more invasive surveillance networks" (Markoff 1999a). What if governments throughout the world attempt to mandate the deployment of such invasive identifying numbers in order to keep better track of their respective citizens? According to security expert Vernor Vinge, "The ultimate danger is that the government will mandate that each chip will have a special logic added to track identities in cyberspace" (Markoff 1999a).

The Intel incident also graphically illustrates the difficult dilemma faced by policy makers involving an unavoidable trade-off between security and anonymity or privacy. Security and anonymity seem to be mutually exclusive goods. If we really want to make the Internet a more secure environment it is necessary to suppress anonymous transactions and hold users accountable for what they say and what they do. For example, thanks to a tracking mechanism installed in Microsoft's Office software, the rogue programmer who released the destructive Melissa virus was swiftly apprehended. But the cost of security and better accountability is a loss of privacy and perhaps the termination of untraceable Internet communications.

But why is anonymity worth preserving? Perhaps cyberspace is not a place where one should be allowed to operate in secrecy. However, in the United States the First Amendment right to free speech has always included the right to speak anonymously. In the Supreme Court decision of *New York Times v. Sullivan* (376 U.S. 254 [1964]) the Court stated that "an author's decision to remain anonymous . . . is an aspect of freedom of speech protected by the First Amendment." This has been affirmed in several key court decisions, such as *McIntyre v. Ohio Elections Commission* (115 S. Ct. 1511 [1995]), where the U.S. Supreme Court affirmed the right to conduct anonymous political leafleting. In a more recent and relevant case that involved the Internet, *American Civil Liberties Union v. Miller* (977 F. Supp. 1228 N.D. Ga. [1997]), a federal court in Atlanta voided a Georgia law that outlawed anonymous online communications. An elaboration of the legal rationale behind these decisions is beyond the scope of this discussion, but these consistent judgments reflect a deep-seated respect for the value of anonymity.

There are a number of cogent reasons why anonymous free expression deserves strong legal protection. Social intolerance may require some individuals to rely on anonymity to communicate openly about an embarrassing medical condition, an awkward disability, or even their sexual preference. Whistleblowers may be understandably reluctant to come forward with valuable information unless they can remain anonymous. And political dissent even in a democratic society that prizes free speech may be impeded unless it can be done anonymously. Anonymity then has an incontestable value in the struggle against repression or in social situations where tolerance appears to be in short supply.

Similarly, anonymity is important for the sake of privacy. Recall that Gavison's (1984) definition of privacy included three key elements: secrecy (or confidentiality), solitude, and anonymity. In other words, individuals can lose their privacy when information becomes known about them, when others gain physical proximity to them, and when they become the subject of another's attention. According to Gavison, "Attention alone will cause loss of privacy even if no new information becomes known." If all of my movements in cyberspace become "traceable" it will be possible for someone to ascertain to whom I have sent electronic mail, which Web sites I have visited, and so forth. Clearly, this loss of anonymity is tantamount to an invasion of privacy, since this information can thrust one into compromising situations. Without the ability to remain anonymous in some contexts on the Internet, my privacy rights will be potentially undermined every time I connect, since I could become subject to this sort of unwanted surveillance as I travel through cyberspace. As Nissenbaum (1997) observes, this loss of "privacy in public" is a serious matter, and hence we must "conceptualize privacy in ways that would extend even to public surveillance."

Thus, while there is a cost to preserving anonymity, its central importance in human affairs is certainly beyond dispute. From a moral perspective, it is a positive good, and it is valued as highly instrumental in helping to realize two other goods that are vital for human fulfillment, freedom and privacy.

Anonymous communication in cyberspace is enabled largely through the use of anonymous remailers in conjunction with cryptography. A brief word about these is in order. According to Lohr (1999), an anonymous remailer functions like a "technological buffer." It strips off the identifying information on an e-mail message and substitutes an anonymous code or a random number. By encrypting a message and then routing that message through a series of anonymous remailers a user can rest assured that his or her message will remain anonymous and confidential. This process is known as "chained remailing." The process is quite effective, because none of the remailers will have the key to read the encrypted message, neither the recipient nor any remailers (except the first) in the chain can identify the sender, and the recipient cannot connect the sender to the message unless every single remailer in the chain cooperates. This would assume that each remailer kept a log of their ingoing and outgoing mail, and that is highly unlikely.

According to Froomkin (1996), this technique of chained remailing is about as close as we can come on the Internet to "untraceable anonymity"; that is, "a communication for which the author is simply not identifiable at all." If someone clandestinely leaves a bunch of political pamphlets in the town square with no identifying marks or signatures, that communication is also characterized by untraceable anonymity. In cyberspace things are a bit more complicated, and even the method of chained remailing is not foolproof: If the anonymous remailers join together in some sort of conspiracy to reveal someone's identity there is not much anyone can do to preserve anonymity.

There are other anonymizing tools that do not rely on the use of multiple intermediaries such as chained remailing. Instead, the user relies on one intermediary to protect his or her anonymity. The company known as Zero-Knowledge makes available a product called Freedom 2.0. This product provides firewall protection to keep the network secure, filters cookies, and allows users to work with pseudonymous digital identities.

Anonymous communication, of course, whether facilitated by remailers or by other means, does have its drawbacks. It can be abused by criminals or terrorists who seek to communicate anonymously in order to plot their crimes. It also permits cowardly users to communicate without civility or to libel someone without accountability and with little likelihood of apprehension by law-enforcement authorities. Anonymity can also be useful for revealing trade secrets or violating other intellectual property protections. In general, secrecy and anonymity are not beneficial for society if they are used improperly. According to Brin (1998), "Anonymity is the darkness behind which most miscreants—from mere troublemakers all the way to mass murderers and would-be tyrants—shelter in order to wreak harm, safe against discovery or redress by those they abuse."

Thus, anonymity can be exploited for many forms of mischief. There are concerns about anonymity abuses from both the private and public sectors. In the private sector there are worries about libel, fraud, and theft, while the state is worried about the use of anonymity to launder money, to evade taxes, to manipulate securities markets, and so forth. Hence, there is the temptation for governments or even digital infrastructure providers, such as ISPs or companies like Intel and Microsoft, to develop and utilize architectures that will make Internet users more accountable and less able to hide behind the shield of anonymity.

In response to these concerns, there are several options available for more comprehensive digital identity systems. The most thorough system would ensure that there is always an indissoluble link between one's cyberspace identity and one's real identity. This is accomplished by somehow mandating the traceability of all Internet transactions. As we have illustrated, the use of technologies such as chained remailers helps protect anonymous communications so that they are untraceable. But what mechanisms might be adopted to mandate traceability; that is, to make the untraceable traceable? One way to achieve mandatory traceability is to demand a user's identification as a precondition of Internet access. For example, traceability could be facilitated by technology; that is, by means of a digital identity architecture that would prevent users from accessing the Internet unless they properly identify themselves. The government might also implement such a system by law, by requiring that all ISPs demand verifiable identification as a prerequisite for access to the Internet. There are many variations on these two broad approaches. According to Covell, Gordon, and Kovacks (1998),

> The basic idea behind any system of mandatory traceability is that speakers entering cyberspace would be required to deposit (e.g., with the ISP), or attach to their communications, a means of tracing their identities. One can conceptualize mandatory traceablity by positing a regime in which an encrypted fingerprint automatically would be attached to *every* transaction in cyberspace. In such a regime, the fingerprint could be encrypted with the government's public key such that properly authorized law enforcement officials could access the private key necessary for decryption while participants in the cyber-transaction would not be able to strip away the speaker's anonymity. (emphasis added)

Digital certificate technology could also play some role in the development of such an identity infrastructure. It would provide a feasible method of authenticating individuals and verifying the integrity of their transmissions. Recall that digital certificates allow individuals or organizations that use the

Internet to verify each other's identity. They can function as an electronic version of a passport but without the drawbacks of a physical document. These certificates are normally issued by certificate authorities and are based on public-key cryptography. CAs certify that a particular public key is associated with a particular user, and this establishes an electronic identity for that user. In other words, it binds a public key of an individual to his or her true identity. Within a Public Key Infrastructure (PKI) digital certificates are issued as follows: The subscriber provides proof of identity to the Registration Authority (RA) which verifies that identity and informs the Certificate Authority (CA). The CA generates and signs the subscriber's unique certificate. The CA then transmits the private certificate to the subscriber and posts the public certificate in the repository (Higgins 2000). If user X (the certificate holder) wants to communicate securely with user Y, he or she sends his or her digital certificate and uses his or her private key to authenticate the communication. User Y verifies the name on that certificate by applying a copy of the public key held in the CA's repository. According to Garfinkel and Spafford (1997), while not tamper proof, "Digital certificates are a substantially more secure way of having people identify themselves than the alternative: usernames and passwords." It seems evident that these certificates can form the basis of a digital identification system. How that might work is a matter of some complexity, but one possibility is that a digital certificate would be necessary to complete any online transaction or transmission. Thus, this electronic identity certificate would become the basis for all of a user's online communications and transactions. Certificates with pseudonyms could be used (in order to protect one's identity at a Web site or for some other reason), but the CA would need to know the user's real identity and log any transactions completed by the pseudonym so that the user could be identified if necessary.

It should come as no surprise that the adoption of digital certificates is not without controversy. While they may safeguard against fraud and other crimes on the Net, these certificates also imperil privacy. Depending upon exactly how they are implemented, digital certificates will permit the traceability and linkability of a user's transactions. All of an individual's communications and transactions become easily traceable if they have been verified by a digital certificate, and this implies that a profile could be constructed based on the aggregation of those transactions. Also, according to a Zero Knowledge White Paper (2000), "Each verifier can store all of the certificates presented to it, and can link them on the basis of their key holder identifiers, public keys, or CA signatures. Different verifiers can exchange and link their data on the same basis. Furthermore, all the dossiers compiled by linking and tracing the actions of participants in one PKI can be tied to the dossiers compiled in other PKIs." One other problem is that certificate holders have no control over these data after a transaction is consummated.

There are, of course, other technical frameworks or protocols that provide for authentication and identification in less draconian ways than systems that mandate the traceability of all transactions. These frameworks will make anonymity more difficult but not impossible. Microsoft's Hailstorm protocol, which is part of its new XP operating system, will include a "digital wallet" with a person's address and credit card numbers, as well as authentication of the individual's identity. The use of the digital wallet should help to streamline online shopping and prevent fraud. Windows XP also comes with Passport, which authenticates a user's ID when any Net Web service is accessed (e.g., Net travel service). User data will be stored on Microsoft servers, and the company's access to all of these data would seem to create a privacy hazard. New Internet standards will also create obstacles for anonymous transactions. Unlike the current version of Internet Protocol (IPV4), the new version, IPV6, would prevent hackers from creating phony return addresses on data packets. The ability to falsify a return address has made denial-of-service attacks much harder to trace, but IPV6 will mark each packet with a secure encryption key that presumably cannot be falsified by hackers.

Zero-Knowledge Systems offers a privacy-enhancing product known as Private Credentials, which allows for identity verification without the privacy pitfalls of digital certificates. For a Private Credential, "The CA's signature binds the individual's public key to one or more attributes. For instance, a demographic credential can specify its owner's age, income, marital status, and residence, all neatly tied to a single public key, by means of one digital signature of the CA" (Zero Knowledge White Paper 2000). Thanks to clever mathematical algorithms, this architecture leaves room for anonymity; different actions involving the same Private Credential cannot be traced to the Private Credential holder, and Private Credential can be shown in such a way that the verifying organization has no mathematical evidence of the transaction. Also, individuals can use different "copies" of the same Private Credential to avoid the linkability problem associated with digital certificates. While this architecture is immensely complicated, it may provide a model for how code itself can prevent identity fraud while preserving a user's privacy and anonymity.

Passport, IPV6, Private Credential, and other protocols coming along are all designed to thwart identity fraud. As long as they do not infringe privacy rights and as long as they do not completely preclude the possibility of anonymous interactions, these systems might be acceptable. On the other hand, proposed architectures for mandatory traceability of all Internet transactions, whether implemented by infrastructure providers or imposed by governments, are irresponsible and should be resisted. Authentication and identification architectures must leave open the possibility for anonymous communication like anonymous e-mail through chained remailers. Communications on the Internet should certainly be traceable in some circumstances, and e-commerce sites have every right to authenticate transactions in order to prevent fraud, but responsible architectures for identification and authentication will not create privacy hazards, and they will not deliberately or inadvertently foreclose opportunity for online anonymous expression. Thus, code does have a valid role to play in enhancing online security and in improving our ability to reliably establish our digital identities. But it must do so in a way that manifests respect for the values of privacy and anonymous free speech.

Finally, it should be remarked that there is surely room for the state to play a modest role in regulating digital identity by passing laws that increase criminal penalties for the theft of someone else's identity and other forms of identity fraud. Such legislation should hold the perpetrator liable for any injuries caused by their irresponsible action. Governments may also want to offer appropriate guidelines to the free market as it grapples with this problem and begins to demand the use of identity verifiers such as digital certificates for certain transactions. There are many other reasonable measures the state can take to circumscribe identity fraud and related crimes without implementing a large-scale digital identity infrastructure, which is likely to have a corrosive effect on privacy rights.

POSTSCRIPT: SECURING TRUST ONLINE

In Chapter 4 we briefly alluded to the correlation between trust and the long-term success of e-commerce business models such as B2B marketplaces. Can this trust be realized through more secure systems that incorporate sophisticated encryption and other protective technologies? Or is trust more elusive, a tenuous goal not easily achieved on the Internet, which seems vulnerable no matter how much commercial vendors boast about improved security? After all, the Internet remains a far-flung and loose network with no central authority working to make it more secure. If there is a "trust gap" between the public's expectations and the Internet's capabilities, how can it be addressed?

Certainly, security is part of the answer, and online vendors must be scrupulous about implementing state-of-the-art security systems. They must have sound policies and devote adequate resources to security. The panoply of technologies discussed in this chapter, such as digital signatures, encryption, firewalls, software filters, and private credential-type architectures, all help to make the Net a stable and trustworthy environment, one that is more resistant to hostile attacks. Fortified with these technologies, e-commerce sites have a chance to fight off illegitimate access, DoS attacks, and other security breaches.

Companies like Visa, which have invested in security resources, have enviable information-security requirements that will help breed trust among their customers and clients. All of their e-commerce clients must comply with this set of security requirements, which "include obvious steps such as implementing a firewall, but also include more far-reaching goals such as encrypting stored credit-card data, encrypting data sent across networks, and testing security systems and processes daily" (Levitt 2001).

While security is important, there are obvious caveats about putting too much faith in secured systems to close the widening "trust gap." The challenge, of course, is to make the Internet less vulnerable without using intrusive means that curb freedoms and infringe on privacy rights. There is a need for balance and proportionality; otherwise, security will be realized at the expense of these worthy values. If the architectures of control overprotect the Net and smother it in security protocols, there will be no basis for transactions or relationships based on trust.

Thus, we must realize that security mechanisms will never give us the complete answer. The Internet experience will be attenuated if we aim for and achieve exceedingly high security goals. As Nissenbaum (1999) writes, "The cost of a perfectly secure cyberspace is a limiting and constraining of what people can do online, the range and nature of activities allowed to them, the freedoms they can experience, and the complexity of relationships the community can build."

We seem to be confronted, therefore, with another painful trade-off. If we want to preserve open, decentralized structures with free-form communities and anonymous digital expression, we will have to sacrifice safety and security. But if we insist on tighter security, such as mandated digital identity, the Internet's freedom-enhancing attributes and broad functionality will be impaired. The prevalence of such tight security, however, will by no means ensure that the Internet is a more trusting environment.

Security architectures are only one element of a complex formula for achieving real trust in the online world. The study conducted by the National Research Council's Committee on Information Systems Trustworthiness (1999), *Trust in Cyberspace*, adopts a rather narrow perspective, since the vision presented here equates a trustworthy system with one that is technically secure. Trustworthy systems alone, however, do not lead to trust, which also depends on the intentions and good faith of those moral agents with whom we interact in cyberspace. According to Nissenbaum (1999), "Although trust is related to a pattern of relevant past experiences in an obvious way—positive experiences generally breeding trust, betrayals breeding distrust—the intentions and motivations of the other party can affect the way these experiences are interpreted."

As we have been at pains to insist throughout this book, the key to making the Internet a trusting and humane environment, a true community or virtual polis, is not government regulations or Internet architectures, but responsible moral agency. The Internet's numerous and dispersed stakeholders must strive for that practical wisdom (*phronesis*) described by Aristotle, which gives them discernment and clear-sightedness in judging what is compatible with the common good of the Internet and the interests of others who use the Internet. To be endowed with *phronesis* one cannot care only for oneself; rather, one must have a sense of measure concerning private transactions as well as the public matters of the Internet. Without such prudent behavior, authentic trust will always be beyond our reach, no matter how well we "protect" this vast digital frontier.

REFERENCES

Barlow, J. (1994). "Jackboots on the Infobahn." *Wired*, April, 40.

Brin, W. (1998). *The Transparent Society*. Reading, Mass.: Addison-Wesley.

Center for Democracy and Technology. (2000). "Fact Sheet: Administration Implements Updated Encryption Export Policy." Available: http://www.cdt.org/crypto/admin

Committee on Information Systems Trustworthiness (National Research Council). (1999). *Trust in Cyberspace*, edited by F. Schneider. Washington, D.C.: National Academy Press.

Covell, P., Gordon, S., and Kovacks, J. (1998). "Digital Identity in Cyberspace." Available: http://cyberharvard.edu/itac98/whitepaper.htm

Dempsey, J. (1997). "Communication Privacy in the Digital Age: Revitalizing the Federal Wiretap Laws to Enhance Privacy." *Albany Law Journal of Science and Technology* 8: 43.

Dempsey, J. (2000). "The Fourth Amendment and the Internet." Testimony before the Subcommittee on the Constitution of the House Judiciary Committee, 6 April.

Electronic Frontier Foundation. (2000). "The Fourth Amendment and Carnivore." Testimony before the House Judiciary Committee on the Constitution, 28 July.

Fitzgerald, A. (2000). *Going Digital 2000: Legal Issues for E-Commerce, Software and the Internet*. St. Leonard's, Australia: Prospect Media.

Froomkin, M. (1996). "Flood Control on the Information Ocean: Living with Anonymity, Digital Cash, and Distributed Data Bases." *University of Pittsburgh Journal of Law and Commerce* 395: 245.

Garfinkel, S., and Spafford, G. (1997). *Web Security and Commerce*. Cambridge: O'Reilly.

Gavison, R. (1984). "Privacy and the Limits of the Law." *Yale Law Review* 89: 421.

Hamilton, D., and Cloud, D. (2000). "The Internet under Siege: Stalking the Hackers." *Wall Street Journal*, 10 February, B1, B6.

Harrison, A. (2000). "Civil Liberties Groups Slam Encryption Export Rules." *Computerworld*, 17 January, 10.

Higgins, K. (2000). "Few and Far Between." *Internetweek*, 6 November, 69–70.

Levitt, J. (2001). "Security—The Enemy Within." *Information Week*, 23 April, 67–72.

Levy, S. (2001). *CRYPTO*. New York: Viking Press.

Lohr, S. (1999). "Privacy on the Internet Poses Legal Puzzle." *New York Times*, 19 April.

Markoff, J. (1999a). "Growing Compatibility Issues: Computers and User Privacy." *New York Times*, 3 March, C1.

Markoff, J. (1999b). "Illness Becomes Apt Metaphor for Computers." *New York Times*, 13 June, A18.

Nissenbaum, H. (1997). "Can We Protect Privacy in Public." Computer Ethics Philosophical Enquiry Proceedings 1997, edited by J. van den Hoven. ACM/SIGCAS Conference, 191–204.

Nissenbaum, H. (1999). "Can Trust Be Secured Online? A Theoretical Perspective." Available: http://www.univ.triest.it/-dipfilo/etica_e_politica/1999_2/nissen baum.html

Schwartz, J. (2001a). "Cyberspace Seen as Potential Battleground." *New York Times*, 23 November, B5.

Schwartz, J. (2001b). "Fighting Crime Online: Who Is in Harm's Way?" *New York Times*, 8 February, E1.

Steinhardt, B. (2000). "Statement of Barry Steinhardt, Associate Director of the ACLU, on the Fourth Amendment and Carnivore before the House Judiciary Committee on the Constitution," 24 July. Available: http://www.aclu.org/congress

Tavani, H. (2001). "Defining the Boundaries of Computer Crime: Piracy, Break-Ins, and Sabotage in Cyberspace." In *Readings in Cyberethics*, edited by R. Spinello and H. Tavani. Sudbury, Mass.: Jones and Bartlett.

Yasin, R. (2000). "Cyberterrorists Crash Web Party." *Internetweek*, 14 February, 12.

Zero Knowledge Systems, Inc. (2000). White Paper: "Private Credentials." Available: http://www.ZKS.net

10

Epilogue

We have covered much territory in this book, and this brief concluding chapter will give us an opportunity to climb to higher ground to see how far we have come. We began this journey with an overview of the Internet's positive attributes, such as its democratic ethos and the openness of its architecture. The Net can still provide a horizontal, inexpensive channel of communication, a global soapbox to almost anyone with a personal computer. The Internet is also a remarkable catalyst for innovation and creativity. It decentralizes the creative process, and it destroys distance, allowing people to communicate instantly across cities and countries. But the Internet of the present is not necessarily the Internet of the future, since this universal, global network has no fixed or immutable nature. There is no guarantee that positive features such as the Net's prodemocracy consequences will endure. We now realize that those sounding the death knell for the state's sovereignty have been premature in their prophecy about the government's impotence in cyberspace. As a report by the Carnegie Endowment for International Peace concluded, "The diffusion of the Internet does not necessarily spell the demise of authoritarian rule" ("The Internet's New Borders" 2001). As countries try to get control of certain activities on the Internet through enforcing local laws and introducing new architectures (like geolocation software), there is a danger that the Internet will become increasingly balkanized and subjected to distinctively antidemocratic values.

What prompts the state's concern and intervention are the detrimental effects of Internet interactions that plague cyberspace. Offensive forms of expression like pornography and hate speech, the dilution of traditional protections for intellectual property thanks to programs like Napster, a steady loss of privacy, these are some of the social ills we encounter in cyberspace. There are less-obvious negative effects, such as the political polarization that can occur when individuals go too far in filtering and tailoring their information sources. What can be done about these social harms? Can we do anything to solve the pervasiveness of pornography or the incessant dissemination of spam? Some states have taken decisive action, and others, like France, have overreacted to these problems. Recall the ruling by a French judge to forbid the auction of Nazi memorabilia on Yahoo's Web sites to French users. That ruling sets a dangerous precedent, since one local jurisdiction is imposing its rules across the entire Internet.

In the Yahoo case the cure seems worse than the ailment. Perhaps the libertarians are right when they argue for a hands-off approach to many of these problems. Perhaps government should have no sovereignty in cyberspace? This unnuanced viewpoint, however, fails to see that regulation of some sort is probably inevitable. It will most likely come from different sources, such as software code, but the effects will be the same. Also, some level of regulation and control is essential, since the alternative is an anarchic environment where fraud and other asocial behavior could get the upper hand.

The dilemma is how to preserve the positive attributes of the Net while responsibly curtailing its more egregious social harms. How do we achieve the right interaction between technology and policy so that the Internet does not lose its promise as a liberating technology of borderless free markets? As Levy (1995) observes, "One of the great conflicts in civilization will be the attempt to reorder society, culture, and government in a manner that exploits this digital bonanza yet prevents it from running roughshod over the checks and balances so delicately constructed in those palmy pre-computer years."

It becomes evident that one cannot make informed judgments about the regulation of cyberspace without understanding the technology of cyberspace. As discussed in Chapter 2, it is vital to appreciate the history and evolution of the Internet's technology, since that technology expresses social values such as freedom and openness. Its earliest features embodied the military's need for a survivable network: "flexibility, absence of a command center, and maximum autonomy of each node" (Castells 2001). If we alter the Net's technology in certain ways, we change its value structure. The key design principle at the heart of the Net's construction is known as end-to-end, and it has unquestionably promoted the Net's free-wheeling and spontaneous innovation. End-to-end simply means that the intelligence is not built into the network itself but is placed at the endpoints. The network's only function is to move packets from one place to the next. According to this principle, the Net is competitively neutral with respect to content, so it treats all packets in the same manner.

There is little substance to the Internet beyond its basic protocols, such as TCP/IP, but those protocols and the software programs layered upon them have a tremendous impact on the Internet's basic character. It would be difficult to exaggerate the central importance of the insight that in cyberspace "code is law." Lessig and others have developed this notion that computer software code such as filters or privacy protocols can have a significant regulatory impact. Software developers can write programs that respect privacy rights or programs like cookies that minimize those rights by tracking and monitoring users online without their knowledge or permission. In cyberspace code may be a more important constraint on behavior than law, the market, or community norms.

Beyond any doubt, while code can control certain social harms or protect privacy, it can also yield deleterious consequences. Filters can suppress free expression and geolocation protocols can lead to new barriers and virtual fences. However, code can be a tenable way to help solve these social harms as long as it is designed and used responsibly. We must learn how to build and deploy code with moral competence. There is good reason to be worried about the sovereignty of technology unless the development of that technology is guided by ethical principles and a respect for the rights and interests of others.

Further, while code can sometimes be a surrogate for the law, it does not replace the law. Most regulatory solutions will involve some interaction of policy and architecture: The issue is what's the right mix, and which constraint takes priority. Of course, we must also emphasize the central role of ethics in all of this. Permanent moral values, grounded in our common human nature, should guide the development of code and law, determine the cybercommunity's norms, and serve as a limiting force on marketplace interactions.

From an economic perspective we can characterize many of the problems in cyberspace as market failures; that is, as negative externalities, costs imposed involuntarily on others. When massive volumes of spam are transmitted by irresponsible corporations or individuals the costs are borne involuntarily by ISPs, by the recipients, and by other Internet stakeholders who suffer because the Net's "pipes" are clogged with useless e-mail. Government intervention in order to fix these failures can sometimes create value, but it is not a foregone conclusion that all market failures are best solved by government intervention. We reject Pigou's (1962) conclusion: "Where there is reason to believe that the free play of self-interest will cause an amount of resources to be invested different from the amount that is required in the best interest of the national dividend, there is a *prima facie* case for public intervention." Sometimes the transaction costs of government intervention are excessive. We cannot assume that government intervention will be free from imperfections and inefficiencies. At the same time, waiting for market forces to equitably resolve these problems is unacceptable, since the market is often not the best forum for addressing social problems.

According to the Coasian theorem, it is preferable to rely on private solutions to these failures if rights are clearly assigned and transaction costs are not a factor. We can adapt this insight to cyberspace. Some social harms in cyberspace can be resolved by private parties without high transaction costs thanks to the power of code. If filters or similar technologies function properly, concerned parents or schools can control offensive content without the need for intrusive government regulation like CHIPA. This will not work, however, unless these architectures of control are developed and used conscientiously. Ethical self-regulation facilitated by code is preferable to reliance on the visible hand of government or the invisible hand of the market.

Thus, we have sought to make the case in this book that the optimal modality of regulation for many of the social ills in cyberspace is the ethical use of code, and we have attempted to provide some insight into how code can be used and designed in accordance with fundamental ethical principles. We contend that this regime of self-regulation, focused on solving problems at the ends (that is, at the level of the end user), will tend to preserve the Internet's original e2e philosophy and basic value structure better than many other alternatives.

However, this model does not imply that government intervention is always counterproductive or superfluous. When there are broad infrastructure issues at stake, such as open access or interoperability, or when a corporation like Microsoft engages in defensive monopolization that could harm innovation, there may be no alternative other than reliance on the government. In these situations end users do not have the tools or the wherewithal to resolve such market failures. For example, government intervention may be needed to preserve the Net's core values such as those embodied in its end-to-end principle. As argued in Chapter 5, regulations imposed on the AOL–Time Warner merger seem appropriate in order to preserve open access and competitive neutrality. Government regulators must be particularly sensitive to infrastructure providers who control all three layers of the information infrastructure: the physical, logical, and content layers. As this infrastructure grows in significance the struggle for ownership and for access control could become a struggle for the Net's basic liberties. Consequently, the need for measured government involvement is imperative.

On the other hand, other social harms can be handled with less emphasis on regulation and more reliance on responsibly designed architectures. In this regard we considered four main areas of social concern, beginning with the issue of free expression. Although the Internet makes possible ample opportunities for expression, there are also offensive forms of speech: pornography, hate speech, threatening speech, and spam. In the United States regulatory attempts to deal with online pornography have been misguided and futile. However, the architectures of control, filters, zoning mechanisms, and labeling infrastructures such as PICS, can help to resolve these problems in the least restrictive way and without violating the e2e philosophy. Decisive is the fact that these architectures must be designed and used responsibly or they will cause collateral damage. Among other things, this implies that those who develop this code must support a high level of transparency as a manifestation of respect for the end user's autonomy. Code that controls content should only be used for a narrow specific purpose (such as preventing young children from exposure to indecent speech), and it should never interfere with legitimate forms of expression on the Internet.

In a world where intellectual property is the greatest source of value, the challenge to protect that property takes on greater significance. Digital music, DVD files, or other online content are more vulnerable, since it is trivially easy to make perfect copies and transmit them across the network. The distribution of digital music provides a good illustration of the intellectual property challenges that have become a familiar problem in cyberspace. It is difficult to balance the rights of songwriters and music producers to control the distribution of their work against the desires of music lovers to use music-sharing technologies such as Napster. The Napster paradigm worries all content providers and this could impede the distribution of digital content.

But in their zeal to protect digital content, U.S. regulators have overreached, as exemplified by problematic legislation such as the Digital Millennium Copyright Act. Here the threat to the Net's integrity seems to come not from architectures but from law. These copyright laws, for example, have been tightened, increasing the possibility that too much content will become enclosed and made off limits to aspiring creators. When ideas are "enclosed," creative recycling is precluded and creativity tends to become more concentrated in the hands of those who own the content. The key is to fine tune intellectual property laws so that, in Aristotelian terms, they "hit the mark" and provide just enough protection to induce innovation and creative ingenuity. There is no reason to accept the premise of many in the entertainment industry that more protection is always better than less. Finally, there may be some place for protocols such as digital rights-management systems that encrypt media files but allow metered access to licensees. DRM can supplement the law and ease the burden of developing and enforcing new regulations, but these architectures must be constructed in a way that preserves long-standing "safety valves" such as fair use and first-sale, as they provide for a reasonable degree of privacy.

Privacy advocates have sounded many alarms about the steady encroachment on privacy rights in cyberspace. There are certainly valid concerns about the state of Web privacy. The impetus to collect so much information about consumers stems from the perception that such information reduces risks because of its predictive power. In Chapter 8 we discussed at some length the threats posed to privacy rights from surveillance technologies such as cookies and Web bugs that collect information about consumers' surfing and buying habits. There are many definitions of privacy, but essentially privacy means being able to restrict access to and exercise some control over one's personal information, so that the right people have the right information at the right time. We can go a long way to protect privacy either through establishing regulations that codify data-protection standards or through reliance on architectures supplied by the market. The European approach epitomized in the comprehensive European Union Directive has been heavily reliant on the law. It is a command and control model that offers unambiguous protection for consumer data. On the contrary, we argue that code, such as P3P and other privacy-enhancing architectures, can play a significant role in defending personal privacy. However, in this case code cannot be an effective surrogate for the law unless commercial Web sites begin to act responsibly by subscribing to sound and fine-grained privacy polices and individuals begin to assume some personal responsibility for protecting their privacy. This approach also assumes that there will be some baseline level of privacy that will be protected by the law; this would include particularly sensitive information such as medical and financial data. Once again, the key is to find the right blend of policy and technology to protect personal privacy while minimizing the burden of regulatory costs.

Finally, we considered the use of various architectures to make the Internet a more secure environment. The Net's inherent vulnerabilities have been exploited by hackers and other miscreants who frequent cyberspace. If e-commerce is going to thrive in the future and the efforts of cyberterrorists thwarted, security issues must be taken more seriously. Among the architectures that accomplish this goal, we find firewalls, powerful encryption software and digital identity systems.

Paradoxically, some of the architectures like encryption code that secure the Net and safeguard privacy obstruct the efforts of law-enforcement authorities to deal with cybercrime and computer-related crime. The protection of public safety can sometimes conflict with respect for basic civil liberties. The search for the right balance between order and liberty has taken on greater significance in the aftermath of the September 11 tragedy, and many citizens are willing to shift the balance away from liberty for the time being. In this context we reviewed the topic of responsible government surveillance and the problems associated with technologies such as the FBI's Carnivore. We also saw that there is a tension between a perfectly secure Internet, where all transactions are traceable and users are held accountable, and an Internet that respects the values of privacy and anonymous free expression. As argued in Chapter 9, anonymous expression is an important social value worth preserving in cyberspace. Therefore, architectures and technical standards utilized to implement a digital identity system or other security mechanisms must not preclude the possibility for anonymous expression or create serious new privacy hazards. We highlighted an architecture called Private Credentials, which enables authentication without the need to sacrifice anonymity or privacy. This is one more example of how code designed with respect for basic values can be relied upon to address a social problem in cyberspace.

Finally, this book clearly assumes that we can preserve the integrity of the Internet as a tool of autonomy and a forum for creativity if we comport ourselves in cyberspace in an ethical manner. Each member of the cybercommunity must engage in activities that support the collective values of that community and refrain from activities that regard it as a commodity. The Internet, like all public goods, is vulnerable to abuses and excesses that can endanger its fragile ecology and some of those abuses can be the result of poorly crafted code. To sustain the Internet's culture of freedom and technological creativity, there is a need for ongoing reflection and dialogue about how to design the Internet's future architectures with moral competence. It is my hope that this book has made a modest contribution to that dialogue.

REFERENCES

Castells, M. (2001). *The Internet Galaxy*. New York: Oxford University Press.
"The Internet's New Borders." (2001). *The Economist*, 11 August, 9.
Levy, S. (1995). "Random Access." *Newsweek*, 27 February, 69.
Pigou, A. (1962). *Economics of Welfare*. 4th ed. London: Macmillan.

Index

ABOUT THE AUTHOR

Richard A. Spinello is Associate Research Professor at the Carroll School of Management at Boston College. Prior to joining the faculty of Boston College, he worked as a programmer, consultant, and marketing manager in the software industry. He has written and edited four books on computer-related ethics, as well as numerous articles and scholarly papers on ethics and management.